Pat Lipscrap

SHELLEY KLEIN

Shelley Klein was born in Scotland in 1963, the youngest daughter of textile designer Bernat and knitwear designer Margaret Klein. She left the See-Through House in 2017 and now lives in London where she works as a writer.

The See-Through House

MY FATHER IN FULL COLOUR

Shelley Klein

VINTAGE

1 3 5 7 9 10 8 6 4 2

Vintage is part of the Penguin Random House group of companies whose addresses can be found at global.penguinrandomhouse.com

Penguin
Random House
UK

First published in Vintage in 2021
First published in hardback by Chatto & Windus in 2020

'A Dying Race' and 'In the Attic' by Andrew Motion (*The Pleasure Steamers*, 1978) are reprinted here by kind permission of Carcanet Press Limited, Manchester, UK

penguin.co.uk/vintage

A CIP catalogue record for this book is available from the British Library

ISBN 9781529111545

Text design by James Ward

Printed and bound in Great Britain by Clays Ltd, Elcograf S.p.A.

The authorised representative in the EEA is Penguin Random House Ireland, Morrison Chambers, 32 Nassau Street, Dublin D02 YH68.

Penguin Random House is committed to a sustainable future for our business, our readers and our planet. This book is made from Forest Stewardship Council® certified paper.

To my mother and father,
who travel with me, always

One need not be a Chamber – to be Haunted
One need not be a House
  Emily Dickinson, *c.* 1863

For the memoir is a repository of truths, as each discrete truth is uttered, but the memoir can't be the repository of Truth which is the very breadth of the sky, too vast to be perceived in a single gaze.
  A Widow's Story, Joyce Carol Oates, 2011

Colour was all around me, pursuing me, cajoling me, asking to be admitted into my life and the lives of many others.
  Eye for Colour, Bernat Klein, 1965

Contents

HIGH SUNDERLAND

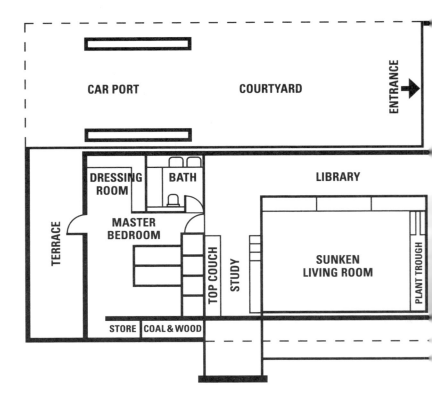

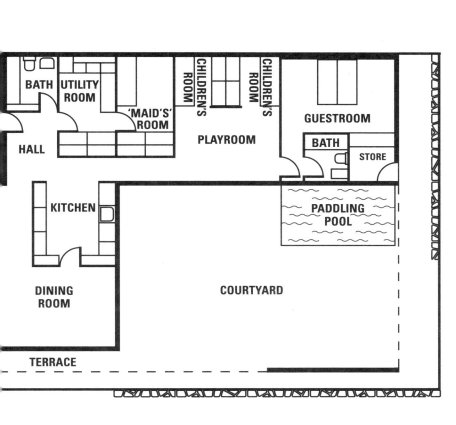

BATH

UTILITY ROOM

'MAID'S' ROOM

CHILDREN'S ROOM

CHILDREN'S ROOM

GUESTROOM

HALL

PLAYROOM

BATH

STORE

KITCHEN

PADDLING POOL

DINING ROOM

COURTYARD

TERRACE

Return To High Sunderland

Requirements: On an isolated site between Selkirk and Peebles, this house known as High Sunderland was required to be easily run and to provide maximum comfort for a household of five. Kitchen and dining room were to be separated and special provision was required for children and weekend guests.

Architecture & Building, 1958

I am sitting in a van alongside all my worldly possessions, driving north on the M6. Four hundred and fifty miles behind me is the tiny fishing village of Port Isaac in Cornwall where I have lived for the past twelve years. Sixty miles ahead of me is a house called High Sunderland in the Scottish Borders. This is where I was born and grew up.

I turn off the motorway on to the A7. Night has fallen, but even so I don't need to see the landscape to know what it looks like. I have driven this road hundreds of times, know its hills and valleys scoured with gorse, its forests and fields sutured together by dry-stone walls. This region has a brutal history, with clans from either side of the border invading each other's homesteads, stealing livestock, slaughtering one another, acts that still echo through the countryside in names such as Bloody Burn and Slain Men's Lea.

But this place is also about farming, about uplands and lowlands and the sheep that graze on them. About wool and water and weaving. It is no accident that for centuries the Borders relied on the textile trade because the rivers that score this terrain once turned the wheels of this industry while the rain that filled those rivers not only produced some of the finest grazing in the whole of the country, it is woven into the landscape in the way trees stream across hills and rivers flow down the valleys.

Snow begins to fall and I start to wonder whether, when I get to High Sunderland, I will make it up our driveway or whether I'll get stuck and have to abandon the van and walk the rest of the way on foot. I know my father, Beri, will be worried. He'll be standing in the hallway, hovering around the front door, waiting to spot my headlights.

Sure enough, fifty minutes later as I spin and slide dangerously up the drive I spy a small figure standing in the doorway, beaming from ear to ear while a flurry of snowflakes drifts past his nose.

Ever since my mother died a year ago, I have known that Beri wanted me to come back and live with him. This is not because he can't cope on his own, for despite being eighty-five years old he is still very capable. But he's lonely and isolated and my older brother and sister (Jonathan and Gillian) have families to look after and jobs that they can't just up and leave, which leaves only single, self-employed, childless me.

I jump out of the van and crunch my way across the front court-yard, where Beri gives me one of his great big bear hugs. There are thirty-nine years between us, one world war, five languages and two countries, but Beri and my mother, Peggy, have given me the only two things truly worth having: love and security.

'This is nice, isn't it?' he beams and I nod because it's true. It is nice to be back, for despite leaving High Sunderland nearly twenty-seven years previously to go to university in London and despite having lived in numerous rented flats throughout the city and more recently my fisherman's cottage in Cornwall, I still consider High Sunderland the only real 'home' I have ever had. I was born here and I grew up here and every year since, no matter what was happening in the rest of my life, I have spent at least one or two weeks here during the summer and every Christmas with the exception of two.

I step into the hallway and immediately breathe in a mixture of familiar smells: paprika, woodsmoke and freshly ground coffee. It is the most relaxing smell in the world. A smell that says I am back where I belong.

But ten minutes later, just as I am carrying all my stuff into the hallway from the van, my mood takes a turn for the worse.

> BERI: Darling, what's that?
> SHELLEY [carrying a battered Victorian chair in her hands]: My furniture.
> BERI: But we have furniture here –
> SHELLEY: I know but this is my furniture.
> BERI: Why's there so much of it?
> SHELLEY: I haven't lived at home since I was seventeen –
> BERI: What's your age got to do with bringing back furniture?
> SHELLEY: What do you imagine I've been sitting on for the past twenty-seven years?
> BERI: I can't say I've thought about it –
> SHELLEY [increasingly irritated]: It's a nice chair –
> BERI: But we have nice furniture here.
> SHELLEY: Not my furniture –
> BERI: Doesn't matter –
> SHELLEY: It does to me, besides you might grow to like it –
> BERI: I won't.
> SHELLEY: How do you know?
> BERI: Because your furniture is GHASTLY.

This was a typical Beri-like comment of the type that drove me around every bend this side of Hadrian's Wall because, besides being one of the kindest, most generous men I knew, my father was also one of the most difficult. So why, you might ask, had I agreed to come back to live with him? The answer lies at the heart of the second argument Beri and I had, which took place barely twenty-four hours after the one regarding my furniture, only this time it involved six little pots that I had brought with me that were planted with thyme, rosemary, chives, parsley, lemon thyme and marjoram. Just as I began arranging them on the kitchen windowsill, Beri appeared at my shoulder.

BERI: Would you mind putting those somewhere else?

SHELLEY: Why? They look nice here.

BERI: Why don't you put them in your bedroom? If you wouldn't mind?

SHELLEY: But they're herbs. They're for cooking with –

BERI: They'd be better off in your bedroom –

SHELLEY: I'm not trotting through to the bedroom every time I need a bit of thyme.

BERI: Suddenly you can't walk a little?

SHELLEY [irritated]: What have you got against herbs?

BERI: They're messy –

SHELLEY: They're plants –

BERI: They're messy plants. Except for the chives.

SHELLEY: And the chives have what going for them that the others haven't?

BERI: They're vertical.

SHELLEY [through gritted teeth]: All plants are vertical.

BERI: But some are more vertical than others –

SHELLEY: You're joking, right?

BERI: They spoil the line of the house –

SHELLEY: The WHAT?

BERI [patiently, as if explaining something to an imbecile]: The line of the house.

And that was that. I knew immediately there was no point continuing to fight the herbs' corner (or, in this case, windowsill).

For as long as I can remember, it has been understood within our family that High Sunderland is not simply a house. One close friend, Jenny, described it as 'a Mondrian set within a Klimt' because with its series of colourful glass panels set against a backdrop of birch and fir trees, it is like living within a work of art. Not only that, but the house, which was built in the modernist vernacular, dictates *how* one should live, what one should pay attention to and what one should ignore. It is a deceptively simple structure yet ultimately a highly complex amalgamation of ideas and ideals, a timepiece and a time machine as well as a combination of two men's ambitions: that of the architect – Peter Womersley – whose first proper commission this was, and a young Yugoslavian émigré to Britain – my father – who commissioned the project. Over the next fifty-six years Beri was to become so attached to High Sunderland it was almost impossible – to my mind, at least – to separate the two things out from each other.

My father was the house.

The house was my father.

Built in the late Fifties, High Sunderland makes no apologies for looking towards the future rather than gazing nostalgically towards the past. Like Beri himself, whom an acquaintance once noted was 'far more modern than any of his children', High Sunderland is more up to date than most contemporary housing. As you approach it from the driveway through a thick forest of pine trees, it appears at the top of the hill as a low-slung series of interconnecting boxes and grids.

Planes of both clear and coloured glass are interlaced with white, horizontal beams that in their turn are balanced between sections of ridged Makore wood that because they don't lie flat, lend each panel a tactile quality normally reserved for fabric. At night, when the internal lights are switched on and you are standing outside, the effect is of a light box effortlessly floating above the ground while during the day the various panels of yellow and green have all the luminosity of boiled sweets. But although as an adult I appreciate the unique beauty of High Sunderland, this was not always the case.

When I was about six or seven years old I recall the plumber, Mr S—, coming up to the house to fix a blocked drain. As he subsequently explained to my parents, when he clambered out of his van Mr S— couldn't locate the front door. All the different glass panels confused him, added to which when the sun slipped out from behind some clouds, the light bounced off these panels reflecting the beech and pine trees and made it twice as difficult to work out where an entrance might be. Finally Mr S— was relieved to spy a small courtyard to his right, on one side of which stood the door. It was a hot summer's day so he wasn't surprised to see the door had been left open.

When glass shatters the sound splits the silence into a million pieces. First there was a tremendous bang as the full weight of Mr S—'s considerable bulk hit my parents' bedroom window. Then came the horrific shattering of glass quickly followed by the sound of Mr S— crying out in shock.

'Was there a lot of blood?' I immediately demanded to know because, sensibly, my mother had denied me entrance to the scene of the accident. Not that I was a bloodthirsty child, but as far as I was concerned this was the most exciting thing ever to have happened at the house save for the time my father slipped on some ice in the garden and broke his leg. I was used to birds smashing into the walls, falling to the ground with dull thuds, but now I pictured Mr S— lying limp and broken on the paving stones, a telltale trickle of brownish-red blood escaping from his mouth. Fortunately for all concerned, Mr S— remained unscathed. There was not so much as a scratch on him, although if I'm honest I found this disappointing. At my friends' houses bloodcurdling incidents seemed to occur on a regular basis. One girl, whose parents' place boasted a 'gun room' that always smelt strongly of wet dogs and saddle soap, told me how her elder brother had accidently shot himself in the foot while cleaning a shotgun and blown off two of his toes (I never knew whether this tale was true despite watching said brother hawkishly every time he removed his shoes and socks). Another friend told me how her aunt had once got so drunk on neat gin that she'd fallen over in the kitchen while holding a carving knife and stabbed herself in the stomach. Stories like this used to cheer me up enormously – as well as leave me a tiny bit jealous because the houses they occurred in were all satisfyingly Gothic or Victorian by design with names such as Ashiestiel, Glenmayne, Auchenblae. It was around this time that I therefore began (secretly) calling High Sunderland the See-Through House because it seemed so much more romantic than plain old High Sunderland. Words were important to me, even back then. How they sounded on the tip of the tongue, their colour and texture, not to mention the images they inspired. Descriptions such as 'ghost-ridden', 'moon-clad', 'twisted with madness' seduced me as a child. Anything might and quite often did happen with imagery such as that. It was the stuff of my favourite novels: of *Midnight is a Place*, *Jane Eyre* and *Rebecca*.

These days I think differently about old houses. Particularly the type of places crammed to the rafters with knick-knacks. Over-adornment panics me: rooms decorated with William Morris wallpaper, flurries of birds and butterflies so dark and dense they make me want to take flight myself. But as a child, houses like these were enchanting and enchanted. My imagination roamed their corridors, discovered locked rooms and played with dead children whereas, to the best of my knowledge, no one had ever spotted a ghost in a modernist house. Nor did modernist houses feature attics where mad women sat locked up for decades. Indeed, to my childish mind, the only thing to occur at High Sunderland of any true consequence was the occasional fashion show.

During the Sixties my father's career as a textile designer had taken off, as a result of which designers such as Coco Chanel and Christian Dior began using Bernat Klein fabrics in their haute couture collections. Undoubtedly what caught their eye was the unusual quality of his woven fabrics, which evolved by doing things that were 'not done' (as Beri would term it). One dazzling consequence of this was his reinvention of traditional tweed.

Hard as it is now to imagine there was ever a time when yarn and woven fabrics weren't vibrant, full-bodied affairs. Post-war Britain was a dull, muted place particularly when it came to clothing, which was rationed until 1949. Church-hall browns, mustard yellows, sinkhole blues – these were the teeth-grindingly drab hues of the day and they continued to dominate the colour palette for some time to come. Beri introduced something new. Combining slubby yarns with twists of three or more colours he created textiles that popped and fizzed. One length of fabric looked like woven bumblebees; another resembled cherries on fire; a third, gold milk shot through with butterscotch; effects chiefly achieved by – in the case of one exceptional fabric – stringing the warp with velvet ribbon while the weft was created from bundles of brushed, section-dyed mohair. This latter was no small achievement involving as it did many months of collaborative work with different dye houses in and around the Borders. Indeed, so individual were the results that in 1964 Christian Dior produced a coat out of one of them. 'Technically,' wrote fashion critic

Ernestine Carter of *The Times*, 'this is a unique achievement: the fabric looks as if it must be hand woven, but actually it is made on ordinary looms.'

We had fashion shows where all of London's leading fashion editors were flown up to Edinburgh only to be driven to High Sunderland where my father's latest creations were being modelled. The open-plan living room had an elevated gallery that made for the perfect catwalk, up and down which the models strutted.

Week-long photography sessions also took place at the house, with models striking poses against the Mondrian-style exteriors. I loved watching these women as they stalked the rooms: leggy flamingos in flame-pink bellbottoms, peacocks wrapped in dizzy green maxi-skirts. I snuck into the bathrooms to try on the models' vast

Fashion show at High Sunderland, 1963

array of wigs in every imaginable colour and cut. To an impressionable child these were wonderful moments. Yet my interest in fashion never extended much further than this.

If my parents talked 'shop' at lunch or dinnertime I grew bored. More often than not they were chatting about what was happening at my father's textile mill where all the fabrics were woven: dull conversations that involved yarns and dye-works and overseas shipments. On occasion Beri referred to people called Balenciaga or Yves Saint Laurent, people whom he admired or worked with, but the names meant nothing to me.

Strange as it may seem to anyone who knew our family and in particular my father, it also never occurred to me that Beri spoke with an Eastern European accent. To me he always sounded like the rest of us so it came as a shock to hear my father being interviewed on the radio one day, only to realise that Beri sounded different. How could I be deaf to something so obvious? How could something so obvious hide in plain sight?

Shortly after this I asked Beri to show me the photographs of my grandparents, Serena (nicknamed Zori) and Leopold (nicknamed Lipot or Lippi) Klein. I had not met either of them because they had died before I was born. Beri dug out two old, leather-bound albums and there, pressed under semi-translucent sheets of glassine paper lay a whole other world. Men and women with faces smooth as river stones stared up at me solemnly. Ashen light suffused the interiors in which they sat and stood. Here was a world of sailor suits and hair ribbons, of wooden hoops and starched collars. The longer I stared, the more it felt as if the dead were returning to life. A feeling that only increased each time Beri spoke of his childhood. 'One of my happiest memories,' he told me apropos this time, 'was watching my mother sitting at her dressing table brushing her hair. It was the colour of flames.'

Klein family group, c. 1927: Beri could not be persuaded to come out from his hiding place behind the family

I pictured the scene, sensed the room within which Zori sat, the sound of the hairbrush, the pale half-light of a lamp. I was in a house in Scotland, but momentarily I inhabited this other world.

Today I trace my grandparents' faces with the tips of my fingers, examine the rooms they are sitting and standing in. The atmosphere is hatched with silver. My grandmother stands wrapped in a quilted silk dressing gown, admiring herself in a mirror. On the table in front of her lies a lace cloth on top of which are arranged a small collection of glass and silver jars alongside an ornate, silver-backed hairbrush. In the living room more lengths of lace are draped across windows, the floors are tiled, sofas and armchairs upholstered in richly patterned chintzes and velvets. There are candelabras and gilt-framed paintings, tiled stoves and huge potted ferns with leaves curled tight as clock springs.

I stare at the photographs and can smell the heat, dust and darkness of those sequestered interiors. I can hear the ticking of clocks and crackle of silk.

Throughout my adolescence and early twenties I returned to these albums, glanced through their pages, forever intrigued by the unfamiliar faces looming out at me. In many ways these photographs were the closest I would ever come to discovering an attic at High Sunderland, that is to say the only dark, ever so slightly haunted space within an otherwise flat-roofed, brightly lit, modernist home.

But of all these compositions possibly my favourite was of Beri and his younger brother, Moshe, aged about six and four years respectively, sitting studying a picture book together. Both boys are wearing dark-coloured woollen suits and pale stockings with black boots and black yarmulkes (skull caps). Why I like it so much, I am not quite clear, for with its sepia tones and dusty lighting, the boys seem more like something out of *Oliver Twist* than flesh-and-blood children.

Another photograph depicts the two brothers in fancy dress. The occasion is Purim, one of the most joyous of all Jewish festivals, which, according to the Book of Esther should be celebrated '[. . .] as days of feasting and joy and giving presents of food to one another and gifts to the poor'. Purim is also celebrated by dressing up in costumes as a way of commemorating how Esther refused to divulge her true identity to her husband, King Ahasuerus, until he had seen the error of his ways.

The photograph lying on the table in front of me has Moshe in a little girl's full-length ball gown decorated with ribbons and lace while on his head he wears a wig of copper-coloured ringlets. Beri, meanwhile, is dressed in Victorian knickerbockers, white tights, polished black shoes and a black top hat decorated with pink roses.

At the heart of Purim lies the nature of identity. According to Judaism, as someone born of a Jewish mother, Beri would always be

Jewish, but when I stare at that little boy dressed up in Victorian knick-erbockers, I know for a fact that despite his childhood being marbled by religion, my father was no more Jewish than he was Victorian. Nor would Beri ever favour tradition just for the sake of it. Instead, it was the future that held him in thrall, hence his intense love affair with the See-Through House. From the moment my father first saw Peter Womersley's plans for this building, right up until the end of his life, High Sunderland excited him. Hardly a day passed without Beri expressing pleasure at the house's design or his conviction that it was the most exhilarating place in which to live. This often proved complicated for the rest of the family, throwing up as it did a million and one challenges, so much so that sometimes it felt as if Beri had replaced one religion with another.

But in recent years the challenge has been all mine. I returned to the See-Through House to look after my father, we lived together for five years. It's now almost four years since he died and the questions come thick and fast. How can I move on from this house, the house I grew up in, the house where I spent all of my formative years? What is it about High Sunderland and about Beri that keeps me clinging on as if my life depends on it?

In Scotland there's a term used by farmers called 'hefting', derived from the Old Norse word 'heft' meaning 'to bind' (although in other parts of the country the practice can be called lairing, heafing, lyring or heughing). Sheep that are hefted are said to belong to the land-scape in that they carry within them an instinctive understanding of their surroundings. They know where the best places are to take shelter, where they need to avoid because of bogs or cliffs, where the best grazing lies. In some cases hefted sheep also develop immunity from the diseases specific to their immediate environment. Over the years the land becomes mapped in their blood and intuitively they recognise each stony pathway, each hillside and rocky decline. Hefted sheep also pass this knowledge on to their young, generation after generation. It's an ancient way of moving through the landscape, one that some researchers believe stretches as far back as the thirteenth or fourteenth centuries.

I am hefted to High Sunderland. The house lies in my blood. I know every crevice, crack, shift and pattern, every reflection that is thrown, every sound that is made. I know the exact spot where my father stood to make his speech at my sister's wedding, the corner in the library where dust always settles more thickly than any place else and that bit of the living room where Peggy started to tap dance one night while watching an old Fred Astaire movie. I also know the precise tree among the hundred or so other trees in the garden that has a crack in its trunk where wild honeybees nest. I know the place in the forest where badgers build their setts and the mossy inclines where snowdrops appear every January. Not that I have never left High Sunderland. Over the years I have travelled to France, Italy, America, Denmark . . . Serbia, Croatia, Australia . . . but I always return to this house, always find my way home. After all, this is where I am from. The house is what I know best. It explains who and what I am far better than any thing or any place else.

But is it rational to feel like this? About a building? Surely a house is just a volume of space enclosed by bricks and mortar or, in this case, glass. Has High Sunderland some kind of hold over me and, if so, what? It seems ironic that a house built to represent so much that was modern now contains only the past.

*

Senta stands next to the river Tisza in the Vojvodina – a region that used to be part of the Austro-Hungarian Empire but which, in 1918, became northern Yugoslavia (now Serbia). Back in the Twenties, when Beri was a child, the streets were wide and sandy and lined with acacia trees cut into lollipop shapes, while every evening at around 9 p.m. the Paris-to-Bucharest Simplon Express passed by the town. Sometimes, during the long summer evenings when the train clattered over the wooden bridge, boys from the region would gather on the riverbanks to wave at the passengers. As a pastime this was better than stargazing, for the passengers on board were heading to places far more dazzling than any far-flung planet or galaxy. 'One could only hope to emulate them,' reminisced Beri in 1965. 'I often gazed at the Simplon longingly and allowed my imagination full rein ... '

A dreamer as well as a mischievous, headstrong little boy, Beri always recalled Senta and the home his parents created for him and his brother on Stevan Sremac Street vividly. He wrote about the dust-coloured farmland that lay outside Senta planted with maize, wheat and barley and the narrow dirt tracks leading through the small rural villages. He wrote of wild chestnut trees growing by the banks of the Tizsa 'alight with spiky green fruit' and of the vegetable market held each Monday and Friday in the main square with – during the summer – its mountains of sugar melons, apples and plums, while from November onwards cabbages were piled high on each stall, only to be bought by the cartload then salted in barrels for use over the winter.

Textures and sounds; the taste of Eskimo ice creams (the local equivalent of choc-ices) and the scent of mimosa as it tumbled over the walls into the family garden. Days spent tobogganing down the dykes of the Tizsa or collecting stag beetles in bottles. Golden orioles nesting in the giant oaks that grew in the People's Garden, the yellow flash of their wings like streaks of hot butter.

My father always loved trees, but oaks held a particular joy for him or, more particularly, their acorns – ' ... the silky, hard skin of the kernel so different in touch and texture from its rough, grooved cap; the taste of the acorn on the tip of the teeth and the delicious, astringent aroma of the forest with which it explodes when bitten in two.'

Beri also recalled the pale yellow lettering on a deep-green background, 3-feet high, reading, first in Serbian Cyrillic and then in Latin script, 'Klein Lipot Textile Merchant'. This was the family business, one that Lipot and Zori had built up from scratch and one that Beri recalled in minute detail. The carved wooden handle on the front door, smooth and warm as a shoulder blade. The bell overhead that made the sound of old copper coins. Waist-high counters whose surfaces swam with reflections and shelves stacked to the ceiling with cloth, each bolt rolled up so tightly, their selvedge ends resembled cross-sections of oak. In particular Beri loved the silks that crackled like eggshells, but also the thicker, heavier fabrics, the Donegal tweeds with their brambly knops and grained, heathery colours. He also enjoyed watching his parents at work, but especially Zori. The way she dealt and advised each customer in turn. The way she measured cloth with arms outstretched to the exact equivalent of a metre and afterwards folded and smoothed each length with the flat of her hand before wrapping it up in brown paper. The rhythm and precision of her movements and the calmness of her demeanour. All of it was a constant source of pleasure to my father; a pleasure that also extended to the family home that stood next door to the shop and over which Zori also presided.

The house on Stevan Sremac Street was a well-built, one-storey affair with a large rose garden for Zori and a small hexagonal summer pavilion in which Lipot often held prayers during the evenings. There was a dining room that could 'seat 24 people in comfort' and a stone-floored kitchen in which Zori and her four sisters, Malvin, Rezi, Piri and Helene, would sit most days, cooking and chatting. Zori loved preparing family meals and would often conjure up special treats for Beri and Moshe, most of which included melted chocolate sprinkled with hazelnuts. But if work and home-life coexisted, the combining factor was always religion, that is to say the Jewish community in which Beri was raised.

Born on 6 November 1922, Beri was a child of the Thirties; at this time Senta had a population of approximately 35,000 people of which 3,500 were Jewish. Even in a community as small as this, however, there were different Jewish enclaves. For example, there were the ultra-Orthodox Jews who worshipped in the Beth Hamidrash (House of Studies) and whose only purpose in life was to praise God and study His word via the Torah (the Pentateuch) and the Talmud (the 2000-year-old compendium of Jewish law, legends and morals) as well as later Hebrew texts. After them came the Orthodox Jews whose synagogue was called 'The Little Synagogue' despite this building being larger than 'The Large Synagogue', which belonged to the third group of Jews living in Senta during that period, the Neologs, who were the most liberal and modern of the three.

Beri's family were Orthodox Jews and worshipped at The Little Synagogue where Lipot was regularly elected head of the congregation, most of whose male members consisted of business people, shopkeepers and craftsmen such as tailors and pattern-makers, but with not one professionally qualified person among them. 'The idea of spending years exposed to totally non-religious teaching, among gentiles, was unacceptable to members of The Little Synagogue,' wrote my father. Thus Beri, having attended a local primary school until the age of eight or nine, avoided the secondary state school and received daily religious instruction at a local yeshiva (a school where only Jewish subjects are taught) while being privately tutored at home in all other subjects by a Mr and Mrs Czartoryski – Ukrainians who had emigrated from Kiev.

Tuition took place at a large desk placed in the sitting room, the windows of which looked out over the garden where, if the weather were fine, Beri would spend recess playing with his wooden Meccano set or hurtling up and down the pathways on his bicycle. In winter, however, he was more inclined to stay indoors. 'The winters were long, snowy and cold,' he wrote, 'and all the rooms in our house had huge tiled stoves in the corners so that when one entered the living room from the outside it felt as if one had stepped into a warm bath from a cool bathroom.' Beri also recalled the big, velvet armchairs into which he and his brother would sink and the huge feather beds in his parents' bedroom where he liked to curl up in the evenings while Lipot read him stories from *Tarzan*.

But 'above all,' wrote Beri in 1996, 'my memories relate to my mother of whom I did not see much after the age of 14 and nothing after I reached 16, when I was sent away to Jerusalem.'

Every time I read this sentence it strikes me as one flavoured by distance. It's a stopgap film with individual frames labelled: Far, Further, Furthest. The words also strike me for what they don't say as much as for what they do and it's this absence or, more accurately, the presence of this absence that led, I believe, to the creation of the See-Through House.

Hallway

Unless you are speaking of grand country mansions with black-and-white chequered floors or wide-sweeping staircases, hallways are rarely, if ever, of note. People walk across hallways, exit and enter them and occasionally crowd them with boot stands, bags and umbrellas. But the hallway is not a room people linger in. Instead it's the place that tells the owners, once they have crossed the threshold, they are home. The hallway also welcomes visitors (unless you have a doormat that does that job for you). It is, as it were, the foreword to the building, the room that announces what else you might expect from the rest of the house.

The hallway at High Sunderland is nothing if not functional; a word beloved by the Bauhaus, a word that became a creed much like Bauhaus architect Ludwig Mies van der Rohe's famous saying, 'less is more'. In fact, that phrase could have been written for this space because, with its simple strip-walnut panels covering the back wall of the room and with only one piece of furniture gracing it, 'less' is not only the dominant impression, it is also clearly 'more' because this room overflows with nothing but space.

As if to emphasise this point, the single piece of furniture, a chair by Danish designer Poul Kjærholm, is an exercise in frugality. Known as PK25, it is typical of all Kjærholm's work being a simple combination of steel and braided halyard. It reminds me of a harp or, more fittingly given my father's career, a loom with the braided halyard acting as warp. The frame is angular – a geometric Z shape, with the rope strung tightly across both seat and back in such a manner that the tension never decreases. It is a surprisingly comfortable chair, although if you are over the age of forty-five or thereabouts, it is impossible to get up from it without help of some kind because the

seat is nearly at floor level. This, however, is a minor drawback compared to the chair's beauty; besides which, nobody actually sits on it because chairs of this type are not really for sitting on. Nor, God forbid, are they for putting things on, either.

When I was young and came home from school this was not the place to fling down my satchel. Nor were guests encouraged to leave their coats, bags or umbrellas on this chair because in reality this chair was not a chair. It was a sculpture, a finely crafted piece of metal and rope that like a Hepworth or Moore was to be admired for its exquisite shape as well as for the manner in which this shape contained and explained the space around it. 'A well-designed object,' wrote Beri in 1976, 'has an air of inevitability about it, an integrity which can be felt and it fits easily and naturally into its environment. It also brings out and sometimes creates certain desirable features in its environment which would otherwise either not exist or not be noticed.' In other words, what the Kjærholm represented was not only a well-designed item of furniture, but also something that reflected and enhanced the house in which it sat. I don't love this chair, unlike some of the other objects at High Sunderland, but the PK25 instantly explains the rest of the building, as do several other items, the thought of which makes me wonder if I haven't begun making High Sunderland into my own private reliquary. Not that I worship its tables and chairs, but am I instilling them with something so overwhelmingly powerful, so unnegotiable, it now feels impossible to let go?

Unlike my brother and sister, I am the only member of our family who has lived their entire life referring to High Sunderland as 'home', by which I mean I never experienced my parents living elsewhere since they moved in to the house in 1957 and I wasn't born until 1963.

Knowing the house as well as I do makes me wonder how Beri and Peggy felt the first time they walked over the threshold into a building that had been designed specifically for them. Two years previously, in 1955, my parents had been driving along a road near to Holmfirth in Yorkshire when, glancing out of the window, Beri glimpsed a strange geometric structure floating between the trees, which on closer inspection turned out to be a house. Designed by Peter Womersley as a wedding present for his older brother John, Farnley Hey (as the house became known) contained all the passion of a young man whose eyes were firmly set on breaking traditional moulds.

Womersley, who was born in Newark-on-Trent on 24 June 1923, had nurtured architectural aspirations from a young age. 'In my teens,' he wrote, 'I saw photographs of the Kaufmann House "Falling-water" [designed by Frank Lloyd Wright] and this decided me on my career. I still think this is the most beautiful house ever built, although I have never [visited] it, but to me it exhibits this sense of involvement which I am sure is so important.' This sense of involvement was something Peter replicated at Farnley Hey, which combined two of his later signature trademarks: floor-to-ceiling windows and an exuberant use of wood panelling that echoed the trees surrounding the house. My father later recalled that catching sight of the building from the road excited him on a visceral level and that he had to know who had designed it. Consequently he and my mother knocked on the front door. Seconds later they were being invited inside by John Womersley who, after showing them around, gave them details of his brother's address.

Beri wrote to Peter the next week, asking if he would be prepared to design a house for him and his family in the Scottish Borders where he and Peggy had recently bought a plot of land in the middle of a large country estate five miles outside Selkirk. 'We hit it off immediately,' my father recalled almost forty years later. 'We liked his work and then liked Peter. He was shy and quietly spoken yet unostentatiously and firmly self-confident, particularly in relation to his work.

Surprisingly to me he was an admirer of Palladio and had a profound knowledge of classical architecture. His professional commitment to the modern idiom however was total and uncompromising.'

Before starting work Peter and Beri had several discussions about architecture, conversations that – according to my father – included talk about 'some of Frank Lloyd Wright's smaller buildings and one or two others, but the main thing was to explain to him how we wanted to use our house, approximately how big the plan was going to be and how we lived and worked'.

Peter then began by doing a few preliminary sketches on a large pad of graph paper. 'It [the graph paper] has two enormous advantages;' Womersley wrote in 1969, 'areas are easily worked out, and from the very start of planning, a discipline is imposed upon the building. It is invaluable for the integration of the structural system with the plan at a very early date. The grid of the graph usually represents some measurement in the region of 3ft plus [...] The planning

Watercolour design for High Sunderland by Peter Womersley, c. 1956

the house from the south-east

itself attempts to be as simple as possible by eliminating all unnecessary corridors and walls. It tries also to be basically Miesian in that the ultimate simple open volume, derived from the plan, is broken down by a series of closed volumes – storage or sanitary accommodation, for instance – into a series of smaller volumes.'

Peter worked quickly, concentrating first on one plan, then on a second set of more detailed drawings that included references to the materials he might use. In essence he saw the project as a timber-framed pavilion made up of two separate wings within which sat courtyards that, according to a later appreciation by Michael Webb, Peter 'treated as extensions of the interior, being roofed, or covered by pergolas'. Webb added that, 'A plain-sided glass box sitting on a hill could easily seem frail or banal; [however] the contrasts of solid and void, varnished boarding and full glazing, within the white frame, give the house strength and character.'

In fact, the original plans for High Sunderland did not include varnished boarding, but instead favoured local stone. This is how the house appeared in a small watercolour done by Peter to show Beri and Peggy how their finished building would look. At the time of construction, however, stone proved too expensive for my father's limited budget, so African Makore wood was settled upon as the most suitable compromise and in many ways fits the building better than stone as the vertical lines of the wood reflect the vertical lines of the trees surrounding the house.

The first frames of High Sunderland went up in the summer of 1956. Beri visited the site frequently, sometimes taking Peggy with him, at other times driving over by himself after work in order to check on progress. The field was a muddy quagmire of tyre tracks, earth and mounds of rubble laced with patches of thistles. Still it was the most beautiful thing he had ever set eyes upon. Over the following weeks and months, Beri picked his way through what would become the house's rooms. He stepped over areas marked out with string, peered out of windows that were yet to be fitted and walked across invisible thresholds. This was the house's footprint, but in a very real way it was also Beri and Peter's footprint – lasting evidence of a combined vision that culminated with my parents eventually moving in to the house in late '57 with Jonathan and Gillian. I did not arrive on the scene until 1963 during one of the worst snowstorms ever to hit Great Britain.

As luck or forward planning would have it, Beri had taken Peggy to the cottage hospital in Galashiels the night before I was due to be born because snow had begun falling so heavily he was worried they wouldn't get the car down the drive if they didn't leave immediately. Nor were his fears unfounded as a photograph taken

Beri and baby Shelley, 1963

shortly afterwards shows my brother standing on top of a snowdrift, touching the roof of the house.

Winter and winteriness. Blizzards and icicles. I have always loved January's bitterness, relished bleak northern landscapes over softer, hotter climes. Give me a bony, frostbitten forest over a tropical jungle any day of the week; give me the silence of a nocturnal whiteout. Something inside me stirs at even so much as the hint of a snowflake while I cling to an imagined vision of my first few months of life. Hanging on to things prolongs the past, stretches time out. I look at the Kjærholm and see my childhood woven into its structure, all the times I stubbed my toes against its sharp metal frame or watched my mother perch on the edge of the seat, too fearful to lean backwards in case she got stuck. And, no matter where I am in the world, if I hear a similar sound to the shrieking noise this chair makes when its feet are dragged across the marble floor, I am immediately transported back not just to High Sunderland, but to the house's smells and textures, to its atmosphere, the family get-togethers, discussions, disagreements.

> BERI [spying my coat slung carelessly over the Kjærholm]: Would you mind putting that somewhere else?
> TEENAGE SHELLEY: There's no room for it in the cupboard –
> BERI: Then take it through to your bedroom –
> TEENAGE SHELLEY: But I'm going out again in a minute –
> BERI: Sweetie pie, that chair is not for putting things on –
> TEENAGE SHELLEY [sullenly]: So what's your bum got that my coat doesn't?
> BERI: Purpose. My bum, as you so gracefully put it, is for sitting on whereas your coat is for wearing or putting away.

Note Beri didn't say 'or hanging up in the hallway cupboard', which one might think the most logical place in which to leave a coat, for although my parents' outdoor gear fitted the hallway cupboard perfectly, it was too narrow to accommodate anyone else's attire. A design flaw? An architect's failure to grasp the fact that people live in the houses they build? This echoes an argument between Mies van der Rohe and one of his most famous clients, Dr Edith Farnsworth, who commissioned Mies to build her a weekend residence in Plano, Illinois. Noticing no mention of a wardrobe on the plans of this sleek, crystal creation, the client enquired where she was to hang her clothes. The response was not what she was expecting. Infuriated by Farnsworth's enquiry, Mies van der Rohe replied that the building was a weekend residence, ergo she could hang the few clothes she brought with her in the bathroom. The bathroom was an enclosed space whose contents could not be seen when one looked at the house from the outside, but unsatisfied with this reply, Farnsworth insisted a wardrobe be built. The task was undertaken by one of Mies's assistants using timber that didn't match the rest of the house's fixtures and fittings – indicating perhaps that the wardrobe was not Mies's idea and that it didn't belong in *his* unique creation.

Whatever the case, the hallway cupboard at High Sunderland is too small to take more than two or three overcoats at a time, which makes me smile, for in order to appreciate the beauty of a house such as this, its inhabitants must be as passionate about its clean, uninterrupted lines and uncluttered rooms as the architect was himself.

My father was just such a man.

Who else, after all, would take the time and trouble to scrub the trunks of the silver birch trees that were planted on either side of our driveway?

'What on earth are you doing?' I said the day I found Beri, bucket of water and bleach in hand, scrubbing the bark.

'Isn't that obvious?'

'Strangely, no.'

'I'm gardening.'

'You can't garden with bleach.'

'Who says?'

'Everyone.'

'Then obviously they don't know what they're talking about.'

'But why are you gardening with bleach of all things?'

'I'm trying to get rid of the lichen,' he cried, maniacally giving the patch he was pointing at a further good scrubbing. 'We planted these birch trees to reflect the white columns of the house. Now all this green stuff is spoiling them!'

'That's nature, you can't control nature.'

'Of course you can, it's called gardening!'

More recently while I was driving Beri back from our local hospital where he'd been confined during a bout of pneumonia, I spied my father beaming with pleasure.

> SHELLEY: Happy to be going home?
>
> BERI: How do you mean?
>
> SHELLEY: You just seem very happy, that's all –
>
> BERI: I'm always happy.
>
> SHELLEY [rolls her eyes]
>
> BERI [catching me doing this]: What's that supposed to mean?
>
> SHELLEY: Always happy? You're joking, right?
>
> BERI [ignoring his daughter's comment]: Have you noticed the hedges?
>
> SHELLEY: Noooo.
>
> BERI: They've been trimmed! See how neat they look ... it's wonderful, isn't it!

My brother and to a lesser extent my sister were also fanatical about tidiness. However, much to Beri's bewilderment, I was of a different disposition, one more prone to leaving a trail of devastation behind me wherever I went. Sitting at my computer, soon enough there will be piles of books, paper and pens alongside little hills of orange peel, mugs of cold coffee, the occasional half-eaten biscuit, sandwich crust or apple core. Half the time I have no recollection of getting up and fetching these items, they just seem to accumulate or accidently fall into my orbit.

A few months after I moved back to High Sunderland two of my closest friends, Chris and Paul, visited from London. Beri always enjoyed watching rugby and tennis with Chris while Paul shared Beri's passion for all things to do with design together with an almost pathological need for order and tidiness. On the afternoon in question I asked Paul if he would mind fetching some peas from our freezer in the utility room.

> PAUL: Sure, which shelf will they be on?
> SHELLEY: No idea. The top one probably or the second or third shelf down –

Several seconds passed while Paul trotted off on his mission after which I heard the freezer door open and a lot of scrabbling taking place.

> SHELLEY [shouting]: Are they in there?
> PAUL [shouting back]: Yes, they're here … alongside thirty years of psychiatric care for having opened this door –

Variations on this theme have stalked me throughout my life, but particularly during the years I looked after my father.

> BERI [entering Shelley's bedroom, which looks as if a three-year-old child has just that minute thrown a massive tantrum

and chucked everything on the floor]: What on earth are you up to?

SHELLEY [on her hands and knees, frantically searching under her bed]: That book I was reading last night? You haven't seen it, have you?

BERI: No –

SHELLEY [standing up and walking over to her desk, which is covered in scraps of paper and piles of books]: It's got a blue cover – you know the one –

BERI: Perhaps you could try locating a surface first?

SHELLEY: Is that the most helpful thing you can say?

BERI [chuckling]: Okay, how about 'give up now'?

Nor was my mother better at the tidiness business although, over the years, she did manage to adjust her behaviour to the extent that she made certain my father could not witness her messiness. To this end there were two cupboards and three drawers in the master bedroom that were entirely hers, together with one drawer in the kitchen that 'belonged', so to speak, to my mother. Opening any of these was an exercise in – particularly if you were Beri – stress management. Elsewhere in the house my mother tried her best to be tidy, for if not as passionate as her husband about matters of design, she appreciated High Sunderland's unadorned beauty, which was present not only in the simplicity of the wood-panelled walls, but also in the choice of flooring.

Made from Italian travertine marble, each slab has a milky, glazed surface, the texture of which is rough, yet also extravagantly smooth. Sometimes I think it looks like the skin of the moon with every tiny flaw and crater visible. More than that it is vital that you are aware of these flaws so as to remind you that you are walking across a natural surface. Perhaps this is why the marble blends so seamlessly with the walnut wood panelling into which two doors have been set, invisible save for their curved metal handles, smoother than fish fins.

Invisible doors are a theme at High Sunderland because one of the building's guiding principals, some might say laws, is that everything should flow effortlessly from one space to the next without any visual interruptions.

To this end the third door in the sequence, the front door through which Mr S— so memorably did not pass, is an unadorned expanse of lacquered white wood with not so much as a letterbox to its name.

So how did we receive our post?

Fortunately High Sunderland is located in a secluded, relatively crime-free part of the country, which means that the front door has, until very recently, always been left on the latch. This was to accommodate the postman, who used to leave our letters inside on an unobtrusive wooden shelf that floats three-quarters of the way down the front wall, a wall made entirely out of two sheets of clear glass. Of all the features in the hallway, this is perhaps the most revelatory because not only does the glass permit the greatest amount of light to flood into this space, it also announces that this is a house that wants to banish all darkness.

Middle Bedroom

From the hallway it is only a short walk through to what became known within the family as 'the children's end of the house', the main area of which is the middle bedroom.

When my sister and I were children, this space was divided into three sections. Two cubicles like ship's cabins were positioned down one side of the room, each with a bed, dressing table, bookshelf and wardrobe. Bright yellow sliding doors that always made me think of bananas then separated these two cabins off from the playroom that lay on their far side and which was furnished with a couch, table and boxes for all our toys. My brother, being that much older than us, had what on one set of Peter's plans was marked down as the 'Maid's Room', which you entered via the utility room, that is to say it wasn't where you might expect a bedroom to be. I loved that Jonathan's room was tucked away out of sight, yet despite this I still preferred the middle bedroom.

Light and airy, Gillian and I rarely if ever slid the doors closed on our cabins, preferring instead the glassy lucidity that poured in through the two sets of see-through walls. Yet despite this luminosity, the middle bedroom is the only place in which I have ever seen a ghost, or at least imagined I'd seen one.

I must have been about five or six years old and, on waking in the middle of the night – probably after a nightmare – I recall being so terrified I couldn't move. Every muscle in my body was rigid. I could barely breathe, I certainly couldn't get out of bed, and then all of a sudden I saw my mother enter the room. Relief washed over me. Here was my saviour. I leapt out of bed and running straight across to her I flung my arms about her waist only to realise she wasn't there. My arms had wrapped around nothing, a discovery that terrified me even more than my nightmare had done and, as a consequence of which, I began screaming so loudly that my mother really did appear in the doorway.

Of course, thinking about this episode today, I assume my mother's apparition was nothing more than the embodiment of my desire to see her, that is to say it was all in my head. But far from putting me off sleeping in the middle room, I grew to love it more and more. I loved that my sister's cabin was a hair's breadth away and that at night I could hear her breathe. I loved my little wooden dressing table and the bookshelf and cupboard above my bed. I felt safe there. I *was* safe there, cocooned and nurtured. This is the room where Beri read *Winnie the Pooh* to me and Peggy *The Hobbit*. The Snow Queen also put in infrequent appearances alongside Mary Poppins, Mrs Tiggy Winkle and Alice. This is also the room where, one bitter January morning on waking to a power cut, I discovered the middle bedroom's windows completely iced over, both outside *and* in. I'd never witnessed such a phenomenon before. Yes, I'd seen icicles hanging from the eaves of the house and snow piled knee-deep on the roof, but this winteriness had never manifested itself within the building. I touched every crystallised surface, traced every tiny reticulation of ice. It was so beautiful, this frosted interiority, and it showed me something else too. It illustrated how within the ordinary lies the potential for the extraordinary. A bumble bee trapped in a soap bubble? Apples that can turn into plums? Inside this room my imagination grew and expanded. My inner world and the outer world touched. Of course, back then I appreciated none of this; I simply viewed High Sunderland as a house. Nor did it occur to me there'd come a time when the house's future might lie in doubt. As a child you acquire things, you don't let them go. You accumulate knowledge. You learn your address and telephone number, how to tie your own shoelaces and which way to look when crossing the road. You learn to ride a bike, to read and write, to swim, to say please and thank you and how, if you don't want to go to school, to dunk your thermometer in a glass of warm water when your mother's not looking. I learnt all of these things while this room was my room. Then, when I was eight or nine, Beri and Peggy decided the cabins were far too small for growing girls. Consequently the middle room was made into one large bedroom for me while Gillian moved next door to the guest bedroom or 'Pink Room' – so named because originally it had a pink carpet. My new room was more open plan than the cabin rooms, with no door between it and the corridor leading into the kitchen, but it was very grown-up, with a fitted wardrobe, bookshelves and desk, and I really missed it when, aged ten, I was sent (like Gillian and Jonathan before me) to a boarding school in Dorset. Beri said his reason for sending us away (Peggy was always far more reluctant to do this) was because he wanted his children to be as British as the British in addition to which he also wanted us to have the best education, although why this was only to be found at the other end of the country is still somewhat of a mystery to me. Whatever his motivations, the results were the same: terrible, miserable homesickness.

I hated leaving my parents, but also High Sunderland. It was like being kicked out of paradise. Beri and Peggy had woven together – whether they knew it or not – as perfect a world as was in their power to create, a world where order prevailed, beauty ruled, where everything, from what one wore to what one ate, read or looked at, was consciously thought about and chosen. Leaving all this behind came as a terrible shock, a feeling so physically painful it often felt as if my heart was being ripped out. Indeed, so horrific did the prospect of returning to school grow that it prompted one of the stupidest things I've ever done in my life.

Having endured the first term at boarding school and not wanting to return for a second term, I locked myself in my parents' bathroom then rifled through the cabinets until I found some pills, which I subsequently swallowed in handfuls. I don't believe I wanted to kill myself because I don't believe I knew what death really meant. I took them because I didn't want to leave home.

The pills seemed the ideal solution although, in the end, they only made me throw up. Ten minutes after taking them I vomited and then I vomited at ten-minute intervals for several hours until Peggy bundled me into the car and took me to Dr Murray. I never confessed what I'd done and in retrospect I think what I swallowed was most likely a combination of contraceptives together with a whole load of vitamin pills as these were pretty much the only tablets my mother ever kept in the bathroom.

Sadly, however, my 'stomach ache' did not get me anywhere and I continued at this boarding school for a couple more years after which I was sent to a larger one in Kent that I hated even more than the first.

So I ran away.

Twice.

After which in utter desperation Beri and Peggy enrolled me at the local comprehensive.

I didn't enjoy this school much either. Surly and hormonal, I took to spending more and more time in my bedroom, curtains drawn, making lists of all the things our house didn't possess such as no attic, no cellar, no letterbox, no upstairs or downstairs, no gutters or skirting boards ... And why – for heaven's sake – was there no door to my bedroom?

I hadn't worried about this at all, when the room was re-modelled, but at the age of thirteen I suddenly wanted privacy. Besides, what was I supposed to slam when I was angry?

A door was duly fitted, which – I'm ashamed to say – I slammed on a regular basis. Then, aged sixteen, being the contrary, spoilt child I was, I asked to go back to boarding school. Subsequently the middle bedroom was turned in to an enormous storeroom for Beri's paintings alongside hundreds of cones of knitting yarn. There was still a bed in the room, but it was stranded in a sea of mohair and oil paint and this is how it remained until, coming home to look after Beri, I made this space in to my 'living room'.

Adaptable, flexible, the See-Through House could be – and was – easily reconfigured. Yet the changes to the middle bedroom suggest more than this; they recognise that nothing stays the same for ever, that everything exists in a state of flux. Of all the spaces in the house, it is the middle bedroom that best reflects this aspect of life.

But what now?

What now that Beri is no longer alive and I live in the house by myself? The last time my father entered this particular room was about a week before he died.

I was lying on my couch when Beri came in to wish me goodnight.

BERI [glancing around him suspiciously]: I still don't understand –
SHELLEY: Understand what?
BERI: All this. I mean, wouldn't you be more comfortable in the *real* living room?
SHELLEY: This is real.
BERI: *Really*?
SHELLEY: I'm fine here –
BERI: If you say so –

But I could tell he wasn't convinced. After all, why would I be okay in a room furnished not only with a Victorian chair, but in recent weeks I'd bought a small Victorian desk that I'd smuggled into the house under a blanket. Beri, however, was no fool. He knew something was afoot and seconds after the desk's arrival he padded through to see for himself. Not that he said anything; he simply shook his head in the type of deep disappointment parents are prone to display when their offspring do something to let themselves down. How on earth could he have nurtured a child with such wayward tastes? How on earth could she have grown up in this beautiful house, yet still choose to bring home such a hideous item?

My living room, unlike the 'real' one, was a mystery to Beri, something incomprehensible, something he didn't want to acknowledge existed. It was like a bad dream or nightmare that, from the look on his face whenever he entered this room, he couldn't wake up from quickly enough.

Living Room

In one of his rare interviews, Peter Womersley was quoted as saying that he liked to treat the entire interior of the open-plan houses he designed, 'as far as practicable, as one entity, and the various rooms within [them] retaining their individuality by being arranged around natural visual obstacles – chimney stacks, stairwells, ranges of cupboards – which punctuate space and emphasise separation'.

Nowhere is this approach more apparent than in the See-Through House, for if you turn right as you enter the hallway and follow the flow of the building around, it leads you effortlessly into the main living area.

This is a space that condenses three rooms into one – a library, a dining room and a living room. 'There are no disturbing curves to upset the rectilinear austerity of the space. There is nothing convolute, involute, awkward or complex. Here everything is understood as a matter of proportion and dimension,' wrote Simon Mawer in his novel *The Glass Room* describing the fictional Landauer House, which was based on a real house, Mies van der Rohe's Villa Tugendhat, built in Brno in the Czech Republic in 1928. Mawer's fictional description of the glass room in Villa Tugendhat could equally describe High Sunderland's central living area, so precisely does it replicate it. Not that High Sunderland's living room, with its 'rectilinear austerity', isn't suffused with a sense of warmth, although in less expert hands than Womersley's it might well have felt very impersonal. Instead, what washes over you is a mixture of intimacy and calm.

You enter this room much like one might enter a swimming pool, that it to say by descending three shallow marble steps into a space measuring eight metres by five. Also, much like entering a pool, the room swims with light created for the most part because the entire

east-facing side of the space is constructed out of five floor-to-ceiling, single-ply sheets of clear glass. The effect this has on the viewer, especially on first entering the room, feels paradoxical because straightaway you are beckoned inside by having your gaze drawn outside.

Beech and pine trees sway gently against bright green lawns providing a backdrop of shivering emerald. This is a room in which to relax, in which you can float, in which you can allow your mind to drift and here, in turn, is another trick of the house in that during the day it expands to encompass the outside landscape while when night falls and the curtains are drawn, the house retracts, draws into itself and exudes only warmth.

Warmth is also achieved by the house's soft furnishings. Three cream-coloured sofas pebble-dashed with bright cushions are set against cream-coloured curtains whose froth-like weightlessness resembles foamy oceans of milk. The curtains bubble with sunshine, the trees glitter while the only other furniture in the room, two glass tables, reflect a white chimney stack floating above an open fireplace.

This stack or column dominates the living room, drawing the eye towards it principally, one feels, because it occupies such a large volume of space while at the same time remaining resolutely unadorned, a statement piece in and of itself. Whatever else is happening in the room by way of colour or ornament, this column remains unaffected. The only time this wasn't true was on those evenings when my brother used the column as a giant cinema screen on which to project Super 8 films he'd made of the family. Curtains drawn, lights dimmed, suddenly the chimney stack, smooth and white as a peppermint cream, would light up and flicker with granular Kodachrome images. Hot summer holidays spent in France, Christmas drinks parties, school fêtes, snowball fights, New Year's Eve walks and on one memorable occasion footage of a stoat killing a rabbit. But of all the films I remember, the ones that stand out most vividly are the *Bat Baby* chronicles. Each of these films was storyboarded by my brother, who cast me in the title role of Bat Baby while my sister played Robin and our maternal grandmother, Hilda Soper, played Cat Woman.

I loved watching these movies playing out against the chimney. Modernist houses make for ideal cinemas. Where else would you find enough empty wall space on which to project your material? But nowadays the whole of High Sunderland seems like a *tabula rasa* with my mind projecting memories everywhere.

Beri stands at his easel squeezing bright yellow oil paint on to a palette knife. Peggy sits by the fire reading a newspaper. Beri stands at the window observing a fox slip into the shadows. He watches as leaves scumble through the late-afternoon sunlight.

I also recall standing by these windows as a child with Beri beside me admiring the beech trees.

'Those leaves,' Beri explains as the trees shake and glister, 'are made up of hundreds and thousands of colours. They aren't just flat and green. Remember that. You have to look, really *look*, beyond what is there.'

I stare upwards at the toppling greens. There are not enough words to describe all the colours I'm seeing, let alone the ones I can't see.

'It's extraordinary,' Beri continues, 'how many colours a single blade of grass can contain, or a feather or pebble.'

I remember his words and I also remember how afterwards I stopped thinking of colour as something to be applied like nail varnish or paint. Instead, it was to be explored, entered into, felt. The world suddenly looked very different; it expanded and achieved unknown depths. Looking at yellow I discovered all kinds of words and emotions and sounds. Yellow was scrambled and fruity and lobed. It was soft, gassy and golden. Occasionally it was sluiced, frequently it was high-pitched, sometimes it was sour as lemons.

When I was older Beri and I would stand and admire the parrot tulips he planted each year. Like ice creams they glowed against the lawn, licks of pink adorned with cream ruffles, scarlet hussies streaked with thin bands of emerald, cones of what looked like coconut ice topped with pistachio glacé. If we could have eaten them, we would have gobbled them down. Instead, Beri would take out his paints and, over the years, he translated their shapes on to canvas via gobs of fat, juicy oil paint. To me Beri's hands were like jewel boxes from which he could conjure up rubies and sapphires.

His was a naïve, childlike joy in colour; a joy that possibly owed something to the agrarian society in which he grew up, for whenever he spoke or wrote about the Vojvodina, his reminiscences were always prefaced by a description of the colour of the dust or the hue of the acacias.

As children, Beri and Moshe enjoyed weekend trips to their maternal grandparents' (Sharlota and David Weiner's) farm that lay approximately eight miles outside the town of Senta. Here the two boys helped out with the horses as they ploughed the fields. The straighter the furrow the better the crop, or so their grandfather said, but more important to Beri was the joy he experienced as a pattern of ridges and troughs began to appear across the entire plain. In summer, when the crops were waist high, Beri watched the wind eddying across their surface creating reefs and ribs of ochre and gold; blood-orange sunsets and fields streaked with red poppies. Later, after the crops were harvested, he'd wait for the stubble to be burnt in order to watch the columns of blue-black smoke curling upwards forming vertical stripes across darkening skies.

The weekends Beri spent at the farm were among his favourite memories alongside reminiscences of his mother. With eyes closed he could describe Zori's face perfectly – her strawberry-blonde hair, her eyes the colour of sea glass, her mischievous smile. She had a heart-shaped face and, 'on the rare occasions when she attempted to control our wilder misdeeds we all soon ended up laughing for we knew that all we had to do to counter her stern mien was to look at her and smile and her anger would be gone'.

Rarely did my father speak of his mother without his facing lighting up. If Zori was in the room then all was right with the world. He also told me how he liked bringing his mother gifts from his adventures outdoors: a blue egg no bigger than a coat button, a fistful of windflowers, a pebble gold as a cat's eye.

This idyllic existence came to an end, however, when Beri turned fourteen. Lipot had decided that his eldest son should be sent to a larger yeshiva in Galanta, Czechoslovakia. The regime at the school was strict. Pupils had to be up at 5 a.m. and studied until 7a.m., at which point the more pious amongst them took a cold shower before attending prayers led by the rabbi that could last over one and a half hours. Breakfast followed, after which there would be lectures (with a short break for lunch) until around 5 p.m. More prayers were said before supper and they were in bed by 10 p.m. Schools such as this – noted Beri later in life – served a precise purpose in that they were only concerned with the preservation of Judaism. As such the hours of study were confined not only to reading the Talmud, but also the hundreds of thousands of commentaries that had been written by former scholars with reference to each sentence in the Talmud. As Beri later expounded, 'This mental honing produced razor-sharp minds exercised in counting the number of feathers in an archangel's wings glimpsed in rapid flight, but minds ignorant of the atom or the molecule. It produced men capable of sustained and concentrated mental effort concerning the hidden meaning of a single sentence [...] yet incapable of writing simply and grammatically in any language; for they had never heard of grammar, not even of Hebrew grammar.'

But these insights into what my father perceived as Judaism's shortcomings came much later in life. At the time, as he himself admitted, he was far more preoccupied being homesick. He missed his friends and his parents and in particular Zori, who'd packed him off to the yeshiva with several sets of extremely smart suits the colour and fabric of which he could still recall almost thirty years later. 'I arrived [at the yeshiva] in a Donegal tweed suit of predominately brown knops and green specks on a light beige ground, matched naturally by a brown tie, shoes and trilby hat. The overcoat was also unusual, a rough-textured heavy herringbone in shades of navy and lighter blues.' Nor were Beri's memories of clothing confined to what he wore, for he clearly recalled Zori's outfits in great detail too. The ploughed browns of a winter skirt. Greenish-gold dresses and blouses with pearlescent buttons.

Beri could feel colour much like the Hungarian André Kertész expressed textures in his early black-and-white photographs depicting the peasants and landscapes of the Hungarian Plain. Kertész showed the grain of wood, the pattern of cobbles, whereas Beri translated the landscapes of his childhood into some of his brightest, boldest tweeds, fabrics that combined the rolling oranges and ochres of the fields at harvest time with paprika-hot reds and dark pickled greens. Not that the landscape of the Borders didn't influence Beri too. It did and in no small measure. The churning pinks and golds of a copper beech spiked by spring sunshine. The hard cobalt blues of an evening hike around St Mary's Loch, shots of drenched violet across the hills above Ettrick. Beri saw and *felt* colour everywhere. And this way of seeing affected how he painted. For example, he never just replicated a tulip, but instead wanted to capture its burn and flare. I have one of these paintings on my wall now – a jug of insanely yellow tulips. I gaze at it and feel my father is in the room with me. He *is* in the room with me. Parrot tulips were his favourite flower, their splashes of colour, sometimes subtle, frequently vibrant. When he died there was no question we would place anything else on his coffin. Several of his closest friends also sent large bouquets of parrot tulips because, as one of them put it, 'no other flowers would do'.

Anyone who has ever experienced the loss of someone they love will know how heavily grief is freighted with a whole range of emotions: guilt, anger, love, regret – they all feature at some point, usually in a giant smash-up that leaves you feeling numb or conversely as if you've swallowed barbed wire.

After my mother died, I recall friends asking what it was like, as if I were a traveller exploring debatable lands.

But it was impossible to describe.

No words were remotely adequate.

I thought of the moon with its Sea of Crisis and Lake of Fear. It was easier naming places a million miles away than trying to communicate the intricacies of bereavement.

Nor did my father speak very much about the effect my mother's death had on him. Beri and Peggy had been married fifty-seven years and had known each other approximately six years before that, so what was there to say? What words could encompass the depth and breadth of such loss? Instead, Beri seemed to mark Peggy's death by all the things he stopped doing. He no longer bought flowers for the house (something that had given him pleasure every week of the year for as long as I could remember), he stopped reading books because the person he wanted to share them with was no longer there and he stopped painting for similar reasons.

Death is bewildering, grief equally so, but as humans we've become deft at avoiding our suffering. No one actively enjoys feeling sad. Almost all of us shy away from physical and emotional pain. But this is the contradiction of grief, that in order to process it, we need to live with the discomfort and feel the disorientation of which it is part.

This thought overlaps with another. In a letter to his brothers, George and Tom, the poet John Keats coined the phrase 'Negative Capability' and wrote that ' . . . that is when man is capable of being in uncertainties, Mysteries, doubts, without any irritable reaching after fact & reason.' Being capable of 'being in uncertainties' rather than struggling against them seems impossible in a world where we treat uncertainty as the enemy and shore ourselves up against it with work, alcohol, drugs, amongst other things.

After Peggy's death, whisky became my best friend. I relied on it to numb the pain and help me to sleep. But when Beri died, things were different. A few days after the funeral, once my brother, sister and friends had finally left to go back to their own homes, I lay on a couch in the living room terrified to move, petrified of confronting Beri's absence yet at the same time reassured by the fact he was every-where around me. Confusingly that which I was finding most painful was also that which was of most comfort. For days, or so it seemed, I stayed in the living room absorbing my surroundings, running my hands across tables and shelves. The room looked like my father, sounded like him, felt like him; was the closest I could get to Beri now that he was no longer alive.

'Is it not possible,' wrote Virginia Woolf, 'that things we have felt with great intensity have an existence independent of our minds; are in fact still in existence?' In this sense perhaps Beri does still exist? Per-haps all the intense experiences of his life are still present within this room and these are what I am touching. For instance, the chair in which he sat shell-shocked after Peggy's death; maybe that chair absorbed his devastation? Or the spot in which he stood year after year in front of his easel; perhaps that space is infused with his frus-trations and joy?

These were the thoughts that whizzed through my mind hour after hour, day after day, as I lay in the living room. I watched as the sun scattered shadows across the glazed marble. I watched the flames in the fireplace. I listened to the ticking of the clock and asked myself: why do I feel so cheated? Am I grieving for myself or for Beri? I told myself that he was ninety-one years old; he'd led a fulfilling life, a life filled with achievements. So why did I want to curl up and die when I knew he would have given anything to carry on living?

I couldn't see any future. It was April and the leaves outside were just beginning to unfurl, the daffodils about to split open. This was the start of a new year; everything was bursting with the present, yet all I could think of was the past.

> BERI [beckoning Shelley towards the living room with urgent hand gestures]: Come! Come and look at this –
> SHELLEY [only half awake]: Can I make myself a coffee first?
> BERI: It won't take a minute –
> SHELLEY [groggily following her father into the living room where he stops and stares through the window]: I can't see anything – what are you looking at?
> BERI: There! Look! They're doing it deliberately! There were none there last night and see now –
> SHELLEY [resigned]: You're talking moles again, aren't you?
> BERI: It's incredible! Look how many fields they have to run around in, but no! They choose our garden –
> SHELLEY: It's a Moley War!
> BERI: Not funny.
> SHELLEY: It is ... a little bit –

Beri makes an indescribable harrumphing sound. Over the years he has tried to remove the moles from our garden with just about every gadget imaginable: traps, gas, windmills, poison – even some odd-looking contraption Peggy bought from the *Innovations* catalogue that came free with the *Sunday Times* magazine that is supposed to emit a high-pitch whining noise that moles dislike, although our moles must have rather enjoyed it as the molehills began multiplying rapidly.

In fact, it is not so much moles Beri dislikes as these hills. They are untidy and disrupt the natural flow of the lawns. There are no flower-beds in the garden at High Sunderland, no herbaceous borders, no benches to sit on or hanging baskets. Instead (with the exception of the springtime tulips under the beech trees) the acres of lawn look if not neat then at least uninterrupted. Only Beri never factored in the presence of molehills, which he takes very personally.

Seconds after our conversation, Beri removes himself to the garden. Sporting a white woolly hat that stands bolt upright making him look like the Pope, he also wears sunglasses and a pair of bright yellow rubber gloves. He couldn't find a trowel in the shed so in his right hand he is brandishing a large serving spoon while in his left is a mole trap. I sit drinking my coffee watching him dig. He knows I am finding it funny and in a way I think he finds it funny too. There is no way he will ever win out against the enemy. Fifty-six years of experience have taught him that. I remember the time when I was about thirteen or fourteen years old and we owned a large ginger cat (chosen by my father specifically because the colour of his fur complemented the furnishings). The cat was called Krampusz, which in Hungarian means 'devil'. One day Krampusz brought a live mole into the house and proudly deposited it on the living-room floor. I remember that for the first five minutes or so, Beri was intrigued by the creature, fascinated by this plump little fellow's velvety body, although he wouldn't touch it or go too close as he had a phobia of mice and all things mousy. So I put on some thick leather gloves and picked the mole up.

It was exquisite. I was mesmerised – so much so that I failed to notice Krampusz about to take a giant leap from the sideboard on to my back in a bid to regain his dinner. As Krampusz's claws dug into my shoulders I screamed and let go of the mole, which flumped to the floor and, in a desperate bid to escape, found its way to a corner of the living room where it began digging. Seconds later it had dug its way through the carpet. This is when I remember Beri ordering me to pick the mole up before it dug under the house.

'It'll ruin the foundations,' he shouted. 'Why did you drop it? We'll have molehills in the middle of the living room!'

These are the memories I played with while I sat in this room in the weeks and months after Beri's death. The past became something solid. A thing I could touch. A thing I could punch or sink into or push up against like a wall. The past was so real I could sit there watching myself as a child, bouncing up and down on the sofas, giggling at something my mother or father had said, while the present was so unreal I could barely recall what I had done only moments before.

Friends and family phoned on a regular basis.

What have you been up to today?

Have you eaten something?

What's the weather like there?

Have you taken Henry for his walk yet?

But I couldn't remember the last time that I had got up from the couch let alone taken my dog out. I must have done, but the present was slippery, it kept evading my grasp. It was like a stone sinking to the bottom of a pond while the past rose up from the mud, not Excalibur, but a kaleidoscope of everything that had gone before.

Weeks and months went by and summer arrived. Before Beri died I had booked to go on holiday with a friend to an island off the coast of Sicily, but when the moment for departure arrived, I felt physically sick, most probably because, ever since childhood, departures from High Sunderland have been linked in my mind with boarding school. Even as an adult I have stood in our hallway, tears coursing down my face and, as my parents grew older, these partings grew increasingly difficult. Mum and Dad would stand arm in arm in the doorway, smiling and waving, while I crossed the courtyard before climbing into a taxi, all the time wondering if this might be the last time I would see one or other of them alive.

Mercifully, going on holiday was not the same as being sent away to school. Even so, as the date of departure grew closer, I couldn't bear the thought of leaving the house unattended because Beri – or so I felt – would be lonely. I knew my father was dead yet the thought kept haunting me that Beri would feel abandoned and upset at being left on his own and so eventually – on the pretext of security – I asked a friend to look after the place while I was gone. But even with this friend in situ, these feelings did not abate. I loved being in Sicily, waking up to the sound of the waves crashing against the rocks, watching as the sun went down on the blue and pink fishing boats, but at the same time I yearned to get back to High Sunderland, yearned to keep the house company, cook meals, light the fire.

On the third or fourth day, my friend and I hired bicycles and headed out of town, following a road that took us across mile after mile of windswept countryside. Scraps of litter blew under our wheels. Occasionally we came across a building or two consisting of nothing more than a few concrete slabs and piles of weed-ridden rubble. Then, halfway around the island, a hot sea wind began to get up that made it impossible to go anywhere quickly. Not a great cyclist at the best of times, the more I pedalled against this wind the more exhausted I grew and the more exhausted I grew the more desolate and rocky the landscape became. I felt as if I were in *L'Avventura*, Antonioni's bleak film about a woman who goes missing during a boat trip to the barren Aeolian Islands. In that instant I wanted to go missing too. I did not want to be there. I did not want to be anywhere. Except home.

I returned to High Sunderland a few days later, but the barren, rocky landscape didn't disappear. Nor did the sensation of needing to move forward only to feel myself standing still. I dreamt of trying to run up hills, but found my legs turned to stumps. I dreamt of house fires and of getting lost in the woods – all of which were completely unoriginal themes. I also dreamt of walking through one of our plate-glass windows although the glass didn't shatter. I had passed through it as if I didn't exist.

Not existing was a feeling with which Beri was also very familiar. By 1938, having spent two years studying in Galanta, Lipot decided his eldest son was to continue his studies even further afield, this time in Jerusalem where he would be taught by the chief rabbi of the city, Yosef Tzvi Dushinsky. Beri was given no choice in the matter. There was no question of disobeying his father, no question of Beri staying at home despite his longing to do so. Burying his feelings was the only way to survive. So he did. He pushed all his misgivings and panic at being sent so far away from home as deep down as he could. Somewhere they couldn't be seen. Out of sight, out of mind, as it were. Besides, the decision to send him to Jerusalem was, he concluded later in life, more than likely influenced by two major factors.

Firstly the events taking place in Europe during that period, which included not only the annexation of Austria by Germany in 1938 but later that same year of the Sudetenland – neither of which augured well. Secondly Lipot, who had served in the trenches during the First World War on the Austro-Hungarian side, nevertheless felt he and his family would always be treated as second-class citizens. 'Lipot made it very clear,' my father said, 'that as Jews, we could not expect equality no matter how we behaved in the service of the country and that therefore we should, among other withdrawals from the national community, avoid military service if at all possible.'

Goodbyes are rarely if ever easy and this one – because it was to be a separation of at least two to three years – was more difficult than most. In particular, Zori found the idea of her eldest child being sent so far away from home almost unbearable, so she insisted that rather than living in the yeshiva, Beri was to board and take all of his meals with the rabbi's own family, becoming, so to speak, part of his household.

Zori also made sure that Beri took certain items with him from home. This included a framed family portrait of herself and Lipot

Zori, Moshe, Beri and Lipot, c. 1930

with Beri and Moshe sitting in between them and a second item, a blue and white cotton counterpane, which up until this point had always decorated her bed.

Finally, in December 1938, Lipot and Beri set out on the long journey south, first by Soviet ship to Piraeus then on to Haifa and from Haifa by car through the hills to an area of central Jerusalem called Mea Shearim.

Mea Shearim was (and remains to this day) the ultra-Orthodox Jewish courtyard neighbourhood of western Jerusalem. Consisting of a labyrinthine network of shabby alleyways and streets, small quads housed different Jewish communities according to the inhabitants' country of origin, that is to say there was a Hungarian courtyard, a Rumanian courtyard, a Polish courtyard. But although each quad was divided by country, what bound this district together was religion. '[...] in the middle of this new country,' wrote Gabriele Tergit in 1938, 'lies an island of eternal Judaism, of two-thousand-year-old Judaism: the ghetto of Jerusalem, Mea Shearim. Wall-like buildings and gates, always prepared for attack. Prayer house after prayer house. Life was nothing but an interruption from prayer and the study of the Talmud.'

Mea Shearim was not a wealthy district and Beri recalled it having what he called a 'gravy-brown' odour from all the different cooking pots on the go, mixed together with the smell of gas and pickled vegetables. Each courtyard also had a water pump at its centre from which the women could fill their buckets and drinking vessels every morning and night. Washing was hung out to dry on long strings that zigzagged from building to building. Most families lived squeezed together in one or two rooms that meant each room had to double up as a bedroom. So cramped were the living conditions, they came as a shock to the young newcomer who many years later wrote about his first impressions saying that it felt as if he had travelled back to the Poland or Russia of the eighteenth or nineteenth centuries.

This impression was informed mainly by the way in which the Jews of Mea Shearim dressed. Even the ultra-Orthodox Jews in Senta didn't wear such old-fashioned garments, whereas here the men all wore the tall, fur hats that Russian noblemen used to wear, they had long black overcoats, black buckle shoes, white stockings and flowered, eighteenth-century waistcoats. In the heat of a hot Jerusalem summer, beads of sweat trickled down their foreheads. The children too were dressed in eighteenth-century garb, the little girls in long brown smocks while the boys wore black, knee-length trousers and white tights and all had the telltale pe'ot or long twisted locks of hair at either side of the face.

Beri stood out like a sore thumb. Wearing the type of suits that wouldn't have looked out of place in any European city of the period, within Mea Shearim his clothes showed him up as an outsider. Only when he walked through the more cosmopolitan districts of central Jerusalem did he feel less conspicuous.

Nor were the shops within Mea Shearim less restrictive. There were bookshops, but they offered only religious texts; there were food shops, but they sold only kosher food, and the few clothes shops that existed were confined to selling traditional garments. Slowly Beri began to feel not just physically uncomfortable, but something more than this.

Confusion?

Uncertainty?

Disillusionment?

He could not put his finger on it because, for the time being at least, he was as serious and religious a young man as any of his fellow students, added to which he wanted more than anything else to make his family proud. But it was a struggle. Beri dreamt a lot about Senta during this period. He was back in his own bedroom, back in his own bed from where at night he could hear the Paris-to-Bucharest train trundling across the bridge. But when he got up and went through to the rest of the house, Lipot and Zori didn't recognise him. They kept saying he was a stranger. That he didn't belong. Beri would wake up sweating and disorientated, not knowing quite where he was, in what room or city.

His mattress smelt of mice. And the rabbi's wife wasn't a very good cook. Added to which his studies were dull. Everything depended on what the words said. But the words had to be dissected, split, broadened, diminished. One interpretation overlapped with another. Ambiguities and clarifications, regulations and explanations, until all of a sudden, Beri felt consumed by a never-ending ocean of text. He needed an escape and so, hesitantly at first and then with increasing confidence, he began slipping out of the yeshiva, skipping lectures in order to walk around the 'other' Jerusalem, the wider city with its Arab and Christian quarters, its extravagant food markets, hotels and bookshops.

> BERI: I began to feel as if I didn't exist – that all I was was a conduit for ... I just began to feel a strong antipathy towards ...
> SHELLEY: Towards?
> BERI [shaking his head]: It's difficult to explain – towards religion ... towards Judaism. The way it percolated ... ruled every aspect of my life. You can't mix this with that, you can't harness animals together of two different kinds – an ox and a donkey, you can't cook or eat meat with dairy, you can't wear fabric composed of both wool and linen –
> SHELLEY: Why on earth not?
> BERI: I don't know ... it's something to do with not wanting to imitate non-Jews, with wanting to keep things unsullied, separate –

But the real separation, the one that really counted and meant something, was the one between Beri and the family back in Yugoslavia.

A few months before Beri died, a journalist visited High Sunderland to interview my father and brought with her her six-year-old son, who was about to be sent to his grandparents in Switzerland for seven to eight weeks.

'And how do you feel about that, Max?' Beri asked, smiling at the boy gently.

The little boy frowned and then gripped hold of his mother's hand.

I watched him do this and I also watched how Beri nodded as if acknowledging something.

Looking at Max's mother he said, 'You'll be visiting him regularly, though, won't you?'

'No,' she replied. 'It's not possible – I've been asked to do a lecture tour in the States for a book I've just finished and my partner can't look after Max either. But he'll be fine,' she added. 'He loves my parents and the time will pass very quickly.'

Again Beri looked at Max and, in turn, Max looked at Beri.

'So it's very important to keep contact; you must ring him every day,' Beri said, as if handing out an instruction rather than forwarding friendly advice, so much so, in fact, that the journalist looked somewhat affronted. Then Beri changed the subject and asked what Max thought of the house.

The little boy smiled. 'I love it,' he said. 'It's an inside-out house. I can touch the trees if I want to.'

'Let's go for a walk then,' Beri said, holding his hand out and then – over his shoulder to the journalist – 'We can talk later.'

The interview did take place, but it was perfunctory. It wasn't so much that my father had taken a dislike to the journalist, needs must and all that, but there was something in Max's predicament that I knew made Beri if not sad, then thoughtful. Besides which, Max's comment about High Sunderland being an 'inside-out' house had impressed Beri for whether Max knew it or not, he had just described not only the precise nature of High Sunderland, but also the contradictory nature of glass, that it is both here and not here at the same time, an invisible substance that makes other things visible. In relation to the house and to my father, this strikes me as profoundly appropriate because Beri's entire career was predicated on looking – so much so that when he came to write a book explaining how he designed, he called it *Eye for Colour*. The See-Through House was also the lens through which Beri viewed the entire world or, to put it another way, it was a mode of perception as well as a piece of architecture.

Nowhere, according to Beri, was more beautiful or more comfortable than High Sunderland. Nowhere gave him the same degree of pleasure or could complement his designs architecturally. Other houses were compared and contrasted with this one, but consistently fell short. Art, literature, music – everything had to be pared back, had to be unfussy, uncomplicated. But if the See-Through House was the lens through which Beri saw and judged the world, to me its glass walls offered the perfect conduit for daydreaming.

Often I sit in this room and feel my mind floating outside, drifting off into one hundred and one different places. Gaston Bachelard in his book *The Poetics of Space* declares that 'inhabited space transcends geometrical space'; in other words, inhabited space has all the elasticity of the human mind, which constantly blooms outwards far and beyond the bony vessel containing it. Glass too surpasses its own, unyielding surface. In this respect the See-Through House is a direct descendent of Villa Tugendhat where trees and sky rather than bricks and mortar act as boundaries. At High Sunderland the lawns and trees rather than stonework mark the house's perimeter. The whole mood and character of the place depends on the trajectory of the sun, on whether it is morning or evening, autumn or winter, fine weather or foul. Nature and the Scottish countryside are the house's interior designers.

I am sitting in front of the open log fire in the living room. The landscape outside is wet and smoky with the angular shapes of branches transposed on to the living-room walls like arboreal wallpaper. The sun slips out from behind a bank of grey clouds and the wallpaper explodes with raindrops. The trees seem more like chandeliers than living organisms. The branches glister. Rain sluices the windowpanes and the interior walls of the room grow fluid as interior and exterior blend into one.

Over the years I have sat here and watched deer wander through this inside-out room, their supple bodies quivering as they bend their heads to nibble the grass. I have spied red squirrels climbing the curtains, swinging across rich, golden leaf-patterns. Pheasants, bedecked in every shade of autumn, sit like scatter cushions on couches of moss. In summer, swallows and house martins skim the ceilings; in winter, the full moon lies brooding in the corner next to the TV – a celestial sculpture.

An owl fell down our chimney once. Fat as Father Christmas, it landed in the fireplace with a dull thud, none the worse for its sooty descent although noticeably dazed. Much to my sister's horror, for she had a fear of all things flappy, my father gently scooped up the owl and together we carried it outside. I can still recall its stone-gold eyes and when I touched it, the mothy softness of its breast. It came from another world.

In summer when the glass walls were slid back, birds and butterflies flew in to the living room only to become trapped. I found a pheasant in the hallway once, contentedly pecking the marble floor, and one night three toads flopped into my bedroom.

Then there were the bats.

A few years ago, when Beri was still alive, some of his friends came around for afternoon tea. We were mid discussion about Gordon Brown's efforts to dissuade Scotland from voting 'Yes' to separation from the rest of the UK when to my horror I spotted a tiny, walnut-shaped object clinging to the curtains directly above the head of one of our elderly, female guests.

> BERI: What do you keep staring at?
> SHELLEY [quietly, not wishing to cause alarm]: A bat.
> BERI [turning around and squinting up at the curtains]: A cat?
> SHELLEY [whispering]: A bat. 'B' as in Brown.
> FIRST GUEST: Very moody man –
> SECOND GUEST: What about Sturgeon?
> BERI [still peering up at the curtains]: Why are we talking about fish?
> SHELLEY [whispering more loudly]: No, it's a BAT.

After everyone had gone I found a ladder and climbed up towards the furry gargoyle, only to discover it was dead. We had a dead bat. This appalled Beri even more than the fact that the creature was there in the first place.

> SHELLEY: It must have been in the folds of the curtain. Hidden from view –
> BERI: You don't clean properly, that's the trouble –
> SHELLEY: Who looks upwards when they're cleaning?
> BERI: People who care.

But perhaps the strangest creature to enter High Sunderland arrived just a few months after my father died.

A 'vulture'.

It was his eyes I noticed first. They were cold, emotionless, greedy. This hook-necked scavenger sat in the living room as if he owned it, as if he had every right to be there in order to pick the flesh off my bones.

That morning it had taken me more than two hours to get out of bed. I had not wanted to wake up, had lain with my eyes tightly shut, aware only of wave after wave of anxiety washing over my head. When I did finally open my eyes it was to stare at the ceiling, willing myself to fall back to sleep. That was all I wanted. Oblivion; non-thinking, un-breathing oblivion because even the simplest tasks felt insurmountable. Brushing my teeth. Showering. There was no point to any of it. Outside everywhere was cold and grey and when I eventually left the house to walk Henry, the wind cut my face.

If you're one of those people who read a lot, you'll have noticed the frequent use writers make of the landscape to reflect their characters' moods. It's a useful literary trope. When Tess falls in love with Angel, for instance, she conveniently does so in the lush, over-ripe surroundings of the Frome Valley. By contrast when Angel abandons Tess, she ends up digging potatoes in the rain-lashed fields of Flint-comb-Ash.

On the morning the vulture descended, the woods and fields surrounding High Sunderland were my Flintcomb-Ash. Saucers of ice creaked and burst underfoot. I looked towards the hills. They were looped with wreaths of mist. I clambered over a fence, all claws of barbed wire that ripped not only my jacket but also the back of my shin. Blood soaked into my jeans. Even the sight of Henry jumping up and down as if on pneumatic springs could not make me smile. The effort of putting one foot in front of the other seemed impossible and more than once I thought about lying down in the hope that I would be encased in a thick overcoat of ice so cold it would numb the pain.

Half an hour later I found myself back at the house. I made a mug of coffee, wanting more than anything else to climb back into bed. But

I couldn't because I had visitors coming, a man and his daughter who had phoned earlier in the week wanting to buy some of my father's work. Although a textile designer by trade, Beri had painted on and off from his early twenties, finding a symbiotic relationship existed between the two disciplines. The one fed in to the other so that embedded within many of Beri's paintings lie swatches of fabric while the fabrics and the yarns were frequently inspired by colours he had experimented with within his art. Reflecting on the importance of this interwoven relationship alongside the rejuvenating qualities of painting itself, Beri once wrote: 'To reactivate my faculties I started to paint again and continued to think of my new cloth. Indeed I could not help but think of it for as I painted the gentle Border countryside in the spring, absorbed the blue evenings of its late summers, caught my breath at the indescribable richness of its clear coppery autumn and finally brooded along with it in its morbid winters I kept on seeing everything in terms of colour and cloth. Colour was all around me, pursuing me, cajoling me, asking to be admitted into my life and the lives of many others.'

For the most part Beri worked in oils and, apart from a few brief years in the Nineties when he concentrated exclusively on still life, landscapes and a few interiors, his work was almost entirely abstract. Occasionally he'd sell a painting; there was a small group of collectors who appreciated his work, the succulent pigments, the saturated reds and drenched blues. Not that Beri's work had a market value, he was not a well-known artist, but to his family and this small band of collectors the paintings had worth.

I was still feeling the same dread dullness after my walk as I had when I'd awoken that morning. I couldn't shake it off, for despite going through all this after Peggy died, what little I'd learnt back then by way of coping amounted to nothing now. The pain was not more or less excruciating; it was simply different. It had its own torments and horrors. Julian Barnes describes grief as if you've been thrown out of an aircraft and 'suddenly come down in the freezing German Ocean, equipped only with an absurd cork overjacket that is supposed to keep you alive. [...] you can never prepare for this new reality in which you have been dunked.' You cannot get your bearings. Your compass – in this case my father – had disappeared and I felt as if I was stranded in the 'freezing German Ocean' not knowing which way to turn. Leastways this goes some way to describing how I felt the morning the vulture descended.

He arrived at 11 a.m. I opened the door to him. That's how vultures gain entrance; they walk in through your front door. I showed him and his daughter the twenty or so paintings I had laid out for him to choose from. His unblinking, vulturey eyes barely glanced at them.

VULTURE: How much for the lot?

SHELLEY [flustered]: They vary from about £6,000 down to about £500 or so depending on—

VULTURE: Those are gallery prices – they're not worth a tenth of that.

SHELLEY: It's what the family wants –

VULTURE: I'm telling you they're not worth it. I'll take the lot off your hands, but I'm talking hundreds not thousands.

SHELLEY [beginning to shake slightly as she feels her flesh being attacked]: This isn't a house clearance –

VULTURE: Are you planning on staying here?

SHELLEY [blood begins to pool on the floor]: Currently I'm—

VULTURE: If you want to sell it, I'll buy it. Needs work, of course. What was it valued at?

SHELLEY: That's private –

VULTURE [staring round the room]: Needs thousands spent on it –

SHELLEY: But I'm not moving –

The vulture shifts in his chair.

> VULTURE'S DAUGHTER: It's a beautiful room, very warm –
> SHELLEY: I love this room. I think the architect was very clever to make such an open space so intimate –
> VULTURE: It's derivative –
> SHELLEY: Everyone's influenced by someone ... Peter would have been the first to admit he admired Frank Lloyd Wright, Mies van der Rohe –
> VULTURE [swiftly changing the subject]: That's a Poul Kjærholm in the hallway, isn't it?
> SHELLEY: Yes –
> VULTURE: How much for that?
> SHELLEY: Nothing.
> VULTURE [frowning]
> SHELLEY: It's not for sale.
> VULTURE: Pity –

But the real pity was I did not demand the vulture leave the house immediately. Instead, I was politeness itself while inwardly I was screaming, FUCK OFF, FUCK OFF, FUCK OFF! Eventually they did fuck off, but the vulture couldn't resist a parting shot.

> VULTURE: I'm sorry you didn't get £50,000 out of me –
> SHELLEY: I wasn't trying to fleece you –

Quite the contrary, it was the vulture who was trying to fleece me. I closed the front door and went and sat down in the living room. I felt raw, exposed and achingly sad. I wanted Beri. I wanted to put my arms around him, or more precisely, I wanted him to put his arms around me. But Beri was dead and tears rolled down my cheeks. I took a deep breath and drank in the quiet of the room. Another deep breath and my ribcage expanded as if the room and I were one.

I have always thought this room the perfect space for meditation. There is something profoundly calm about it as well as kind. Can you say that about a room? That it is kind? I can say that about this room. His room.

Originally the living room boasted a wooden floor beneath which was laid – as it was throughout the house – under-floor heating. Extraordinary as it seems now, back in the late Fifties energy was cheap; not only that, it was believed it would only grow cheaper thanks to nuclear power. Walking into our house was like arriving in the tropics. The heat enveloped you. The floors were a living creature, their surface warm as skin. If windows are the eyes of a house, floors are its flanks. Even as an adult I love lying down on them, find comfort in the way the heat seeps through my body.

My childhood friends loved these floors too, especially during the cold winter months when they could remove their shoes and socks and feel the warmth caressing their toes. Most of these children lived in old stone houses where most of the heat escaped out of ill-fitting windows or attics that hadn't been insulated. Their parents would swaddle them in thermal knickers, thick woollen jumpers, cardies and socks. I recall one girl whose feet and hands were swollen and cracked with chilblains from November to May every year. Her parents hardly if ever switched the heating on in their house because, even at full blast, it made no difference.

High Sunderland's under-floor heating therefore assumed legendary status and was as foreign to my friends as my father was with his gentle, Herbert Lom accent or his collection of bizarrely shaped cacti that swelled and bloomed at the opposite end of the living room in a purpose-built, marble trough. Not that as children we spent a great deal of time in the living room. For one thing we had our playroom, but more significant than this, the couches (that were designed by Womersley specifically for High Sunderland) were so uncomfortable that it was almost impossible to lounge on them or sit by the fireplace with even a modicum of ease.

Of course, as deprivations go, being made to suffer uncomfortable furniture is not up there with malnourishment or homelessness. But as a symbol of both the good and less good aspects of living in a modernist building, the couches are a perfect example.

> TEENAGE SHELLEY: Couldn't we replace them with something more comfortable, less narrow perhaps?
> BERI: They're fine as they are. They're extremely beautiful.
> TEENAGE SHELLEY: But they're not relaxing. You have to admit that at least?
> BERI [shaking his head at his daughter's failure to grasp the significance of good design]: They were designed by Peter. You couldn't ask for more beautiful items of furniture –
> TEENAGE SHELLEY: That doesn't make them comfortable.
> BERI: But it would make me uncomfortable if we replaced them with something else.

And it would. It most definitely would have upset my father's sense of how things should look if we had gone out and purchased some big squishy things on which to wallow.

An earlier bone of contention when it came to the living room was the Christmas tree. I've never asked either my brother or sister what they felt as children regarding this subject, but for me, as a small child and later as a stroppy teenager, it was a travesty, for every year I pleaded with Beri to grant the tree entry into this room and every year the answer came back a resounding 'NO'.

During Beri's childhood the only celebratory festival during the long winter months was Hanukah – the Jewish Festival of Light. But given that by the time Beri was living in Scotland he had turned his back not only on Judaism but on all religions, it was little wonder that Christmas and by association Christmas trees (not that these have anything to do with religion) were not to his liking.

> CHILD SHELLEY: Why can't we just try it? You never know, you might find it looks good.
> BERI: It won't –
> CHILD SHELLEY: Please?
> BERI: If you really want a tree, have one in your playroom. That's what it's there for – to fill up with things you like.
> CHILD SHELLEY [whining]: But we don't unwrap our presents in the playroom. We unwrap them in the living room and our presents should be under the tree.
> BERI: Why should they?
> CHILD SHELLEY: Because that's where everyone puts them –
> BERI: We're not everyone –
> CHILD SHELLEY: I know we're not, because they'll have a great Christmas and we'll –
> BERI: Sweetie pie, stop being so silly –
> CHILD SHELLEY: But the tree would look really pretty in the living room –
> BERI: It disturbs everything –

I didn't understand.

'Disturb' was a word one used if one felt upset or perturbed and to my childish mind Christmas trees could not cause either of the above. Far from it, they were one of the prettiest things on earth, all fairy-tale colours mixed up with tinsel and green and pink lights. What on earth was so disturbing about that?

But no amount of cajoling could persuade my father he was in the wrong, nor would Peggy intervene. Instead, she made certain that we enjoyed wonderful Christmases with all the trimmings, including the most beautiful tree in our playroom. Unlike other children, she would point out, Gillian and I could enjoy looking at the tree from our bedrooms and fall asleep watching the lights.

Yet despite the joy of this magical sight, I never relinquished the 'Battle of the Christmas Tree' and over the years I did achieve small victories.

One year I succeeded in getting the tree as far as the hallway. I was about fifteen years old by then and no doubt my father, worn down by years of hearing me moan on and on, gave in just enough for the tree to come within twenty yards of where I thought it roughly belonged.

Another time I managed to get the tree erected outside in the front courtyard overlooking the living room. A single pane of glass separated us from it: surely this would be as good as having the tree adorning the living room itself? But it was a disaster because the only decorations I could use were garish red and blue waterproof light bulbs so in the end it didn't appeal at all.

Only when Beri was in his late eighties and I had returned home to live with him, did I at last succeed in my mission.

> BERI [in a resigned voice]: Anyone who puts up an argument for nearly fifty years should win at least once.
> SHELLEY: That's very generous of you –
> BERI: It is, isn't it?
> SHELLEY: I was being sarcastic –
> BERI: I know you were –
> SHELLEY: Oh –

BERI: Actually, it really looks quite nice –
SHELLEY: Seriously?
BERI [with a twinkle in his eye and snorting at his own joke]:
No, I was being sarcastic.

Despite, however, being desperately disadvantaged in both Christmas tree and sofa departments, neither detracted from my love for this room. And, as I've grown older, this love has only deepened. Womersley's skill at redefining the word 'room' using only invisible prompts is, at least to my untrained eye, a kind of alchemy.

Over the years surprisingly little, if anything, has been written about Womersley's professional or personal life. In fact, most of what is known about him comes from a paper he delivered at the Royal Institute of British Architects in January 1969, which was subsequently printed in their journal. In it we catch a fleeting glimpse of Peter's father opposing his son's 'architectural aspirations' – a stance echoed by Peter's headmaster – after which Peter was bundled off to an occupational psychiatrist in London for three days' worth of tests for no other reason than that, in Peter's own words, 'he was a difficult child' – that is to say he wanted to do something of which his father strongly disapproved. Unsurprisingly the psychiatrist agreed with Womersley Snr and 'diagnosed a lawyer, a solicitor, or an economist – but, alas, no signs of an approach to architecture'.

With no other choice, Womersley knuckled down to his exams and won a scholarship to Cambridge University to study law, but this had to be postponed due to the intervention of the war. Consequently the next five years were 'spent ingloriously in sundry English watering places, ostensibly as an infantryman, but actually making good my educational deficiencies. Five years of hard cultural square-bashing during the war got me through the AA [Architectural Association] entrance exam at the ripe old age of 23.'

At this point I'd like to ask Peter what this 'cultural square-bashing' consisted of, what was he reading, for instance? What buildings might he have visited and been influenced by? Museums? Art galleries? But of course I can't because Peter died many years ago. Instead, and more by luck than design, I stumble across a small pamphlet on Womersley's work published by Historic Scotland in which I notice that one of the first tutors Peter met at the AA was a German Jewish architect called Arthur Korn. Korn was a student of Erich Mendelsohn – another German Jewish architect who was an early exponent of the International Style – a movement begun in the late Twenties in mainland Europe that sought to distance itself from the more decorative practices of Gothic, Romanesque and even Renaissance architecture. Coincidentally Mendelsohn also designed the Hadassah hospital on Mount Scopus in Jerusalem, a building Beri visited and photographed several times while studying in the city.

In 1929 Korn wrote *Glass in Modern Architecture*, a book described by many as 'prophetic'. 'Glass,' wrote Korn, 'is noticeable yet not quite visible. The great membrane, full of mystery, delicate yet tough.' The influence his teaching had on Peter is not difficult to appreciate – particularly as Korn was also an early advocate of Mies van der Rohe, whom Peter described as being 'a god of my younger days'.

It was not until a few years later, however, while visiting the Festival of Britain, organised by the government to inspire post-war architects and the public alike to look towards designs of the future, that Peter realised 'we were all going to be called upon to recreate this type of twentieth century environment'. And what an environment! For a start there were the exhibition buildings themselves, the names of which conjured up images of spaceships and cosmic exploration – the Dome of Discovery, the Skylon, the Sea and Ships Pavilion. It was an architects'

Peter Womersley, c. 1961

utopia, a playground of the imagination, much of which was indebted to the type of European Modernism that Peter had already come into contact with via his tutor as well as sojourns in Europe. Peter spent a great many holidays on the continent, drinking in its art and architecture while, in later life, he bought a house overlooking Lake Garda in northern Italy to which he often invited family and friends.

Much like Beri, however, Peter also fell in love with the Borders. Travelling up to discuss what my father had in mind for his new house, Peter eventually relocated to Gattonside village on the banks of the river Tweed where he was to design and build not only The Orchard, a private house for a Mr and Mrs Schofield, but also his own modernist home, The Rig, which was completed in 1958. From Gattonside it was only a fifteen-minute drive across to High Sunderland, a journey Peter (who by this time had become such a close friend of both my parents that they'd made him our legal guardian should anything untoward happen to them) did most Sunday evenings throughout my childhood.

Arriving in his silver Alfa Romeo Spider, he would nearly always be dressed in what I now think of as the uniform of a young, Sixties professional working in the Arts, that is to say beige trousers with either a checked shirt or a tight-fitting polo-neck sweater.

'His aperitif,' wrote my father, 'was a dry Martini (never spirits); his favourite main dish: steak and kidney pudding.'

From my child's eye view, Peter was a curious character. My strongest memory of him is the day when, on finding Peter, Beri and Peggy sunbathing in the garden, I commented on the fact that Peter's skin was the colour of tinned frankfurters for it had an extraordinarily smooth, nuclear orange glow to it. Peter wasn't amused. I hadn't meant to be cheeky, I'd thought I was simply stating a truth, but his reaction made it very obvious I'd offended him deeply.

Peter was a complicated, diffident individual, less approachable than most adults I knew, someone who didn't suffer fools gladly. He was also someone who would never (if he could help it) miss an episode of *The Muppets* – added to which he always loved a good party, revelled in gossip yet when he laughed, nine times out of ten this laughter would be followed by a barbed observation, usually at somebody else's expense. As a child his sexuality meant nothing to me, but in my twenties when he occasionally visited High Sunderland (by this time Peter was living and working in Hong Kong) I took it for granted he was gay. It's only in recent years, however, that I've caught myself wondering about the paradox of such a deeply private individual designing a see-through house. Perhaps I'm wrong to suggest this has anything to do with Peter's sexuality. On the other hand, if you consider that homosexuality wasn't legalised in England and Wales until 1967 and not in Scotland until 1981 and further consider how hiding or not being allowed to publically voice such a vital part of yourself must affect you then surely it's not so far-fetched to believe this side of you will express itself in some other way. Suppression versus expression. Inhibition transformed into (in this case) exquisitely executed modernist exhibition.

I wonder too if the strong friendship that sprang up between Peter and Beri might have been based on the fact that both men, although welcomed into the Borders, still felt like outsiders. Did the young gay architect and the Yugoslav émigré feel drawn towards each other because neither of them quite fitted in or wanted to fit in to the prevailing cultural landscape?

'I'm glad I came from somewhere else,' Beri said to me once. 'Being on the outside makes you look at things differently. I was paprika in a large British stew.'

I felt something similar when, in 1997, I moved to Cornwall from London where I had been working as a book editor for a small publishing company. I needed a break from the city in which I had been living ever since studying English Literature at the University of London. I was tired of the push and shove of urban life, of spending all my money on rent and none of my time doing the things I loved most: walking, reading and writing. As luck would have it a friend of mine's family owned a cottage on the coast that had stood empty for years. 'Perhaps I could rent it?' I said, an offer they swiftly snapped up.

Arriving in mid-summer Port Isaac was flooded with tourists, which meant I remained hidden for months. I floated under the radar, watching, but not being watched. Then, at the end of the season, the crowds began thinning out until all that was left was a tideline of fish and chip wrappers, worn-out locals and a couple of people like me, who had decided to stay on and make the village their home. Suddenly the anonymity I'd enjoyed vanished. I was an emmet (a pejorative word for someone of non-Cornish descent) and a 'blow-in' (a pejorative word for someone from outside the community). Not that it's so bad being an outsider, but for every welcoming person you meet there are five times as many who'll let you know in a variety of subtle (and not so subtle) ways that you'll never belong.

Yet even then, I was used to this type of reception. In my teens, having succeeded in escaping boarding school, I attended the local comprehensive. My victory, however, was short-lived because, with my 'stuck-up' English accent and boarding-school demeanour, I couldn't slip under anyone's radar. Not only that, there was no bus service along our stretch of the valley, consequently Peggy had to drive me in to Selkirk in our 'posh' car. It was humiliating. I wanted to curl up, disappear, fade into the background, but instead I tried to fit in. Beri had done the same; that is to say, he took great pains to learn English before he entered the country and later on spoke and wrote it better than most natives. But unlike myself, my father never felt the need to be part of the crowd. Instead, he revelled in bringing an outsider's sensibility to his designs and way of life. Beri didn't want to copy or imitate what had gone before; he wanted to create something new, and this same modus operandi applied when it came to building a house. He and Womersley were adamant they were not in the nostalgia business. 'For it seems to me,' Beri said once, 'that a strange disease struck the nation about 100 years ago; that this disease had a special effect on the eyes and that the inhabitants of these isles have been going around in a grey haze ever since, barely noticing what was around them.' This 'disease' was, of course, tradition, something that afflicted neither Peter nor Beri. Quite the contrary; anything they designed had to look to the future – an attitude that carried over into the second building Peter designed for my father, The Studio.

The Studio, 1970–1992

The Studio was commissioned in 1970 (completed in 1972) in order that my father might have a place close to the house where he could work and entertain business clients.

It is an extraordinary piece of architecture, a building that demonstrates Peter's enthusiasm for Frank Lloyd Wright's 'Fallingwater' with a first-floor 'bridge', or gangway, that disappears into the surrounding pine and beech trees. It also has a winged appearance and resembles someone standing with arms outstretched, a sort of Angel of Brutalism.

Like the See-Through House, the structure of The Studio incorporates huge planes of glass that bring the outside inside, however this time Peter – working alongside structural engineers Ove Arup & Partners (and builders M. & J. Ballantyne) – used soaring, cantilevered concrete horizontals and bone-thin verticals as his framework. In addition, as noted by Peter and Beri's friend, the architectural critic Peter Willis, the corner windows were 'frameless and mitred so as to enhance the views and to accentuate the suspended, floating character of the upper studio'. The result is a building that is as grounded as it is airborne, the larger second floor hovering among the branches of beech and pine trees while the smaller space of the ground floor is rooted to a plinth of workmanlike, blue-black brick. It was these bricks that, while The Studio was under construction, Beri painstakingly sorted through because on delivery from the manufacturer he discovered they were not the same colour as the sample bricks, but instead many of them appeared more red-black than blue-black, a detail my father couldn't let pass. The red ones were thrown to one side and returned to the manufacturer 'not fit for purpose'.

Details mattered. How something looked mattered. Down to the tiniest thing: be it the type of thread used in the construction of a garment, the colour of a brick or the composition of a yarn.

To this end, at one time or another Beri installed both a handloom and a spinning wheel in The Studio so that he might experiment with different colour-ways and weaves, for ' ... unlike the architect, who knows what his raw materials are, his bricks, glass and precast concrete units ... it is not often I can use established yarns if I am constructing a new cloth. I must construct a yarn first. This might sound simple enough, but it is not. In fact yarn spinning is such a complicated business that most weaving firms avoid it and depend for their yarns on other firms who do nothing but spin.'

Purchasing fleeces was usually – for these very small runs – a matter of negotiating a deal with one of our farming neighbours after which the raw pieces (often raddled with ticks) were sent out for scouring, carding and dying in Selkirk before being returned in thick bales of colour. The spinner then discussed which of these colours were to be blended and whether my father might want a woollen or worsted yarn. There were also (what seemed to me then) hundreds of different terms for all the different ways the wool might be carded and therefore end up; for example, you could opt for rolags or batts or slivers or rovings depending on what type of yarn you wanted to create, but the fact is I never really got my head around any of these terms, nor what each one meant for the spinner. What did interest me was watching the fat cushions of fibre being transformed on the wheel into a product that could subsequently be knitted or woven up into samples. It was a mesmerising process, like sugar being spun into candyfloss, only this was wool being wound on to old wooden bobbins. More often than not knops and slubs occurred, crushes of raspberry, bubbles of blackcurrant. I recall one yarn looking as if it was strung out of snowballs. Sometimes Beri dismissed a yarn as 'not being up to much', at others times he'd spend weeks experimenting with different tensions and twists to get the exact look or texture he required before moving on to the knitting or weaving process.

Stringing a warp could take hours, sometimes days, with hundreds of threads gathered into hanks in a specified order according to what idea Beri had in mind to create. Cathedrals of wool, that's how the warps appeared to me. Cathedrals of wool with choirs of colour

Beri with loom at Netherdale Mill, c. 1966

embedded within them. Beautiful, delicate structures that, when I think of it, also suggest another basis for the friendship between Beri and Peter, that is to say that architecture and weaving are both structural practices – that the views from within a loom and within a building disclose multiple connections, cross-overs, layers. In Peter's case this resulted in what Neil Baxter (former Secretary at the Royal Incorporation of Architects in Scotland) termed 'woven architecture' while in turn Beri produced textiles that worked on a variety of different planes thus exhibiting a wonderful three-dimensional quality.

But as much as Beri experimented with the spinning and weaving processes, there was a third way he approached matters of design, that is to say, through his painting and his appreciation of other artists' work. Going to exhibitions was a way of life for both my parents and wherever we travelled as a family there was nearly always a stop-off to visit a nearby gallery. Beri admired many artists, but in particular Nicolas de Staël, Paul Klee, Ivon Hitchens, Oskar Kokoschka, Graham Sutherland, Karel Appel and Jean-Paul Riopelle. These painters had a profound impact on him, not only in the way he saw and experimented with colour, texture and form, but also in their single-minded approach to the work. '[They] have,' wrote Beri, 'a personal view of the world and do not compromise in expressing it' – a sentiment that could apply equally to himself. Perhaps that's one of the reasons he commissioned not one but two rigorously modern buildings and when it came to his artwork, the same was also true. Painting was as uncompromising an activity as any other in his life, most particularly because it fed directly into his textiles. 'I paint,' he said in a BBC documentary, 'because I get excited by the things I see around me and I feel I have to do something about it. And that something usually turns out to be painting it. I play around while I paint. I experiment while I paint and then I find it's quite natural and easy to use the same combination of colours next morning or the next day, when I design some textiles or some other object. So that the two are very closely connected and if you look at my painting of any one period and compare it to my designing activities of any one period you can see the connection clearly even though it is not a deliberate one.'

The interdependence between his paintings and his design work is also expressed by the fact Beri hung The Studio's inner core with some of his most spectacular oils so that while he worked on designing his yarns and fabrics, the fox-fire reds and bloody crimsons of his paintings glowed in the background. At night when it was dark outside and the lights were switched on, the work blazed as if the building were burning alive. Even in daylight the effect was spectacular, so much so that drivers often slowed down or parked up at the side of the road in order to work out what it was they were seeing.

Not that The Studio was universally admired.

It wasn't.

It was a Marmite building.

You either loved it or hated it.

And plenty of people fell into the latter category. On one occasion, when Beri and I needed some repairs made to a chair, the upholsterer on arrival at the house immediately enquired what on earth 'is that frightful building on the far side of the wood'?

Beri chuckled. 'What sort of buildings do you like?' he asked.

'Balmoral's beautiful,' came the reply.

Needless to say, the upholsterer departed High Sunderland without the chair.

Both The Studio and High Sunderland are extensions of who Beri was and what he believed in. Modernist buildings brought out the best in people, their emphasis on natural light and well-proportioned, airy living spaces promoting not only optimism and good mental health, but also a demonstrative curiosity in the world and open-mindedness. It therefore puzzled him why more people didn't warm to these buildings in the way they did, say, to Victorian or Georgian architecture. And why was it modernist architecture was so often portrayed as inherently suspect? King Vidor's 1949 classic film *The Fountainhead* (adapted from Ayn Rand's novel of the same name) being a prime example. Here at least Gary Cooper, who plays modernist architect Howard Roark, is seen as 'the good guy', the individual who stands up to the crowd, but the mob mentality portrayed in the film very much reflects the common attitude towards modernist buildings even today and the suspicion in people's minds about an architecture that doesn't reference the past and stubbornly refuses to add frills. For example, The Elrod House by John Lautner in Palm Springs features in *Diamonds Are Forever* as the house in which arch villain Willard Whyte lives. And the fictional Vandamm House in Hitchcock's *North by Northwest* (modelled on Frank Lloyd Wright's work) signals – if nothing else quite does – that here is the home of someone who doesn't play by the rules, ergo they are most likely untrustworthy and morally corrupt. In *Exhibition* – a more recent film by Joanna Hogg – the modernist building in which the main protagonists live seems to have been chosen by the director to represent an emotional impasse. From the off the two main characters are distant and disengaged from one another, operating on different emotional planes. Any intimate dialogue that occurs doesn't do so in face-to-face encounters, but via an intercom system linking their two separate offices. Even the couple's names are stripped back, the woman is called D, the man H. At night D whispers erotic fantasies into a tape recorder while H sleeps next to her in the bed. Not that the couple don't express their love for the building, but there are hints that it's as much a prison keeping them separate from the outside world (and each other), as it is a refuge. There's also a dinner party where a neighbour (who lives in a Georgian house opposite) expresses horror at the thought of living in such a structure. 'Who,' she says to her husband, 'would want to live

... it's very odd ... it's not really a family home, it's an artist's home, but it wouldn't be right for us' – or words to that effect. The building, in other words, is not a space where real life is lived. It's 'other'. It's alien; it's a place where art can be created, but not life.

This feeling is echoed once again by the Farnsworth House, for not only did Edith Farnsworth fall out with Mies van der Rohe over (among other things) the non-existent cupboards – refusing to pay the final bills until he took her to court at which point she counter-sued him for going over budget – but after it was completed, she stated that her overriding feeling while in residence was one of alienation from the building. 'The truth is,' she said in a 1953 interview – given anonymously – to *House Beautiful* for an incendiary article entitled 'The Threat to the Next America' by editor, Elizabeth Gordon, 'with its four walls of glass I feel like a prowling animal, always on the alert. I am always restless. Even in the evening. I feel like a sentinel on guard, day and night. I can rarely stretch out and relax ...'

I sympathise with Edith Farnsworth having, on occasion, felt exposed at High Sunderland, however both it and The Studio have always been inviting spaces. More importantly, their architecture promoted a far warmer, more intimate way of living than the small, boxed-in rooms of most conventional buildings. Yes, it was like living within a work of art and, with reference to The Studio, like working within one too, but far from experiencing this as alienating, it was exhilarating and these feelings only increased the longer Beri and the rest of us lived and worked in these two magnificent structures.

Beri loved walking to The Studio every day in what he called his morning commute to work. Approaching it via a small section of woodland, the first glimpse he would have of it was through a fretwork of branches. Even on days when it was pouring with rain, the effect of walking through the trees with water shattering the leaves before briefly glimpsing the glow of glass floating on outstretched arms of white concrete was like the glimpse of a photograph emerging through a fog of developing fluid. It was both 'of' and 'not of' the place. A revelation and obfuscation. Hard to read, challenging yet always eerily beautiful.

Of course, like the upholsterer there were (and still are) many people who loathe The Studio and will never accept that it adds anything to the landscape in which it sits. But ruffling the feathers of any prevailing norm never worried Beri and in this he and Peter were cut from the same cloth. The two men developed a strong friendship, one based not only on a mutual respect for each other's visions, but also on admiration for their respective talents. 'I did not interfere with how Peter worked,' Beri would say when interviewed about commissioning Peter to design High Sunderland. 'A professional such as Peter is entitled to design what he or she believes works best, without anyone else putting their half-penny's worth in.'

Bernat Klein Scotla

Bernat Klein 2 / Mohair/Wool

Living Room, continued

The sound of ice being dropped into a glass of whisky & soda. Gin & tonic with a slice of lime. Maraschino cherries. Forty or so voices all chattering and laughing together. Chicken liver pâté served on thin fingers of toast. The chink of an oh-so-large diamond against the edge of a champagne flute, the aroma of Gitanes or Woodbine mixed with Chanel No. 5.

When it came to designing High Sunderland, Beri and Peggy's only stipulation was that the house be both a family home and also the type of place they could entertain guests. To this end the sunken living room, bordered as it is on two sides by the library, was ideal for the type of lavish drinks parties and get-togethers so typical of the Fifties and Sixties.

In my memory these occasions are giddy, high-octane affairs that combined a heady mix of perfume and lipstick with gin and cigarette smoke. Peggy and her friends would wear wonderful cocktail dresses together with fabulous jewellery and bouffant hairstyles. But it was the shoes I loved most. My mother had a vast array of Charles Jourdan stilettos that had been hand-dyed in every colour imaginable to match her different outfits. There were shoes in turquoise, emerald, apricot, rose, lime, olive, lemon, cerise and one glorious pair in burnished gold that she wore with a gold shot-silk cocktail dress that shimmered whenever she moved.

Sometimes when the parties were over I'd examine the empty glasses to see if I could find one with lipstick on its rim that I would then rub off with my fingers before smearing it over my lips. Peggy's lipstick was always the same bluish-pink; it made me think of hydrangeas or those most English of flowers, delphiniums.

Peggy stands in front of me. She died over nine years ago, but she is dazzlingly present. And the perfume she wore, I can still catch its essence. There's a drawer in my parents' bedroom where she used to keep chiffon scarves. I have never emptied it. It's my 'go-to' place when I want to be close to her. All I have to do is slide the drawer open and bury my nose in its soft, silky perfumes and suddenly she is with me again.

Ever-present throughout my childhood, even when she was at work or I was at boarding school, I would be thinking about her. In that respect, leastways up until my teenage years, High Sunderland was the perfect house for a child because its open-plan interior meant I could see or hear my mother even when I was in the living room and she was in the kitchen, or when I was in the playroom and she was in the dining room. The downside only struck me when I hit adolescence and needed some privacy. Suddenly there was nowhere to hide or conduct private phone calls. There were only two rooms in the entire house that were not either open-plan or open to prying eyes due to their glass walls: my parents' bathroom and the guest bathroom. Between the ages of twelve to twenty I therefore spent a great deal of time locked in one or other of these rooms, either sobbing my eyes out over some minor drama or chatting to friends on the phone because my parents' bathroom was the only room in the house that had a telephone in it on which you could talk and not be overheard.

Privacy came at a premium in the See-Through House. There were no under-stairs cupboards or rooms into which you could slip and remain unseen. Perhaps that's why I spent so much of my time playing in the pine forest buttressed next to the garden. Crow Wood was a favourite haunt of mine, especially for building hideouts and dens; its intricately dark interiors a blessing. High Sunderland was too transparent. In places you could see right through it, from one side of the building to the other, as if you were looking at an X-ray with couches, tables and chairs in the place of heart, liver and lungs. Little wonder, then, that as a child one of my recurring nightmares was – if an intruder broke in – where would I hide?

Over the years I have visited houses with priest holes and secret stairwells that lead into rambling gardens. Houses that boast attics and cellars and snugs. By contrast, at High Sunderland there is not so much as a dark corner. Rinsed by sunlight, it's as clean and well lit a space as a Nordic snowscape. No wonder I yearned for a window seat with curtains drawn across it such as those behind which Jane Eyre hides.

Recently I was asked by an architectural student if I thought growing up at High Sunderland had had any particular effect on me as a child. In retrospect things often mean more than they do at the time, but sometimes I wonder if I'm more secretive, more withholding, than I might otherwise have been because so much of my early life was, for want of a better word, transparent. When I played with my dolls, I kept all their voices inside my head so no one could overhear me and for a couple of years I became convinced our gardener was deliberately mowing the lawn directly outside my window just so he could watch what I was up to. Secretiveness became my default position; in my late teens I snuck off to Vienna for two weeks when I was 'supposedly' staying with friends in Yorkshire. I skipped the country, first to Brussels and then to Austria, phoning Beri and Peggy every now and then from my hotel room. And during my early twenties when I met and fell in love with an older man who flew light aircraft for a living, I kept that to myself too. Luc and I would fly across the Channel to Paris, exhilarating trips that I wouldn't or couldn't share with anyone else because I needed to keep these bits of my life private. Perhaps it's a long shot to say I did so because I grew up in a house made of glass and therefore needed certain things to remain unclear, but there's a kernel of truth within that idea. I wanted to be opaque, clouded, un-see-able through. Once, apropos of something I failed to tell Beri about, God knows what, I recall him saying that 'secrets have no place within a family'. Beri liked to talk openly about everything. He liked to share his thoughts and by return wanted to know ours as well. I hesitate to say he was as open-plan as the house he lived in, but in many respects this is true. Of course children, and in particular teenagers, keep a lot from their parents; it's part of growing up, part of becoming an adult and separating yourself from your family. It is a perfectly normal thing to do.

But my secret self went deeper than that. Often it felt as if it was the only way to survive. Beri was so overwhelming. Yes, he liked to encourage other people to contribute their ideas and sometimes he even adapted his own to take these views on board – but more often than not he stuck to his own. There was no alternative reality for him. To keep things hidden therefore became a means of defending my own vision, my own way of seeing and interacting with the world. Trespassers were definitely not welcome. This line of thought suddenly leads to another. My head fills with 'Keep Out' signs and 'No-Go' areas, places that should not be traversed, things that cannot be spoken out loud, and I start thinking of a programme I first heard on Radio 4 called *The Glass Piano* by Deborah Levy about a nineteenth-century princess, Alexandra Amelie of Bavaria.

Found one day wandering sideways down the corridors of the family palace, when asked what she was doing the princess replied that as a child she had swallowed a glass grand piano. She couldn't touch any walls or allow herself to bump into furniture in case these objects shattered the delicate instrument. As glass delusions go this is fairly extreme and is open to multiple interpretations, the most obvious being that she wanted to protect or keep from being heard something very fragile relating to her own music, that is to say, relating to her 'self'. Hearing this story makes me wonder if the See-Through House hasn't swallowed me? If living inside it hasn't turned me into the thing that feels vulnerable? Is that why I feel the need to be secretive because I don't want anyone seeing or judging me? The most painful realisation, however, is that I rarely if ever felt this away about my mother. Peggy was far less intrusive or judgemental, which meant that often with her I was the open book Beri always wanted me to be. I hate myself for writing that. The guilt attached to that sentence is overwhelming.

'Do you think he knew how much I loved him?' I repeatedly asked my sister after Beri died. But no matter how many times she said 'Yes', I could not or would not believe her.

The phone is ringing. When I pick it up, I hear the vulture's voice on the other end of the line.

> VULTURE: Is that Susan?
> SHELLEY: Shelley, yes –
> VULTURE: Yes, Shirley, Sherry . . .
> SHELLEY: Hi –
> VULTURE: I was wondering . . . someone told me . . . that High Sunderland is up for sale?
> SHELLEY: It's not –
> VULTURE: They said they'd seen it on the Internet or something?
> SHELLEY: Like I said, it's not up for sale –
> VULTURE: I didn't think it was, not just yet anyway . . . only this person said they'd seen something somewhere –

SHELLEY: It's not up for sale. I can't say it any clearer than
that –
VULTURE: If you do decide to sell it, though, you would let
me know, wouldn't you? You'd give me a call?
SHELLEY: Of course, absolutely . . .

The words come out of my mouth and I surprise myself at how
genuine I sound because the vulture is the last person on earth
I would contact if High Sunderland were being put on the market. I
loathe the vulture and anger burns inside me like acid.

I am still seething the following morning. How dare this man call
me up out of the blue, put me on edge like that? Seconds later I find
myself grabbing my laptop and trawling through the Internet to see
if there's any mention of High Sunderland being on the market. Perhaps someone is pretending to be me? Is someone trying to con my
brother, sister and me out of our home? But of course the search
reveals nothing.

Still, a niggling feeling burrows away at the back of my mind.

I am very unsettled.

That night I dream of molehills in the middle of the living room.

*

Memory conceals itself in the quietest moments, in the tiniest, most
mundane details. The smell of turpentine, the taste of Victoria plums,
a pile of orange peel, a freshly ploughed field.

Writing at the table this morning I glance up from my computer
and stare through the dining-room windows. Perhaps it is the way the
light hits the fields or perhaps it is the striated pattern the shadows
make on the wall, but suddenly I see Beri sitting on one of the couches
holding up a length of cherry-pink silk. His love of colour was possibly
the most romantic thing about him and definitely the only Romantic

thing about him. Lyrical, poetic, emotional, expressive. Colour was texture. 'Those leaves. They aren't just flat and green. Remember that.'

Earth is never just brown.

In my early twenties, having already taken my BA in English, I went on to study photography for a year at Goldsmiths College in southeast London. I had a small Ricoh camera, something I bought for about £80 at Jessops on Oxford Street. I took this camera everywhere. One Easter weekend I caught the train up to Scotland, only to be met at Berwick-upon-Tweed by Beri. I'd thought Mum was going to pick me up, she always did, but on this occasion she wasn't feeling well so had sent Beri instead. As soon as we got into the car he handed me a pack of smoked salmon sandwiches.

'You've missed lunch. You'll be hungry,' he said. I hadn't the heart to tell him I'd bought a sandwich on the train. Instead, I munched the ones he'd made me, at the same time noticing he'd brought his camera with him, a beautiful, extremely expensive Hasselblad.

'The type of camera they took to the Moon on Apollo 11,' he explained proudly the day he bought it.

Halfway back to High Sunderland Beri drew in to the side of the road.

'Why are we stopping?' I asked.

'I thought we could take some photographs? Who are the photographers you most admire?'

'Can't say I've thought about it.'

'You *must* have!'

I began racking my brain. The pressure to name someone was monumental. Beri's interrogations were notorious amongst my friends. I recall bringing a new boyfriend home once when, almost before said boy was over the threshold, Beri began:

BERI: So, Mark, if money were no object and you could buy any work of art in the world, what would it be?

BOYFRIEND: Oh! I don't know ... that's really quite difficult ... uhmm –

BERI: Come on, *any*thing – sculpture, painting –

BOYFRIEND: Yes I see, uhmmm, perhaps something by Michelangelo?

BERI: *SERIOUSLY*?

BOYFRIEND [glancing towards Shelley in search of a life-jacket]: Okay, perhaps not Michelangelo as such ...

SHELLEY: You like more modern stuff too –

BOYFRIEND [looking rather blank]: Yeah, I do, don't I? More modern stuff ... definitely, yeah ...

BERI: Such as? Remember, money's no object –

BOYFRIEND: How about Joseph Cornell? He did some pretty great stuff, didn't he?

BERI [incredulous]: You mean the man who collected RUB-BISH and put it in BOXES?

Parked up at the side of the road, I felt the same pressure Mark had been under. I racked my brain for the name of a photographer, some-one Beri would like rather than someone *I* liked, not because my father's approval made me feel good (although it did), but because I was lazy and didn't want to go to the bother of justifying my choices.

'Ansel Adams's okay.'

'Just okay?'

'Diane Arbus?'

'Are you asking or telling me?'

'I like Arbus.'

'She's good,' Beri said, clambering out of the car. 'Not the best, but definitely quite good.'

'She is, isn't she?' I agreed and then before he could think of any more questions, I swiftly changed the subject back to what we were doing parked up at the side of the road.

'Over there,' Beri explained. 'I saw it the other day when I was passing.' He nodded towards a field.

'It's a field,' I said.

'Yes! It is! Come on, hurry up, we won't need your camera. I want to show you how the Hasselblad works.'

Minutes later we clambered over a gate into several acres of recently ploughed mud.

'Change that lens for the fisheye,' Beri instructed as we squeezed along a tight little path towards the far end at which point we stopped. 'Now hold the camera down at your waist and look into the viewfinder. Can you see?'

'Yes.' I nodded and then, 'Oh, wow!' Because suddenly the field had become at that angle something with such a rich, chocolaty texture it looked more like a length of knubbed tweed through which loops of velvet had been woven. For Beri the warp of a ploughed field, its rumpled, earthy furrows, were nothing if not a study in brown; the texture and grain of it, its raw physicality. Not only that, the Hasselblad's lens was so powerful, I could see how fibrous the soil was, how each clod glinted with hundreds of thousands of tiny threads, each one knuckled and knotted together with stones.

'Can you see it?' Beri said.

'I can.'

And I did.

I saw it and felt it like a punch to the stomach.

But Beri was not the only one who had me falling in love with this landscape. When I was small, Peggy and I spent long afternoons visiting local landmarks – Cauldshiels Loch, the Devil's Beef Tub, the Grey Mare's Tail – trips during which she taught me how to identify wild flowers, insects and birds. Memorably, Peggy also took me hunting for agate. We'd roam the hillside streams and riverbeds searching for small pitted rocks that, when split apart with a hammer and chisel, revealed blood-red interiors clittered with bands of orange and violet. It was cold work. Often, by the time we clambered back into the car, my fingers would be aching and raw, my trousers wet-legged and clingy, but the wonder of being so in touch with water and rock, the wonder of tapping and cracking open something so dull-looking to reveal those stone-bright interiors, always left me feeling as if the landscape and I were as one.

Knitting. Weaving. Plaiting. Braiding. In his book *Waterlog*, the nature-writer Roger Deakin wrote that sheep 'are the makers of their own landscape. By grazing the moors and mountains, they keep the contours – the light and shade – clear, sharp and well-defined.'

Beri was also a maker of his own landscape, one he created with his eyes; his use of colour nothing more or less than an extension of his generosity of spirit, of his ability to embrace the excitement and vibrancy of life and incorporate it into huge skeins of yarn that were subsequently woven into bolts of extraordinary fabric. Not for him the lurking greys or malnourished blues of austerity Britain. He wanted to set textiles ablaze.

I look at some of my father's early designs and they steal my breath away. The finished garments were often presented in leaflets and catalogues that were also meticulously designed. Stylish photographs of the models graced the front covers while the back covers were composed of a still-life picture of the yarn alongside complementary fabrics that the home-knitter could purchase in order to sew a matching jacket or skirt. Each separate knitting wool was also given its own name: Lindean Blue, Selkirk Green, Abbotsford Orange. Naming the yarns became a family game, with each season presenting a fresh challenge. Sometimes we'd choose names from operas or ballets (Carmen, Figaro, Giselle) at other times it was foodstuffs (Paprika, Poppy Seed, Nougat).

A favourite front cover was photographed in our living room with the two female models reclining on one of our sofas. The image is as familiar to me as a family snap; indeed, one of the models wears a necklace belonging to Peggy and which now belongs to me. Of course, no one in our family would be posed with such style or grace, but the fact that my father's designs were photographed within the house spells out how strong the symbiosis was between the building in which Beri lived and the work he created within that building. They were all one and the same: a weaving together of ideas and practice, albeit that the practice of knitting was always Peggy's domain.

The sound of my mother's needles. The satisfying click click of the long metal pins. The way her fingers wrapped and looped and twisted the yarn. Peggy had infinite patience when it came to designing garments; while the yarn itself described her nature, for Peggy was a warm, nurturing figure just as wool and mohair are warm, nurturing yarns. Peggy drew people together, she had a wonderful ability to put visitors at their ease, keep the house and our lives within it harmonious. Perhaps that's why my parents' marriage was successful because, while Beri's temperament was fiery, headstrong and at times downright belligerent my mother's was more accommodating, measured and calm.

The garments she created reflected this. Not that Peggy didn't have edges or complications, for, again, like the patterns she created with their talk of purl stitch and plain stitch, of skeins and cones, of stocking and moss stitch, casting on and binding off, Peggy was as complicated as the next person. I'd find little scraps of paper scattered

Peggy knitting with Shelley, c. 1967

around the house with her workings peppered across them, pages full of tiny dots and dashes, crosses and numerals, as though she were composing sheet music. To me these notations were (and still are) as foreign as Chinese and as complicated as Morse code, but from them Peggy cooked up storms of cardigans and jumpers, hats and scarves.

I stare down once more at the picture on the front cover of the knitting pattern, only this time I'm reminded of another symbiosis, that of inner and outer landscape. One of the models is wearing a dress made out of a tweed the colour and texture of moss prickled with turquoise. Beri was always bringing the outside in: lichen that grew on the larch trees, mushrooms with undersides soft as crabs' lungs. Puffballs, oak apples, buzzard feathers, wasps' nests and birds' skulls. 'I have looked at and have had my sense of touch stimulated,' he once wrote, 'by the silky texture and subtle colours of our Tibetan Wild Cherry and by the pinky-white beige of our silver birches. Some of my textile prints were based on them.'

Even when Beri chose to dye yarn in solid colours the results seemed to vibrate and linger in the mind's eye longer than colours by other designers. But of all the yarns he used, the one he liked to work with best in both hand-knitting and woven textiles was not lambs' wool or cashmere, cotton or silk, but mohair.

Nicknamed the 'diamond fibre' because of its light-giving, lustrous qualities, the true origin of the word is 'Mukhayyar' from the Aramaic for 'choice' or 'quality'. And it was for mohair's very particular qualities that Beri prized this yarn so much and worked with it in his textiles almost as passionately as he did oil paints in his paintings.

Introducing mohair to the rather conservative Borders' textile industry was like introducing parrotfish into a tank of brown trout. Strictly speaking, however, it was the Czechoslovakian textile and fashion designer Zika Ascher who, in the mid-Fifties, first introduced mohair fabrics to the British public, but unlike Ascher, who used flat-finished mohair, Beri favoured teasel-raised yarns that gave the finished product a silkier, fuller, brighter appeal. He also worked in close collaboration with a local dye house, Kemp, Blair & Co, to invent what became known as 'resist dip-dying', which in effect meant a single yarn could contain up to four different 'intended' colours and four 'seepage' colours or tones that when woven together with four other, separately dip-dyed yarns would then produce a fabric containing thirty-two colours. Beri's inspiration for this, however, far from being rooted in textiles, came instead from art.

Some time during 1954–5, my father and Peggy visited the Tate in London where they saw Georges Seurat's *Une Baignade, Asnières* (1884). As my father later explained, the painting was created by 'breaking down the basic colours of nature into tiny dots of their component colours and leaving it to the viewer's eye to put them together again'. Intrigued and stimulated by this technique, Beri began trying to replicate it within his woven textiles although, had he known what a long, laborious task this would turn into, he might have had second thoughts. Suffering knock-back after knock-back, disaster after disaster, eventually with nearly all of the technical issues resolved – the design work proper began. 'For months,' wrote my father, 'we sat and prepared colour combinations – each yarn dyeing had to have four colours in different proportions; these colours had to be basically different and yet they had to be of the same weight visually. Each had to have something definite to say and had to say it in just the right strength without getting lost amongst the other colours and without out-shouting them [...] Often dyeings were spoilt and we had to find out how and why and to decide how to replace them and what to do next. The dyers were very helpful as indeed was everybody else of whom at one time or another I asked the most impossible seeming, ridiculous sounding and most definitely "not done" things. At last our colour card containing twenty colour combinations was ready.'

Eureka!

The seemingly impossible had been achieved.

Library, Workspace, Top Couch

First and foremost this is the place where I danced on my father's feet. My small, cold hands held tightly in his much larger, warmer ones while my feet were placed firmly on top of his polished brown shoes. Slowly we began to waltz up and down the L-shaped walkway that wraps around two sides of the living room. There was no one else in the world I wanted to marry except Beri. How could there be anyone else better than him?

Does every little girl decide at some point that they want to marry their father? Jung labelled this the Electra Complex, but it never seemed that complex to me, rather it was real and overwhelming. No one was as kind or as funny or as wise as my father. Why would I want to look anywhere else for a husband? I loved only him.

Fortunately for all concerned it did not take too many years before this puppy-like adoration metamorphosed into undiluted teenage rage. Then, rather than wanting to wed Beri, I wanted to murder him.

'How on earth have you stayed married for SO LONG?' I hissed at Mum.

Or, 'Doesn't he drive you UP THE WALL?'

Or, worst of all, 'If he dies before you, I'll look after you. But if you die before him, HE'S ON HIS OWN!'

As a teenager it often felt as if I was an only child; Gillian and Jonathan, six and ten years older than me, had already left home by then to live elsewhere. No longer could I rely on their presence to dilute Beri's attention. Instead, living with my father was one long, intense battle. I would growl under my breath at him while he would growl, not so quietly, back at me.

I was a surly adolescent with a black cloud hovering over my head, a mixture of love, loathing and hormones.

I close my eyes and think back to when I was five or six. I can still feel Beri holding me, moving my body about in wide, waltz-like circles up and down the length of the library, the warmth and weight of him keeping me upright, swinging me round. I tilt my head back so that now the room is not only spinning, it turns upside down while all the books on the shelves blur into one.

Books and reading always played an integral part of life at High Sunderland, both Beri and Peggy holding education in the highest esteem. Perhaps this was the reason behind one of the more curious periods of my life, namely that between the ages of seven to ten – that is, before I was sent away to boarding school – I was educated by a governess called Miss Brodie, a name that never failed to make my parents smile.

I shared Miss Brodie with six friends whose parents also decided a governess was just what their offspring required before being packed off to boarding school. To this end Mr and Mrs Y—, who lived in a house the size of Belize, furnished us with an old-fashioned schoolroom that wouldn't have looked out of place in one of my beloved Victorian novels.

I enjoyed going there. And I adored Miss Brodie, for despite being a formidable woman, strict almost to the point of sadism, she took enormous care to nurture each of her pupils' personalities. The only drawback was religion. Miss Brodie religiously encouraged us to praise God every morning. She religiously papered over any sentences in our poetry books she deemed blasphemous, religiously pursed her lips at any notion of disobedience and religiously made us learn long tracts of the Bible by heart.

On the plus side she read to us from Bunyan's *Pilgrim's Progress* most afternoons, a story that set my imagination on fire with its strange-sounding place names such as the Slough of Despond, Doubting Castle, the Valley of the Shadow of Death.

Many happy days, weeks and years were spent with Miss Brodie during which, in between singing 'Jesus Wants Me for a Sunbeam' and learning all the stories from the miracle of the five loaves to the raising of Lazarus, we managed to squeeze in a few Maths, English and Latin lessons. But for the most part it was religion that ruled the classroom and I was completely under both its and Miss Brodie's spell.

How Beri did not drag me away from her clutches astonishes me to this day. Particularly as I'd race home from school spouting lines such as, 'Miss Brodie says you shouldn't drink alcohol.' (Cue Beri asking if Peggy wanted a drink.)

Or, 'Miss Brodie says we must attend church every Sunday.' (Cue Beri rolling his eyes.)

Or, 'Miss Brodie says you won't go to heaven if you wear lipstick.' (Cue Peggy deliberately applying a thick layer of lipstick to her mouth.)

Or, 'Miss Brodie says you shouldn't swear.' (Cue Peggy quickly putting her hand over Beri's mouth.)

My early education veered between old-fashioned hellfire and modernist militancy. The only thing, in fact, that rescued Miss Brodie from being declared completely insane by Beri was her gifts as a teacher. So long as I was receiving a good education she could spout whatever 'damned nonsense' she pleased.

Nonsense was also a concept Beri extended towards most categories of fiction. A fact that is reflected in the bookshelves where, despite all the books being jumbled together, it is instantly apparent that my father's tastes differed wildly from my mother's.

'Every library is autobiographical ... ' wrote Alberto Manguel in his own wonderful book *The Library at Night* ' ... our books will bear witness for or against us, our books reflect who we are and what we have been.'

This is true of Beri and Peggy's library. For instance, here is a copy of Dickens' *Great Expectations*, a plum-coloured volume of Keats's poetry, *Le Grand Meaulnes* by Alain-Fournier, George Eliot's *Middlemarch*, Anthony Trollope's *Barchester Chronicles*, Kate Chopin's *The Awakening* – all belonging to Peggy, all reflecting her fondness for the Victorians and the Romantics. Buttressed next to them, however, are books on Alvar Aalto, monographs of Francis Bacon and Lucian Freud, Koestler's *Darkness at Noon*, Primo Levi's *If This Is a Man*, *The Art of Colour* by Johannes Itten, a Hebrew dictionary, Ian McEwan's *Saturday*, a book on Scandinavian design and an impressively large volume on the Bauhaus. What do these say about Beri? That reality and functionalism mattered the most? That fiction only worked if it resembled fact?

I scan the bookshelves again, note how many biographies, memoirs and novels there are: J. G. Ballard's *Miracles of Life*, Levi's *If Not Now, When?* Solzhenitsyn's *Cancer Ward*, *Night* by Elie Wiesel, *The Last Days of Hitler* by Sir Hugh Trevor-Roper, Bernhard Schlink's *The Reader*, *Stalingrad* by Antony Beevor, Hannah Arendt's *Eichmann in Jerusalem*. These titles run like a vein through the shelves. But how come I'm only noticing now how many of them refer to the Second World War? Possibly because Beri never talked much about this period of his life and yet he obviously felt compelled to study it closely. Knowledge is power? But knowledge also brings comfort, can help the nonsensical make sense. And there is nothing more nonsensical than death.

After my mother died I devoured any half-decent book I could find on the subject. My normal tipple of choice, fiction, was unceremoniously tossed aside. It was good for nothing. I wanted facts. I needed cold, sobering facts. Consequently I devoured C. S. Lewis's *A Grief Observed*, Paul Auster's *The Invention of Solitude*, Julian Barnes' *Levels of Life* and Joan Didion's *The Year of Magical Thinking*.

I consumed these books one after the other, sucked the marrow out of their bones. Words were comforting, solid like the tick-tock of a clock next to an infant. Indeed, reading about death felt like the most life-affirming thing I could do. So perhaps that's why the library contains so many books on the Second World War and the Holocaust. Throughout his life Beri always preferred fact to fiction, his forays into the latter almost always proving deeply problematic. As an adult, for example, many was the time he shoved a book into my hands exclaiming, 'READ THIS! THIS IS THE WORST NOVEL I HAVE EVER READ!'

SHELLEY: You say that every time you give me a book –
BERI: Well, this novel is.
SHELLEY: They can't all be the worst –
BERI: Who says?
SHELLEY: If you say something's the worst, it kind of implies that there can't be anything more terrible –
BERI: Is it my fault if I read something awful and then find out later that some idiot's written something even worse –
SHELLEY: You're very drawn to bad books, aren't you?
BERI: If it's had a good review, I get the book –
SHELLEY: But some critics won't like the same stuff as you do –
BERI: I like everything – so long as it's well written –
SHELLEY: How about a well-written fairy story?
BERI: Be serious.
SHELLEY: Okay, how about a well-written piece of magic realism?
BERI: That's just a fairy story trying to trick you into believing it's something more highbrow.
SHELLEY: James Joyce?
BERI: You know I hate anything Irish –

SHELLEY: Dickens?

BERI: Now you're just being ridiculous. There's no point in anything pre-1930 –

SHELLEY: Why don't you ever give me a good book to read? Something you've really enjoyed?

BERI: Because you don't like the ones I like –

SHELLEY: I'm not that fond of the ones you don't like either.

BERI: Well, this one is the WORST, WORST, *WORST* ever book. You'll love it. Just read the first page –

SHELLEY [after half a minute]: It's unreadable.

BERI [beaming with pleasure]: YES IT IS!

I run my hands over the bookshelves again. Some of the spines are split while others look as if no one has opened them in thirty years. There are German-language books and books in Serbo-Croat and Hungarian. Beri spoke all three languages, plus Hebrew and Yiddish (none of which he passed down to his children). I enjoyed listening to my father speak these languages. They bestowed a sense of otherness on him, something I loved, just as I loved that he wasn't born in this country. Here was the most familiar man in my life but with keys to a different world.

However, if Beri's languages separated us, there were books we both enjoyed reading.

A slim volume of poetry by Andrew Motion springs to mind. I bought my father a copy of *The Pleasure Steamers* after Motion gave a short talk at my sixth-form college in Oxford in the early Eighties.

By this time, having clocked up two boarding schools plus Selkirk High School (where I stayed for four years), I left home once again, this time for a school in Oxford that was everything I hoped it might be in that there were no uniforms, no dormitories, no sadistic matrons or compulsory games lessons. Instead, the school was co-ed, encouraged students from all over Europe and was slap-bang in the middle of Oxford, which meant that if we weren't in lessons, we could enjoy the town, go to the cinema, art galleries, cafés and restaurants. The education was good too, with outside talks from all manner of people: historians, scientists, musicians and poets.

Andrew Motion's visit left a huge impression on me so I was overjoyed when Beri said he enjoyed his poetry too and in particular a poem that Motion had written about his mother, who had spent several years in a coma after a riding accident. In many ways we both felt it was Motion himself who was in the coma, returning as he did year after year through the same landscape towards the same hospital to visit his mother who was neither dead nor alive.

> It's always the place I see,
> not you. You're somewhere outside,
> waving goodbye where I left you
> a decade ago. I've even lost sight
> of losing you now;

I did not know it then because I had never lost anyone close to me, let alone a parent, that what Motion was describing was grief. But my father knew it. He knew the limbo one experiences after someone you love dies. How death holds you suspended in a virtual Antarctica. How, over time, the feelings of loss gradually grow lost themselves. 'I've even lost sight/of losing you now' – after which you lose the tone of their voice, the outline of their face, the touch of their hands. You want to recall something they said, but suddenly realise it's not possible because they're lost in the windstorm of death.

It's four years since Beri died and nine years since Peggy died. How is that possible? How can that be true?

I pad up and down the library. Each day this room grows emptier while I grow lonelier. This is not an easy thing to admit to, how lonely I am now that my parents are dead. It's not that being alone per se is terrible. I like being alone. In fact, I thrive on having time and space to myself. No, that is not it at all. This type of loneliness is different. It's a peculiar type of vertigo, of feeling unbalanced, while everyone else looks so much more stable. This type of loneliness makes me want to reach out and touch something solid. A table, a chair . . . I need to reassure myself I exist. It's embarrassing to admit this, of course, but then this thought overlaps with another and I begin to believe that when I bump into someone in the street they can sense something is wrong, they can smell my loneliness on me – leastways this is what I start to imagine during one of my long spells of navel-gazing. That's another affliction of the lonely – how introspective we become, how every tiny thought becomes the subject of detailed, daily analysis. Everyone is self-obsessed to some extent, but when you're lonely the world shrinks and you turn into an egocentric giant. It's *Gulliver's Travels*. It's Lilliput. Solipsism on an ugly, unaccommodating scale.

My loneliness is, of course, compounded by the fact that nearly all my friends and family live hundreds of miles away from the See-Through House. The only people I still know around these parts are the parents of friends I grew up with, friends who themselves have all moved away. Now I'm thinking I should perhaps follow suit.

From the second Beri died, it was clear that sooner or later I would need to move out of High Sunderland. Practicality wise, this house is too large for one person. Besides, I don't earn enough money for its upkeep and, even if this weren't the case, I know my life belongs elsewhere. I need more than the past to sustain me. I need to engage not just with bucolic landscapes, with trees and grass and sheep, but also with the fierceness of a city, its bite and kick, its streets and its fumes, its bright lights and its shadows, but most importantly of all, with its people. Yet despite repeating this to myself like a mantra, despite curling up by the fire each night wishing I could pop around for a glass of something or a cup of tea every now and again with a friend, the thought of leaving here remains unbearable. I'm stranded on a glass island, one whose shores I patrol every day, guarding tidelines of pinecones and thistles whilst simultaneously losing sight of reality in the rolling fog of my own fear.

Is that what living in the past does to you? Do you become deaf and blind to the outside world? Am I turning High Sunderland into a place I no longer live in, but haunt?

*

When I lived in Cornwall the sea mists were legendary. Some days it was as if the clouds had fallen into the streets. Any number of mythical creatures might emerge from those vapours. If you stood on the shoreline it was impossible to separate the waves from the haar. Little wonder that this landscape was populated with so many folk tales.

One of my closest friends during this time was a woman called P—, who lost a friend in the 7/7 bombings in London. A few days after this terrible event I visited her – she lived in a ramshackle cottage a few doors up from mine – and while we sat in her garden playing with seashells, drinking coffee, she told me that that morning she'd opened her door to find a white feather resting on the step outside.

'It was a sign,' she whispered. 'An angel left it for me. His angel.'

'Or ... ' I said as gently as I could, 'it might have come from a seagull? After all, there are seagulls everywhere here, thousands and thousands of them?'

But several months after my mother died, what did I do? On a cold, rainy November night I went to Wadebridge Town Hall to see a clairvoyant ex-hairdresser called Clarence Stark.

Peggy's loss had hit me very hard. I was grieving. I was lost. Since her death I had barely slept a single night in my bed, but had decamped to the couch where I kept BBC News 24 on so that I could watch the flickering images of wars and diseases and floods because I didn't want to face my grief.

Sitting in Wadebridge Town Hall felt comforting, hopeful even, but what if Clarence didn't choose me? I wanted to be chosen. I needed to be chosen; however, looking around me I could see at least two to three hundred people, all of whom were as anxious as me for Clarence Stark's attention.

The Town Hall was a down-at-heel type of place that had definitely seen better days. The walls were painted a sickly NHS green while the windows were grubby and the whole place stank of an over-liberal use of toilet cleaner.

Normally I might pop in there on a Wednesday morning when the WI put up stalls selling home-grown vegetables or home-made cakes, but that evening there was no cheerful plate of iced goodies or odd assortment of badly knitted toys to distract me. Was this really a wise way to spend a cold night in November? In an unheated Town Hall waiting to listen to an ex-hairdresser try to contact the dead? Everything inside me screamed, 'Get Out!' Yet there I was, glued to my seat, eyes transfixed on the stage.

Finally Clarence appeared and for the next hour I watched him being contacted by a number of spirits.

'Does anyone here know a Michael?' Clarence shouted into his microphone.

'Does anyone here know someone called Rachel who's recently passed over?'

'Does anyone here know someone called Robert or Bob or perhaps Bobbie or Bert? Rather overweight? Died in a car crash?'

Unsurprisingly, these Michaels, Rachels and Roberts were all 'claimed' by somebody or other in the room. And every time a new name was mentioned a whole bunch more hands would shoot up – all hoping that Clarence would point at them and say the magic words, 'I think it's you they want to speak to –' whilst the rest of us looked on enviously.

Finally Clarence said, 'I have a Margaret here? Does anyone in the room know a Margaret who's passed over recently?'

My hand shot up so quickly I nearly dislocated my shoulder. I was desperate, I was so anxious that Clarence choose me rather than another woman sitting three rows in front of me who's hand had also shot up that I leant forward as far as I could without taking a nosedive and fixed Clarence with my eyes.

Clarence said, 'Margaret informs me that she died at home? She'd not been well for some time ... '

The woman in front of me nodded.

I nodded more vigorously.

'Margaret is saying something about a scarf or a ... a ring?'

My rival's hand reluctantly returned to her lap.

Suddenly all Clarence's attention was focused on me.

'I'm wearing my mother's ring?' I said, holding up my left hand to show him said item of jewellery.

'Margaret was fairly old when she passed?'

'Eighty-five!'

'Hang on ... hang on ... Oh ... she's saying you've had your hair cut recently.'

'Yes!' I said.

'Well ... she's laughing. I think she likes it, but she's laughing –'

'I cut it myself,' I said, astounded that this was actually happening – at the time I had completely forgotten Clarence had once been employed as a hairdresser and consequently would have been able to spot a badly cut head of hair at a hundred paces. Even my friends had commented on how dreadful my fringe was.

'Yes,' Clarence now muttered, as if in conversation with someone behind him. 'Yes, I hear what you're saying. Yes, I'll tell her. Margaret says that you've been up to something you shouldn't have been doing?'

I nodded.

'Oh God,' I said, feeling my face starting to burn, for the truth was I'd begun smoking again – something I'd sworn to Beri and Peggy I'd given up years ago.

'She had difficulty eating at the end, didn't she? She's telling you that she's sorry but she just couldn't face it. And there's something else, something about towels, she keeps talking about towels and a key?'

I shook my head. 'No. I don't recall anything about towels,' I answered, puzzled at the randomness of what Peggy wanted to convey from the other side.

'What about the key?' Clarence pursued. 'She's definitely saying the word "key".'

'Sorry, no.'

Clarence looked rather peeved at this, but then quickly changed tack and said that another person was coming through, someone called . . . but I don't remember his or her name. What I do remember is – about half an hour later, leaving the brightly lit hall and stepping out on to the high street where it was still raining. A short distance away, on the other side of the street, stood Barney's Fish & Chip Shop, its windows all steamed over. As I walked by, I noticed someone had drawn the words 'Every Little Thing's Gonna Be Alright' in the condensation and afterwards a smiley face that had begun to dribble a bit at the corners of the mouth. But I couldn't smile because half of me knew I had been conned while the other half of me didn't mind in the slightest because at that moment even a con felt better than nothing.

Three years later a close friend of mine, Nancy, died and I found myself visiting another clairvoyant, only this time in a cramped booth in the basement of Selfridges on Oxford Street. All that separated me from the thousands of shoppers milling around outside was a thick velvet curtain. I have no idea what colour the curtain was, it might have been racing-silk green or plum red with shiny gold stars scattered across it, but I couldn't tell because I was sobbing so much.

Initially I had wanted to make an appointment at the College of Psychic Studies near the Natural History Museum in South Kensington. This sounded an authentic sort of a place, but when I phoned up I was told that the only person working on Saturday was fully booked and had been for months so my next move was to google 'spiritualists London' on my laptop. Why I chose Selfridges still baffles me to this day. There were hundreds of other psychics I could have seen and yet the following Saturday, after a short bus ride with my friend Jenny, there I was sitting in the 'Psychic Sisters of Selfridges' booth, buttressed between a Nespresso Bar and the Crockery department. Tears and snot streamed down my face, my whole body shook uncontrollably. All I wanted to hear was that Nancy's spirit was out there, that there was still some part of her that was connected to the world in which I lived.

The psychic, whose name I can no longer recall, looked visibly shocked at the state I was in and pushed a box of tissues towards me nervously.

'You're not in a good way, are you?' she said, stating what the majority of people in Selfridges had already spotted.

'No,' I sniffled.

'You've lost someone, haven't you?'

Another nod from me, although this time I like to think my face displayed a flicker of incredulity beneath the snot and the tears.

'All morning I've felt the presence of a little white dog,' she continued.

Oh God! What the hell was I doing here? From outside the booth came not just the murmur of people shopping, but their actual conversations. Someone was trying to decide what plates to buy for her kitchen, white ones or 'those over there with the pretty gold pattern'.

Why on earth was I searching for Nancy here? This was not the type of place she'd have frequented even when she was alive. In fact, it was the least likely place any self-respecting spirit would visit, unless they had a penchant for Wedgwood.

Yet despite these misgivings, I did not leave. I was too polite. Instead, I sat through the next forty-five minutes hoping at any moment the spiritualist might suddenly say something relevant about me and my friend, but all we kept coming back to was the little white dog and the fact that if I committed suicide I would not meet up with her or my mother because killing oneself was frowned upon in spirit circles, which, truth be told, I thought rather mean.

So why am I writing about this? It's definitely not because I want anyone to know how insane I was or how, after the death of both my mother and Nancy, I temporarily lost my mind and subsequently my ability to think in a rational fashion.

I'm writing about it because, after Beri died, I felt absolutely no need whatsoever to visit anybody: not a spiritualist nor a clairvoyant nor a medium.

Because Beri was all around me.

The See-Through House was constructed not of bricks nor of mortar, nor of wood, nor even of glass. It was built entirely out of who my father was, out of his spirit, his soul, out of *him*.

Suddenly I think of all the houses I have visited over the years, houses in which I have tried touching the past: the Freud Museum, Leighton House, the Musée Rodin in Paris with its bruised marble statues, Villa San Michele on Capri, Keats's House in Hampstead.

I recall standing in the latter, in the cramped bedroom, thinking how strange it was to be in such close proximity to the poet's dreams. Similarly, when I stepped into the study, I felt as if I were suffering vertigo. Keats had been dead nearly two hundred years and yet it was as if I could touch him. Is that what I'm doing now, touching ghosts? Am I a tourist in my own house attempting to catch hold of the past? I look at the handles on the doors at High Sunderland and see my father's hands gripping them, the two things inextricably linked. I hear the sound of a kitchen cupboard being opened and immediately my mother is standing next to it. Sights, sounds, smells. The clunk of the electricity meter at five o'clock each afternoon as the heating comes on; the sound the windows make when they glide open or shut on their smooth metal runners; the cold, sour smell that escapes from the wine cupboard and the sweeter, woodier aroma that belongs to the drinks cabinet.

I look at the books on the shelves in the library and catch sight of a novel by Jeanette Winterson, *Written on the Body*. It belonged to my mother: it was a birthday present from me because we had both enjoyed *Oranges Are Not the Only Fruit*. In it the narrator says of her lover that she is translating 'me into her own book'. Am I translating High Sunderland into my father? Are its frames and struts the bones of his body? Sternum, clavicle, scapula, spine. Are the windows his eyes?

This is how my mind is working these days. When I walk through the rooms I think of his bloodstream. The living room transforms into the lungs of the house, the library its spine with each book a vertebra. House and body, body and house, the two are inseparable.

Little wonder, then, that when I leave the building a kind of panic sets in only to be assuaged when I step back inside. Beri's skin has become my skin and with that comes a very real problem because recently I have noticed that leaving the house for long periods causes my whole body to shake. If the house represents Beri, is my reluctance to leave it simply an unwillingness to accept Beri's death? I want him back.

'What are you?' I whisper angrily to myself. 'Five years old?'

But I long for him and for Peggy. My world is diminished without them and dull, for the texture of longing is an absence of texture. A nothingness. An un-texture or non-feel.

> My hands push down between
> hollow, invisible sleeves,
> hesitate, then lift
> patterns of memory:
>
> a green holiday, a red christening,
> all your unfinished lives
> fading through dark summers,
> entering my head as dust.

'In the Attic' was Beri's favourite poem in Motion's collection, with the above two verses striking the most profound chord. Patterns of memory. That was the phrase he lingered over, explaining to me how it summed up the way he recalled Zori; the tints of auburn and gold in her hair, a brown and cream skirt that always made him think of coffee and honeycomb.

'Occasionally,' Beri said once in an attempt to explain how he painted, 'I combine colours in relation to people I know well. The blue-greys and turquoise-blues in this painting [*Turquoise*, 1969] sum up for me the personality of my wife Margaret.'

Biography as colour? Is that what he meant? I scan the bookshelves and notice three flesh-pink volumes by Ernest Jones on fellow psycho-analyst Sigmund Freud buttressed next to Gitta Sereny's *Albert Speer: His Battle with Truth*. For me Speer would be an unedifying grey whereas Sereny is a kaleidoscope of colours: oranges, indigos, golds.

Beri shakes his head at his daughter's flight of fancy.

'For goodness' sake, Shelley, stick to the facts!'

The facts. The facts are: there are no facts. Everything shifts, escapes explanation, eludes my grasp.

I take each book down from the shelves and begin leafing through them. I'm looking for something, but I don't know what that some-thing is. All I know is that I don't want to miss it. I take the books down one by one and flick through their pages, pausing every time I come to a creased corner. These tiny folds feel like footprints in the sand or tracks in the snow – they're ghost-trails of all the places Beri stopped reading, switched out a light, fell asleep. Here and here and here, I whisper under my breath. It's a pointless exercise, of course, but at the same time I also know I'm doing it because at some point in the not too distant future I'll have to pack the library up and because I can't keep all of these books – some of them will have to go to a charity shop – and what if I donate one with something precious inside it? A letter or note?

No sooner do I think this than something slips to the floor. It's a sketch of my mother – one I've not seen until now – and suddenly I feel elated. I've discovered gold. My father never, *never* drew or painted people. Abstracts – mostly; landscapes – sometimes; flowers – occa-sionally; but *never* people. Until this one.

Did Beri make it while the two of them were watching TV? Per-haps while they were reading by the fireside? It's a very private little sketch (I wonder if Peggy even knew he was doing it) and it was obvi-ously done quickly – in biro – but it's a beautiful picture.

I place the sketch on the sideboard – it will need to be framed – then put the book back on the shelf before moving down the line, firstly to *Architecture in Britain Today* by Michael Webb then to *The Virgin in the Garden* by A. S. Byatt followed by several Penguin Classics before my fingers alight on a book that – much like the pen sketch – I've not seen before ... a tiny volume bound in black leather with gold lettering on the spine, some of which has flaked off so that the words are almost illegible. Perhaps this is why the book has escaped my attention? Or perhaps I wasn't interested enough before now in the contents of these bookshelves to take this small volume down to examine it.

The book is in Hebrew except for the end papers stating it was printed in Budapest. Flicking through it several times I notice a scrap of handwriting in the top left-hand corner of one of the title pages, but because the writing is also in Hebrew, I don't have a clue what it says. Frustrated, I pull out my iPhone, take a snapshot then email it across to a relative in Israel to translate.

Deep down I know from the pocket-sized nature of the volume together with the translucent quality of the paper that it must be some type of prayer book. A few hours later my suspicions are confirmed. My relative emails me back that it is a Jewish prayer book and that the writing says, 'Dov Klein, 5 Ramban Street, Jerusalem'.

Dov was a nickname that a handful of my father's friends called him instead of Beri. In Hebrew it means 'little bear'. Confusingly it is also a nickname that applied to my grandfather, who occasionally signed himself Dov on family documents and who, a few years after the war ended, emigrated to Jerusalem. So either Lipot gave the book to my father or it was Lipot's own prayer book, which has somehow made its way here, perhaps after his death? Whatever the case, I find it curious that Beri held on to this volume as it sums up everything he came to reject.

*

Having spent just over a year studying and living with Rabbi Dush-inksy in Mea Shearim, Beri began – tentatively at first and then more rigorously – to question not just his own faith but also that on which Lipot and Zori had built their whole lives. This felt extremely disloyal; however, it was made somewhat easier, or at least did not prey on my father's conscience nearly as much as it might have done, because due to war-regulations all correspondence (letters / phone calls / telegrams) had come to a halt.

Suddenly Beri was freer than he had ever been in his life. Freer to think. Freer to question. Freer to roam the city. Skipping lectures became his norm, escaping the yeshiva for the wider experience of the city. Beri walked and looked and heard and tasted. Aesthetic considerations became uppermost in his mind. Not that he really understood what aesthetics were; he simply knew he had to keep looking because freedom lay in these new discoveries, the pleasure of really noticing shapes and colours and moods. The honeyed yellows of the Jerusalem stone. The glistering blues of an Arabic mosaic. The weave of ancient with modern. Of Christian with Jew and Arab with Christian. Of music and food. Dimpled lemons and bitter black coffee. Everything melded together, this was not just the goodness of life; it was life itself.

It was also during this time that Beri made contact with one of Zori's cousins – an archaeologist employed by the Public Works Department of the Palestinian government – who encouraged him to stray even further from the culture of the yeshiva by lending him novels and persuading him to take an interest in history and politics. More importantly – having spotted a small illuminated manuscript that Beri had painted to decorate a booth at The Feast of Tabernacles (a Jewish festival celebrating 'God's salvation of Israel when he brought the Jews out of Egypt') – this same cousin suggested Beri might apply for a place at the Bezalel Art School.

Serendipitously the name Bezalel rang a bell for Beri because as a child he had spent many a long afternoon listening to one of his teachers read to him from the book of Leviticus in which God chooses Bezalel (the son of Uri) to weave 'curtains to serve as walls for the tabernacle while the Israelites wandered in the desert'. In fact, as my father was later at great pains to point out, Bezalel was a man of many talents, for not only was he chosen by God to weave cloth, he was also tasked by Him to build the tabernacle itself as well as decorate its interior.

'But most illuminating,' recalled Beri, 'is the sentence which follows a detailed description of Bezalel's work. "Him has he filled with wisdom of heart to work all manner of work of the engraver, of the embroiderer, of the cunning worker and of the weaver."' This 'wisdom of heart,' my father continued, 'was applied to all the different tasks so that he [Bezalel] seems to have been an integrated craftsman and artist – certainly the first I was aware of – who designed and supervised the manufacture of not only the edifice itself but, and in great detail, all the furnishings that went into it.'

As the name for an art school Bezalel could not, therefore, have been more apt. It also struck a deep chord for my father, creating a comforting link both to his homeland and to his parents. To enrol at the school, however, Beri had to leave the yeshiva.

But how to tell the rabbi?

How to tell this most holy of figures that he wanted to join the secular world?

Perhaps he could say he needed to try something different? That joining the art school wouldn't mean he'd stop studying at the yeshiva? He could do it part time? Or perhaps he could say that he needed a profession and this was what the art school provided?

The weekly conversations with his cousin began to sound like army manoeuvres. Beri wanted his freedom. Lying in bed at night, he

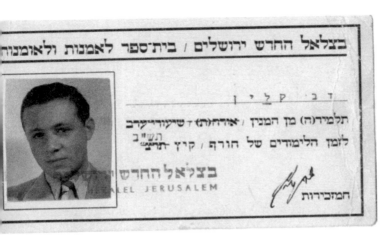

spent hours strategising. Could he do this? Might he do that? Perhaps the rabbi wouldn't be so appalled if Beri could explain himself in terms the rabbi might understand?

In the event it was worse than even he had imagined.

Hitting a brick wall would have been easier.

The rabbi was adamant that only prayer could save him. Beri should take his phylacteries (Hebrew verses hand-written on vellum contained in a small, black leather box) and go to the synagogue to pray.

Beri refused. He would leave the yeshiva with or without the rabbi's blessing.

In the event, it was without.

Beri never saw Rabbi Dushinsky again.

It was many years since my father had lived outside a religious community, many years since he had felt quite so at liberty and yet also on edge. He dreamt a lot during that time. Mostly about home, but also about Mea Shearim around which he would wander, not being able to locate the yeshiva yet never feeling quite lost. Nor, on waking up did he regret his decision to abandon his studies. Quite the contrary. As soon as he began at the Bezalel, he knew this was where he belonged.

Life, when viewed in retrospect, often reveals interesting juxtapositions. I find it fascinating to think that just at the moment when Beri was most at liberty to do with his life as he wished – that is, to participate in the art of weaving things together, of painting and creating something from scratch – that was the self-same moment his family was brutally being ripped apart. In April 1941 the Axis powers had begun their invasion of Yugoslavia. The Hungarians took control of Senta and forced any man under the age of fifty, which included Beri's younger brother Moshe and cousin Ochi Haur, into labour battalions while later, when the Germans took control of the town, the remaining Jewish population was loaded onto cattle trucks and sent to Auschwitz. This round-up of Jews included Beri's parents, grandparents, aunts, uncles and cousins – some of them in their mid-nineties, sick and disabled, others barely old enough to walk. By contrast, Beri, having been released from the yeshiva, began to engage in the making process, in the creating and drawing together of objects and in the excitement of a new life.

The small black prayer book sits in my hands. It barely weighs more than three or four ounces and yet I know that throughout his childhood and into his early twenties, the words in this little book carried tremendous weight for Beri. I also know that even in his nineties my father felt a certain degree of guilt at having turned his back on his religion. Perhaps that's why he held on to the prayer book for so long, although I doubt he ever removed it from the bookshelves once it was placed there. Nor did he believe the words that were written within it; but like the rest of the library, which in so many ways denotes the physical presence of two people's lifetime of reading, it represents how as human beings we are both complex and contradictory. How we can believe one thing yet play with an opposing idea. This thought strikes an echo. I reach back in my mind and for once, I can pin down a precise memory.

In 2000, the British artist Rachel Whiteread chose to represent a library as the most fitting memorial to the 65,000 Austrian Jews who were murdered by the Nazis during the Holocaust. *The Nameless Library*, as it has become known, stands in Judenplatz in Vienna. It is an astonishing piece of public sculpture, one that most probably derived from the long-held concept of Jews being the 'People of the Book'. Constructed from steel and concrete, all the spines of the sculpted books face inwards so the onlooker cannot read the titles or authors' names, nonetheless the books represent humanity in all its glorious complexity as well as individuality. People are made up of stories, and stories are what books contain.

Architecture and sculpture have a great deal in common, namely both practices deal with space. Whiteread's own trademark is that she casts spaces in concrete – the most famous example being *House*, a piece she made in 1993 by pouring concrete into the shell of a derelict building located in the East End of London. Once the concrete was set, the outside shell was removed to display a perfect cast of the empty rooms within. Suddenly what the viewer was seeing in quite literally concrete form was what the viewer would not normally see, that is to say emptiness.

I cannot compare Whiteread's work to Womersley's in such tangible terms, but I would suggest there's a similar concept at play here, namely a dialogue between the enclosed exteriors at High Sunderland and the wide-open interiors which, as Michael Webb points out in his book *Architecture in Britain Today*, highlights the difference between 'solid and void'.

Am I reading too much into Peter's intentions? Maybe. But this house has come to mean so many different things to me. Every day I rifle through memories as if they are pages, flit backwards and forwards in time, discover new footnotes, puzzle over dark chapters while celebrating lighter, funnier ones. Occasionally I want to take out a marker pen and highlight a beautiful scene or a particularly poignant moment. At other times I want to scribble in the margins as if High Sunderland were some kind of palimpsest.

Reading the house has become a daily occupation, something I do both consciously and unconsciously, but although I've known the building for over fifty-four years it can still catch me by surprise. Yesterday, for example, I took Henry for a walk around the garden last thing at night. To start with I walked away from the house down the driveway only to turn back halfway. There in the darkness floated not the house that I knew but something other. A theatre set. A building that had shape-shifted so that what was once a familiar outline made up of walls, courtyards and roof now disappeared leaving only a series of suspended glass panels glowing under a large yellow moon.

Moon and glass. Glass and moon. I have rarely seen anything more beautiful; the glowing disc of the planet floating above three panels of luminescent colour. It made me think of the work of Paul Klee and I hurried back to the house where I knew we had a book of his on the shelf alongside all the other volumes on artists such as Andrew Wyeth, Picasso, Dali, Hopper, Chagall. These were all works Beri had collected over the years, books I leafed through as a child and which recently I have attempted to take down and dust. Only something stopped me.

The same thing had happened a few days previously when I tried to place one of my own books, a copy of *Villette*, in a small gap I had spotted between the Hebrew Dictionary and Philip Roth's *American Pastoral*. But it seemed wrong, as if I were trespassing on someone else's territory. Similarly, ever since Beri's death, I have on occasion attempted to introduce a few of my own belongings such as the occasional framed photograph, rug, etc., into the living room only to realise there is no place for them there. They do not look right. They do not sit well in this space and this reminds me of something Bachelard said about houses being like snails' shells, organically connected to the owner/occupier and as such having no room inside for anyone else. Is this what is happening? Or perhaps it's to do with the fact that I want to keep everything precisely as it was in case Beri comes back?

I think – in this instance – the latter is closer to the truth. I want my father to recognise his home. I want him to know I have kept things exactly as they were so that he can walk back into the house whenever he's ready to resume his old life. Joan Didion calls this 'magical thinking' – when the bereaved are convinced the loved one might return. They have always returned before, haven't they? They have always come back from work, from business trips, from visiting friends or from trips to the shops. So it stands to reason that they are about to walk back into the room now, doesn't it?

Doesn't it?

How can Beri not come back to sit in his chair in the dining room, the one in which he sat almost every day of his life? How can he not come back to plant the tulip bulbs, which he did every autumn? How can he not come back to arrange and rearrange his prized ceramic collection that sits on a shelf directly beneath the bookshelves?

An early black-and-white shot of the library taken circa 1960 shows only three vessels on display on this shelf. Almost sixty years later there are in excess of seventy. All of these pieces are of varying size, colour, material and worth. Beri loved his collection yet he wasn't sentimental or precious about it. Some of the vases are nothing more than old wine or perfume bottles chosen for their particular colour or shape while others are collectors' pieces by artists such as Hans Coper and Lucie Rie. Beri enjoyed and celebrated the bottles' organic forms and varying glazes, although none of the pieces on display are highly decorated or adorned, but reflect the key principle by which he lived and worked, that 'less is more' or as the architect Adolf Loos put it in *Ornament and Crime*, 'The evolution of culture is synonymous with the removal of ornament from objects of everyday use.'

In this respect Beri's collection of bottles is a microcosm of the See-Through House, for like a painting by Giorgio Morandi, they stand testament to the intrinsic worth of simplicity. And it is that simplicity that, over the years, I have increasingly come to appreciate. Everything within and without the house has been pared back to essentials. It is a house in which you can rest. It is a house in which you can breathe or, as Simon Mawer puts it, it is a place where 'the ultimate opulence of pure abstraction' is celebrated.

Simplicity was also a value Beri saw reflected in the type of garments that Chanel, Dior and Balenciaga constructed out of his fabrics. Many of these designers made clothes that resembled textile origami or, on occasion, ceramics; their shape, their fluid lines, their classicism and above all else their purity of form reflecting what my father enjoyed most about his bottle collection.

However, it was not only the bottles that were of value to Beri. It was also how each piece was placed in relation to one another. Not a year passed without him arranging and rearranging the bottles, moving one item a little to the left, another a few centimetres forward or back. When a new bottle was introduced to the mix, it was not unlike watching a dancer practising a fresh routine. Beri would place the bottle on the shelf amongst the others, take two steps back, perhaps tilt his head slightly, take two steps forward, move the bottle to a different position, take one step back, pause, look down the line of older bottles, step forward, move the bottle again and so on and so forth until the right position was found. The way Beri handled each item also conveyed an intimate history or conversation with each. If a bottle got chipped or smashed, which did happen occasionally, Beri carefully glued the pieces together again. Just because the bottle was damaged did not mean his appreciation of it waned. He would never throw a piece out; indeed, sometimes I think he loved the damaged bottles more than those that were perfect. Beri obsessively reassembled each and every one, gathering all the fragments and splinters together, sitting patiently for hours on end, often with a magnifying glass in one hand and a tube of superglue in the other. Perhaps this was a hangover from the 'make do and mend' of the Second World War, but I think it went deeper than that, to the very core of what Beri believed with regards to design. If in the first instance an object or garment was made from good quality materials and if in the second instance there was integrity in its design, then even if the object were broken, it would be worth putting in the time and effort to try to mend it. This is the opposite of today's throwaway culture, instilling not only longevity upon the objects we love but also value. Thus Beri spent hour upon hour arranging these shelves, moving backward and forward in a meditation of sorts, with the space between the bottles creating as many lines, shapes and rhythms as the bottles themselves. Absence was crucial to the picture, as beautiful and as complicated as everything else.

Another absence, although this time on a human level, was the lack of any decorative objects belonging to Peggy.

There were none.

Not in this space, nor anywhere else in the house.

There cannot be many homes where this is the case, where the woman of the house sacrifices her own sense of style for that of her husband. Not that a lot of the furniture and decorative pieces at High Sunderland were not bought and appreciated by both Beri and Peggy, but it was Beri's sense of taste that always prevailed. To this end my mother found a different outlet to express her own, more eclectic nature, namely in Present Time – a gift and kitchenware shop that she owned in the local town. Here she was queen of all she surveyed, which for the most part meant stacks of white china together with shelves of Le Creuset and glassware from Sweden.

But there was another side to Peggy, one that was definitively more Victorian and one that she indulged by buying china decorated with bouquets of pink roses, butter dishes adorned with brown cows, tea towels across which ginger cats strolled. Mum also loved ducks: wooden ducks, china ducks, duck doorstops and ducks woven out of raffia. These were not items she would ever dream of inflicting on Beri, but in the shop they satisfied a silent, more homely part of her self.

Another item Peggy kept at the shop, although this time in a back room hidden from view, was a purchase she made from an antiques shop while staying in Bath some time during the late Eighties.

As far as I am aware Peggy never told Beri she'd bought this 'item'. Not that the cost would have bothered him, but she knew if he ever set eyes on it, his reaction would have been one of utter incomprehension, for the object in question was a small black box containing six cut-crystal, cranberry sherry glasses most probably manufactured at some point in the early- to mid-eighteenth century.

'I bought them on a whim,' she explained the day she revealed her stash to me. We'd been working together in the shop and during a lull between customers she signalled for me to follow her in to the back room.

'I want to show you something,' she whispered conspiratorially before lifting the box out from under a table. 'But don't tell your father ... '

Later, when my mother sold the shop, she smuggled the glasses back to High Sunderland and stuffed them at the back of her wardrobe so there was never any question Beri would discover them. In many ways it would make the perfect short story. Sometimes I imagine Peggy opening the box as if it contained her true nature. At other times I see her opening it because what it contained was rebellion. Everyone likes to kick out once in a while, swim against the prevailing tide. Some people do it on a large scale, others prefer small insurrections that won't damage the status quo, but which nonetheless fulfil a latent desire.

Thinking about them now, however, I'm amazed that I never considered her choice of purchase; that is to say that of all the antiques she could have bought, Peggy chose something made from glass. I'm also surprised that I've never drawn a parallel between my own secretive nature and that of my mother. The fact that she needed a private realm where Beri was not *not* welcome but where he knew it was sensible to stay away, a domain in which she hid her secrets. As early templates go it seems I learnt a lot from Peggy and realising this now makes me feel a little less guilty that I kept so much back from my father.

Of course, seen from Beri's perspective, symbolically speaking the crate of sherry glasses might correspond to Pandora's box, containing all the evils of the world, which in this scenario would be a cut-glass, pre-twentieth-century, over-decorated one. Flowers and flounces were the devil's work according to Beri, who considered the worst swear words ever were 'Pre' and 'Raphaelite', 'cheese' and 'cloth' and never, *never* forgetting 'Laura' and 'Ashley'.

Like most little girls of my era, I loved all things floral. This was the Seventies after all, when a backlash against everything 'modern' was apace, particularly in fashion, but also in the wider world of design. Suddenly people were yearning for a time when they felt more secure. 'The stripped-pine, Laura Ashley-led Victorian revival engulfed the popular British home, while, for the social elite, the country house replaced the sophisticated metropolitan home as a domestic idyll,' wrote Penny Spark in an essay accompanying a V&A exhibition on British Design.

When I was a very small child my mother made Gillian and myself beautiful clothes out of Bernat Klein fabrics. In particular I recall a tweed coat woven with heavenly slubs of pink, green and orange wool that when I think of it today makes my mouth water, the colours were so delicious. But at the time I didn't think much of it. In point of fact, I would have preferred something less colourful, possibly in black, green or pillar-box red, a coat like those my friends wore. Ditto the jumpers Peggy knitted me out of Beri's yarns – all of which seemed too abstract and outlandish whereas I yearned for navy-blue sweaters or, most coveted of all, long pinafore dresses and sprigged maxi-skirts.

Eventually my dreams came true and Peggy bought me several full-length affairs. One particular dress became a firm favourite, sporting as it did a pattern of small yellow rosebuds across a pale mauve background. But when I put the dress on and skipped through to the living room, Beri took one glance at me and rolled his eyes.

'You look like the walls of a Victorian toilet,' he declared, disappointment writ large over his face.

I looked terrible, he continued.

I clashed with everything I stood next to.

Did I really want to be mistaken for a potty?

At this point I don't recall whether I cried or threw a tantrum or both, but I do remember never forgetting those words and when I reached my twenties and thirties I enjoyed quoting them back at him as evidence of the trauma I'd suffered. I was joking, of course, and we would both laugh because I had had a wonderful childhood and then Beri would always finish by saying, 'But of course I was right!'

At the top end of the L-shaped library – that is to say in the top, right-hand corner of the room beyond the bookshelves – is Beri's workspace.

Essentially this corner did not change the whole time Beri lived and worked at High Sunderland.

Marked on Womersley's original plans as the 'Study', the two walls that make up this corner consist on one side of horizontal panels of clear glass while the other side, at right angles, is made of panelled wood. There is no partition between this space and the rest of the living room, added to which, when we were young, one of the rectangular glass panels was an incandescent yellow. Like light pouring in to a church through stained glass, this yellow rectangle brought slabs of buttery sunlight into the room. More than that, even when the sun was not shining, it was luminous. But when one looked more closely at this window you could see that rather than the glass being 'stained', the colour was created by pressing a web of semi-translucent yellow paper between two sheets of clear 'diffusing' ply glass. This trapping of colour is repeated throughout the building in slabs of green, taupe, gold and black; however, over the years, the sunlight has damaged the pigment to such an extent that in places it has been leached of all colour.

One of the first signs of depression can be that the sufferer feels their world dull, without light or shade, without brightness. The world grows dreary as if a cloud has passed over the sun. Even before my parents died, I often suffered low moods. Weeks or months of bleakness were my norm.

As a child I always imagined those struck down by this condition were romantic or noble in their despair. There seemed to be something beautiful about melancholy. Perhaps that's why I was drawn to Millais' *Ophelia* or Wallis's *Chatterton* and repeatedly turned to the poetry of Edna St Vincent Millay and that other favourite of angst-ridden schoolgirls, Sylvia Plath.

But of course depression is not romantic at all.

It's dull, tedious, lacklustre. It's *Groundhog Day* without the laughs. It's the poem by Emily Dickinson, 'I felt a Funeral, in my Brain'.

Every morning begins with the same struggle to surface from the darkness, to put one foot in front of the other and simply exist. But the worst part is the repetition, the morning after morning after morning … of the same dread fear. And the pain. No one ever mentions the physical pain of depression, the feeling that at any moment you might suffocate because the ache in your chest is so bad it prevents you from breathing.

After Beri died things grew considerably worse. Now I was depressed and grieving and it was impossible to know which was which. Was I feeling like death because I was mourning my father or because my depression had returned, or both? Did it even matter which one I was experiencing given that each was equally terrifying?

When playwright Dennis Potter was diagnosed with inoperable cancer he described how, with his days cruelly numbered, everything took on an intensity the like of which he had never experienced. Plum blossom suddenly became 'blossomest blossom', whiter and frothier than anything he'd ever seen before in his life.

When Beri died the opposite happened. My world was suddenly dreariest dreary. I knew I was walking under blue skies, through green fields, yet all I saw was a sort of washed-out, underpants grey. The window in the corner of Beri's workspace reflected this. One day I sat staring at it for hours wondering how many years it had taken for the colour to leach away. How many years had it taken to go from bright, buttercup yellow to nothingness? Nor was the irony lost on me that it was in this small area of the house that Beri had done the majority of his most colourful paintings and design work.

Measuring approximately three metres square, the workspace is large enough to house a desk, a chair and what became known as 'The Colour Box'.

The Colour Box was a large wooden structure designed to hold twenty or so boards on to which were stuck row after row of tiny, plastic pockets. Into each of these compartments Beri would place his samples: tiny twists of yarn, snippets of paper, dimples of wool and fingernails of cloth he'd collected for reference purposes. Whereas the great Victorian naturalists travelled the world collecting beetles and butterflies, Beri collected colours. He would bend to pick up a puff of pink cashmere from the floor at the dye-works or he'd spy a curl of soft, peachy mohair on an old jumper stuffed at the back of a wardrobe. As Dylan Thomas wrote (apropos the Festival of Britain), 'And what a lot of pink – rose, raspberry, strawberry, peach, flesh, blush, lobster, salmon, tally-ho – there is. ' Not to mention the blues, greens, greys, oranges, yellows and purples. Like a proud entomologist Beri also took great care as to precisely where, in the grand sequence of colours, each new specimen should be placed. He would grade them as if they were diamonds and weigh them as if they were gold. It was all to do with balance, he would explain to anyone interested in how he designed his yarns and fabrics. Needing to combine three or four different shades he would pull out sample board after sample board, removing a twist of cherry-coloured wool to hold up against a snippet of cobalt. Then, if this did not work, out would come a different shade of red, something darker or lighter perhaps, then another and another, until finally he hit on the right combination. 'Color [sic] is life;' wrote Johannes Itten in one of Beri's favourite books, *The Art of Color*, 'for a world without appears dead.'

On the easel in front of me sits the last painting my father ever made. It was completed only a few days before he died. It is a beguilingly simple picture, a study in green. The background resembles a thick impasto of avocado flesh on top of which dance four squares, each a different colour, moving from sharp lemon yellow to pistachio, sea green and finally olive. It's a meditation, if you will, one that has

High Sunderland through the birch trees, *c.*1990

'Mace', Bernat
Klein tweed
sample, *c.*1961

Bernat Klein
Scotland catalogue,
featuring High
Sunderland, c. 1964

Bernat Klein space-dyed
mohair yarn sample,
1960–80

Princess Margaret in a Bernat Klein
velvet tweed, 1965

Infinite Blue (oil on canvas),
Bernat Klein, 2011

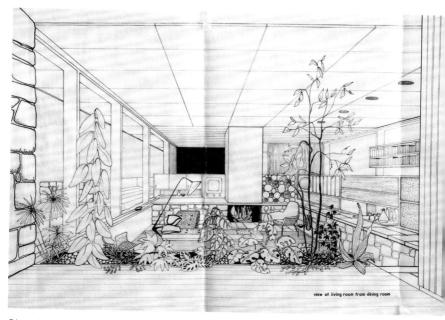

Sketch of the Living Room at High Sunderland, Peter Womersley, *c.* 1956

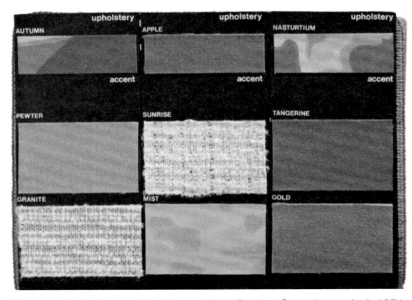

Co-ordinated colour guide, Bernat Klein Design Consultants Ltd, 1971

Beri considering
colour guides
in the Studio,
mid-1970s

Tulips in the Living Room (oil on canvas), Bernat Klein, 1976

Shock them in Terlenka. The girls will never stop raving about this beautifully simple dress by David Gibson.

Buttons in front and at the cuffs, and a tie belt. The fabric design is by Bernat Klein and features a subtle mixture of pink and white or yellow and white. Forget ironing, it's Terlenka. About £9.

Terlenka advert featuring a Bernat Klein fabric design, c. 1969

Bernat Klein tweed with specially dyed, brushed mohair yarn, c. 1962–4: many of the cloths woven at the mills were influenced by the colours of Beri's paintings

Tulips 3, Bernat Klein, *c.* 1961: 'All I wanted to put down was my original excitement at seeing these glowing colours in their full extravagance'

Beri painting
Lichens 2 in the
Library, 1963

Elle Collections cover featuring Bernat Klein tweeds, *c.*1961

Beri in a coat of his own tweed, *c.* 1962

Reflections: the views through the See-Through House, Shelley Klein, 2015

drawn me to it almost every day since it was finished. One that contains the last image my father ever looked at with his artist's eye.

For over seventy years Beri experimented with every shade he could lay his hands on. He dyed, spun, knitted and wove, printed, painted, pulled, pushed, harmonised, juxtaposed, balanced, contrasted and contorted them, as if creating a Kama Sutra of colour. Now, here in front of me, stands the distillation of all that work, the purest of paintings within the simplest of houses, each an echo of the other.

Even the space in which Beri's easel stands is simple. This is not a Romantic's idea of an artist's studio, the type of place where the floor is splattered with paint, where every surface groans with rusting tins, old rags and jars of half-used brushes and palette knives.

Beri had a profound fear of chaos. Faced with disorder he grew anxious and quite frequently angry. Sometimes I wondered if this was a response to the disorder that war had imposed on his family. Was High Sunderland a reply of sorts: a house that exiled confusion, demanded clarity, highlighted reason? Or is this yet again reading too much into Beri's story? Whatever the case, my father could no more live or work in an untidy environment than a polar bear could survive in the Sahara. That being the case, every implement that he employed in his work, be it a pen, brush or paperclip, was always arranged very neatly and never used without being returned to its 'rightful' place.

These tools of his trade still lie on his desk: a vast array of palette knives and plasterer's trowels, brushes, spatulas, an old canvas on which he mixed up his colours, an odd assortment of stained rags, a plastic bottle half-filled with white spirits and several blackened, gummy matchsticks which he would sometimes use to scratch his signature into the bottom right- or left-hand corner of paintings.

And then there were the paints themselves.

'I find,' wrote Lucian Freud, referring to an article that he had written almost fifty years previously, 'that I left out the vital ingredient without which painting cannot exist: PAINT. Paint in relation to a painter's nature.'

Beri's tubes of oil paint are arranged on top of a black towel that has been placed over a wooden cabinet that stands to one side of his easel. Each tube has been placed in order first by size and then by colour. Old and half-squeezed, their soft metal bodies are smeared and indented with fingerprints. 'Manganese Blue' reads the first label. Cobalt Turquoise, Ultramarine Light, Quinacridone Rose, Permanent Madder, Transparent Gold Ochre, Alizarin Green ... So many shades which, when mixed together, produced thousands more shades. In fact, there was only one point in his life when colour was not his main theme.

For a number of years after Peggy died Beri downed tools. I was in Cornwall; my sister and brother were in Surrey and Hampshire respectively. Every six weeks or so I flew up to Edinburgh to make sure Beri was okay. I also rang him every morning to check he was up and about and again every evening to have a chat about the day. My sister also tried to get up to Scotland as often as possible and rang him most evenings, yet despite our best efforts he was lonely, grieving for the person he'd shared his life with for over sixty-one years.

No wonder he didn't have the inclination to put paint to canvas. Explaining his lack of enthusiasm he told one of his oldest friends: 'Without Margaret there's no point. She was my sounding board. I was painting all my pictures for her.'

Painting had been a part of my father's life ever since taking his first steps away from the yeshiva to enrol at the Bezalel Art School. Turning his back on the assurances of religion to embrace the uncertainties of art had not, however, proved easy. Yes, he'd replaced his small black prayer box with a slim wooden case containing ten cakes of watercolour, but other changes weren't so easy to pull off. For example, the students at the art school viewed Beri as a 'Bakhur Yeshiva', which in effect meant 'the outsider', 'the Orthodox young fogey' studying alongside the far more sophisticated, up-to-date art students.

Beri had to learn fast. He was years (if not centuries) behind his contemporaries – particularly when it came to working out practical issues. 'My problems now were not abstract mental exercises to do with worlds that I never knew and with things that could not ever matter to me; they were almost painfully tangible and of the moment [...] the simplicity of a basic idea in a poster which had to convey half a dozen points of information and persuasion clearly at a glance.' The technique involved in threading a warp, 'the smooth gloss and warmth of the bleached bone of a skull' and how to convey this in paint.

Beri lapped everything up. And the joy of discovering that using one's eyes and using 'them freshly every day, was a way of life' never left him. One year slipped by and then two, at which point he realised that if he was serious about a career in textiles, he'd need to leave Palestine to continue his studies in Britain. But Beri didn't speak English (nor had he passed the London Matriculation exams, which at that time were a requirement for entry into Britain) so once again it was back to the books, back to studying until finally, *finally*, having passed the exams and having spent a short time in Cairo working for the British Ministry of Information as a monitor of broadcasts from Europe – he chose a textile design course at Leeds University.

After all his hard work Beri's felt overwhelmed with excitement. This was a real adventure, one he'd dreamt about ever since standing with his younger brother Moshe by the wooden bridge over the Tizsa, waving at the Paris-to-Budapest Simplon Express. Now it was his turn to travel, his turn to go on an adventure.

The year was 1945 and the war in Europe had ended. For the most part Jerusalem had remained unaffected during this period. British troops had been (and still were) stationed in the city, but save for some of his fellow art students joining the Haganah (a Jewish paramilitary organization, an offshoot of which – the Irgun – was later responsible for bombing the King David Hotel in 1946) Beri recalled little other than the buying of his passage to England on board a troop ship, the RMS *Franconia*.

However, days before his departure, my father received the first communication from his family in over three years. The letter was from Moshe, who was living as one of thousands of displaced persons in a refugee camp just outside Senta. In the letter Moshe explained how the family had been rounded up by the Germans. He – Moshe – had somehow managed to escape from his forced-labour battalion and had joined the Partisans, but almost everyone else had been taken away. Except that now Lipot was back! Somehow, he had managed to make the painfully slow journey home from a prison camp called Auschwitz in Poland. The journey had taken him weeks. He'd hitched lifts on the back of lorries and a number of British Army and Red Cross vehicles, but was now in a makeshift hospital suffering typhoid fever. That was the good news. The bad news was that no one knew where Zori was, nor even if she was still alive, but both he and Lipot thought it unlikely.

Turmoil. Confusion. Overwhelming despair mixed with relief that Lipot had survived. But Beri didn't know what to do for the best. Should he return to Yugoslavia immediately? Surely he should? But how to get there? His cousin said travelling through post-war Europe was impossible and reports in the newspapers backed this up. Hundreds of thousands of people were some place other than where they belonged, needed or wanted to be. But to go to England felt callous. Not so, replied his cousin. It was the most sensible action he could take under the circumstances. Moshe would keep him informed and Beri could link up with the rest of the family as soon as things grew more settled.

Standing on board ship Beri's mind drifted between what lay ahead and what he was leaving behind. He listened to the sound of the ship's engines, to the lap of the water, stared up at the enormity of the sky. Dark and then bright and then dark again. On deck the wind scoured his face. Everything felt overwhelming, *was* overwhelming. He threw up, but couldn't tell if this was seasickness or fear. The only thing that helped was keeping busy and so, alongside a group of other passengers (mostly fellow students who were also heading to universities across Britain), Beri helped keep the hold clean, scrubbing floors, cleaning toilets. The last thing on his mind was painting or textiles. In fact, he wouldn't pick up a brush or palette knife for another fifteen years.

The same occurred after Peggy's death; my father had no desire to produce anything new. Nor would he talk about Peggy during this time, about what her death meant to him. He didn't need to because anyone who knew him well could see he was suffering by the fact his easel stood empty.

I tried coaxing him to begin painting again. Perhaps he'd like to start with some roses? I said. The pink ones on the dining-room table? Or how about the view from the dining-room window? The corn poppies in the field below the house? I could go and collect some if he liked? But it wasn't until a family friend asked him to paint a small abstract for her that something inside Beri shifted. At first I thought there was no way he'd agree to her request, but I hadn't factored in how much my father liked and respected this person and also what a pushover he was when anyone, but particularly an elegant woman, requested something of him.

Two days later I was told to go out and buy a small canvas and a selection of oil paints.

Once Beri began painting again his enthusiasm returned quickly except for one curious thing. For over a year he would only use blue. Gone were the fiery reds and hot pinks and oranges. No, the only colour he was interested in was blue, blue or blue. Of course, he mixed the pigments into different shades from cobalt to aqua marine. From lapis lazuli to cerulean, but essentially it was a one-note song.

An outpouring of grief.

An elegy to Peggy.

That is how I interpreted the paintings.

A deluge.

A flood.

Something my father could articulate in no other way than by using the colour he most associated with his wife, the colour most people associate with melancholy.

Eventually, fearing that he would never use another colour again and concerned for his well-being, I asked if he might like to move on to warmer, brighter colours . . . ?

Beri shook his head.

The blue paintings continued.

Canvas after canvas.

I don't believe for one second he ever thought of what he was doing in terms of grief work. He was not the type of man to indulge negative emotions so perhaps I am incorrect in explaining his motivations in these terms, but this was the only time in my father's working life that I can recall him sticking resolutely to one colour, one theme.

Eventually – after almost a year and a half – the blues began to give way, tentatively at first, to greens then to yellows and umbers before slowly melting into cerise and rose pink. The series of small canvases became what he referred to as 'The Colour Circle' and this is how they were displayed in a small exhibition in 2012 with one whole wall of the gallery given over to blue while the remaining three walls accommodated the rest of the spectrum.

Today I pick up a tube of paint, unscrew the cap, sniff it and am immediately transported back to childhood. It's a dark, oily smell that – when combined with the aniseed whiff of white spirit – takes me straight back to lazy afternoons lying on my stomach down in the living room reading a book while Beri stood above me at his easel, palette knife loaded with colours, layers of which wobbled like jelly. Beri's use of paint was always generous, sensual, involving not only an intensity of colour but also a tactile viscidness and plasticity. He used paint much as a pâtissière uses whipped cream, that is to say liberally. Layer upon layer of scarlets and pinks so thick and blancmange-like that a painting could take four or five years to dry. Little wonder that as a child I often wanted to eat Beri's paintings; indeed, it took a great deal of control not to stick my fingers into the deepest, swampiest bits.

There was only one fly in the ointment. A very thin, spindly fly, a friend of my mother's. This person was an artist herself. But one morning I recall her arriving for coffee and during a seemingly pleasant conversation (during which my father was absent) she mentioned how wasteful she found Beri's use of oil paint. Not only wasteful, it was 'depraved'. I was a child and did not understand what the word meant, but from Peggy's reaction I knew it could not be favourable and later I looked it up in our dictionary. How could my father's use of paint be corrupt? How could it contaminate something or someone else? Upset and confused I asked Peggy, who said her friend was most likely still in a 'post-war' frame of mind, one in which she no doubt felt everyone should practise frugality. But this was the late Sixties – over twenty years after the war had ended – so, although I did not push the point, I did not entirely believe her.

The incident left a nasty taste in my mouth. Fortunately, however, it didn't taint the pleasure I took in Beri's work. Even today I feel a shiver of anticipation when I recall the sound his palette knife made as he moved it over the canvas in sharp, downward gestures. Sometimes the sound catches me unawares while I'm sitting in the living room reading a book or standing by the windows looking out across the fields. The scrape of metal on canvas: quick, decisive, inspiring.

Hearing is supposedly the last of our senses to die. Sitting with Beri's body at the hospital I leant as close to his ear as possible and whispered loudly that I loved him. I LOVE YOU, I said. I knew he couldn't hear me because Beri was profoundly deaf by the end of his life. Besides which, I'd missed the actual moment of his death by some fifteen minutes or so. Something I find hard to forgive myself for. This is the type of thought that plagues me. All the things I should or could have done. All the things I did not say and cannot now say, ever. It was the middle of the night and I sat with him for as long as I could because Beri always hated being alone. He needed company. I held his hand, which was still warm.

Even when Beri was painting, he didn't like the idea of working in solitude. I was reminded of this only a few days ago when reading a book called *Night Studio*, a memoir of the artist Philip Guston by his daughter Musa Mayer. In it she reveals that, despite her father's studio standing only a few feet away from the family home, she never once saw him paint. It shocked me when I read this. Of course, Beri did not make a living from painting. In this respect it was a sideline from his 'real' work, but his real work would not have existed in the way that it did without the paintings. Theirs was a symbiotic relationship. As was the relationship between the paintings and the family.

One of the first paintings in oils my father made at High Sunderland was *Lichen 1,* circa 1960. 'On one of our walks,' wrote Beri in 1965, 'on a bright winter morning, we came upon a fallen tree that must have been lying in the same position for many decades [...] The children proceeded to climb it and explore it. This is how we found a most unusual fungus growing on one side of it which was frozen hard and which, with the sun shining on it, looked quite beautiful.'

Using his preferred method of applying paint with palette knives, my father proceeded to paint the lichen and in a later interview commented that it was ' ... the intellectual exercise involved in translating an object from nature into a colour study' that interested him most. But although his paintings over the next six decades were also colour studies, they were in addition personal responses to how he experienced the world, to his joy and commitment to his immediate surroundings and to his family and friends.

I remember Beri standing by his easel with Peter Womersley one evening. I cannot recall the precise painting that was in front of them although I do recall it being a mixture of turquoise and greens. It must have been during one of Peter's infrequent visits to the Borders, some time after he left Scotland to go to work in Hong Kong, because I was in my early twenties at the time. Perhaps my father had asked Peter what he thought of the work. Or perhaps Peter had volunteered his opinion, whatever the case, the conversation soon veered off to discuss the work of Peter Lanyon.

Neither Peter nor Beri were great enthusiasts for hanging works of art in their own homes. For Peter I suspect this was because he thought the purity of the architecture might be compromised whereas for Beri if you hung a painting on a wall, he was concerned the viewer would become so inured to its presence that they'd soon fail to notice its qualities. With this in mind my father, with a few rare exceptions, barely displayed anything on the walls at High Sunderland. Yet despite both men's reluctance to hang works of art in their own houses, they were passionate gallery-goers and could often be heard exchanging views on the most recent exhibitions they had visited. Lanyon was one of Peter's favourite artists, whereas Beri favoured Kokoschka, Klee and Vuillard.

He once purchased a painting by the latter, a small jewel of a picture in a complicated gold frame. It used to sit above what the family call 'the top couch', which – as the name suggests – is a couch that runs along the top section of the L-shaped library.

As with the library and my father's workspace, there are no walls dividing this area from the rest of the living room – only the rectangular block of white chimney that floats like an iceberg above a pale marble sea.

The Vuillard was a beguiling work. I don't recall its title, but if I were to give it one, I'd call it *The Almost-Black Hat*. The background was an impressionistic flutter of greens and golds while in the foreground, a little to the left, as if about to disappear beyond the frame, loomed the back view of a woman wearing a large hat. The hat is mostly in shadow, hence why I recall it being 'almost' black. If there was any more detail in the painting, I do not remember other than to say it enchanted me. Nor do I know why Beri chose to buy this particular work. My guess is not that it was enigmatic or beguiling, but that he was drawn to it solely because of those pulsating greens.

Peter valued Lanyon's work for altogether different qualities. I recall him talking about the several planes Lanyon worked on in his paintings; how there was no single vantage point. This also rings true of his own work: the horizontals and verticals of High

Sunderland making it impossible to stand either within or without the building, without growing aware of its constantly shifting layers and planes.

Simplicity is central to all Womersley's buildings. Coco Chanel once said, 'Before you leave the house, look in the mirror and take one thing off,' but this sentiment could apply to Peter's work in that a lot more was 'left out' than ever 'put in'. A case in point is that between the 'top couch' and the sunken living room is a three-foot drop with no barrier in place to stop anyone falling over the edge. Nor, until recently, has this ever proved problematic. Until recently, indeed, I had barely given this a second thought. Then one day shortly after Beri died, an architect called around at the house. He wanted to take some photographs of the building as he was 'a huge fan of Womersley's work'.

ARCHITECT: Perhaps you should think of putting up some sort of railing to stop people falling over the edge?

SHELLEY [laughing]: No one's that stupid not to notice the drop –

ARCHITECT [very serious face]: I don't entirely agree with you there. Accidents happen all the time. Also, I think you'll find that these windows are very dangerous too. They certainly wouldn't pass building regs today – all those raw edges –

SHELLEY: There's nothing wrong with the windows –

ARCHITECT: There is, I'm afraid, but the drop down to the living room is worse. I'm surprised no one has hurt themselves –

SHELLEY: In sixty years no one's so much as teetered, let alone fallen over the edge.

ARCHITECT: How about something in glass and steel? That might do the trick –

SHELLEY: It's an A-listed building, nothing can be changed –

ARCHITECT [in an increasingly patronising tone]: I'd be surprised if that were the case; it's a well-known fact that listing rules can be flexible … if you know the right people –

But another fact was, had Peter heard this exchange, he would not have reacted half as politely as I (sadly) did. Instead, he would have enjoyed giving this man a piece of his mind. Back in 1960, for example, when East Barnet Urban Council refused to approve plans for a house he designed for Peter Shand Kydd, Peter was quoted as saying, 'Time and time again they [the council] turn down anything that is not conventional. They put up disgusting brick-rendered hovels, with little holes pretending to be windows. Anything dreadful gets past the local council quite easily. But anything with a flat roof to harmonise with the landscape and lots of windows from floor to roof, which reflect all the trees and garden around is taboo. They are a damned nuisance and they are doing much more harm than good. In fact they are quite simply ruining the countryside. Why should a committee of local tradespeople and butchers think they can teach designers what their houses should be like?'

This is vintage Womersley: opinionated, uncompromising, self-assured and visionary – so much so that when Sir Basil Spence, then president of the Royal Institute of British Architects, was asked to choose the best modern house in Britain, he was quoted as saying 'anything designed by Peter Womersley'.

Peter's uncompromising nature was one of his best qualities both as an architect and as someone to whom Beri felt a deep affinity. Neither man minced their words, particularly when it came to matters of design.

Standing beside the architect who I had invited into my home, I conjured up an image of Peter and my father frogmarching him out of the front door. This cheered me up enormously, that and what

Beri would have made of what the architect was wearing – namely a pink, striped shirt with a flowery red and purple tie and pinstripe navy trousers.

Beri's views on the way people dressed were not revolutionary; he preferred classic cuts, nothing ostentatious or sloppy, and the same applied to how people presented themselves, by which I mean their physical appearance. In particular he nurtured a pathological hatred of facial hair. He could not understand how any man could tolerate such an unruly appendage as a beard or moustache, especially if it was a handlebar one or something equally flamboyant. No matter how neatly clipped, Beri would regard it with a mixture of suspicion and mild disgust.

On one occasion when my mother, Beri and I were sitting watching a TV programme on childbirth, I recall Beri suddenly starting to gesticulate wildly.

> BERI [at the top of his voice]: Look at that! Just look at THAT!
> PEGGY [anxious]: What, what? What's wrong, darling? What on earth's the matter?
> BERI [pointing at the screen to where Sir Robert Winston was being interviewed]: Look at him! Look at that moustache! THAT MAN HAS NO RIGHT BEING A GYNAECOLOGIST WITH A MOUSTACHE LIKE THAT!

But all things considered, Sir Robert got off lightly.

On numerous occasions I'd come through from my bedroom to the main part of the house for breakfast only to be met by Beri saying, 'Really? Is that really what you intend on looking like?'

'I'm forty-five, Dad. This might come as a shock to you, but I can dress how I like.'

'Certainly . . . if you want to look like a tramp –'

When my sister chose a Laura Ashley dress to get married in, my mother dragged Beri aside.

> PEGGY: On no account are you to mention it –
> BERI [looking slightly hurt]: As if I would!
> PEGGY: Darling, I mean it. You are not to upset her –
> TEENAGE SHELLEY [piping up from behind him]: Or me –
> PEGGY: Or Shelley –
> BERI: Are you wearing Laura Ashley too?
> TEENAGE SHELLEY: Naturally.
> PEGGY: Just tell Gillian how lovely she looks. This is her big day –
> BERI: I'm not a monster –
> PEGGY [raising her eyebrows]: I'm not saying you are –
> BERI [calmly]: So then –
> PEGGY: So then –
> BERI [at the top of his voice]: But Laura BLOODY Ashley, for GOD'S SAKE!

Memories appear as if out of nowhere, float into mind apropos something somebody says or does. My sister's wedding day is a day I will never forget, but since starting out on this book other memories have snuck up on me, catching me by surprise. This often happens when clearing out cupboards.

Opening one I am hit by a tide of half-forgotten moments; stuttering images that, like old films, keep skipping frames.

Today I look through one of my father's wardrobes. I take out five suits in shades of brown and green, two passports, three hats, a medal he was given by the Queen for services to British industry, four wrist watches, several white plastic shirt collars, a paint-spattered artist's smock and a small bowl containing five padlocks. But it is what I don't find that affects me the most. The item I'm thinking of was usually kept in this cupboard.

'It was a gift from my mother,' Beri said, pulling out the neatly folded, blue and white cotton bedspread. Have you seen it before?'

'I don't think so –'

'When I left Senta ... well ... it belonged on her bed, but she wanted me to have something to remind me of home. Now I use it when it gets too hot to sleep with a duvet –'

'Not too often then?'

Beri smiled. 'No, not too often,' he said.

Beri had used the blue and white bedspread throughout his time in Jerusalem and afterwards had taken it with him to Leeds where it lay across every bed, from one dingy boarding house to another.

Leeds was a shock to his system, for despite enjoying his studies, he found the city cold and damp, added to which he'd only just learnt to speak English, which meant he failed every one of his fourteen first-year exams. Not only that, but at the same time Moshe had begun sending monthly updates detailing his and Lipot's efforts to trace Zori. This was hard work. Forms were filled in, interviews given, letters dispatched. The International Tracing Service alongside other agencies were doing their best to help, but they had informed them it could take months, perhaps years, to discover even the most basic details. Moshe also wrote saying that although Lipot was gaining in strength by the week, he'd indicated that as soon as he was fully recovered he wanted to immigrate to Palestine. In the meantime, he, Moshe, had been back to Senta, to the family home, but it had been ransacked. It was nothing more than a shell of its former self, evidence of which Moshe sent to Beri, who was devastated 'by the shabby, neglected, once so lovely home of ours of which I was sent photographs and now found to be yet another part of my past from which I had to learn to wrench myself free'.

I read that sentence today and a gaping black hole appears. A nothingness. A void. It's the type of fissure people suffering migraines occasionally speak of, where areas of their vision go missing. The dilapidation of the house, its 'shabby, neglected' appearance, is a world without Zori. It also occurs to me that Beri must have destroyed these post-war photographs because none exist in the family albums. The only ones we possess are those Moshe recovered from the debris, that is to say photographs of the family and house before the war blew both apart.

Then, a little over a year after they began their search, Lipot and Moshe received the notification they'd all been dreading. It was confirmed: Zori had been murdered in Auschwitz. All that was left was for Lipot to visit his eldest son in England in order to relay the terrible news. Arrangements were swiftly put in place shortly after which, father and son met for the first time in over eight years. As reunions go, it was subdued, the joy at seeing his father tempered by the change in his physical appearance, the exhaustion and pain of the past few years plainly written across Lipot's face.

'Did Mum ever meet Lipot?' I asked because I'd never heard her talk about Beri's father.

'She did, but she didn't speak Hungarian and he didn't speak English so it was . . . '

'But he knew she wasn't Jewish?'

'He never asked and I never told him. He probably guessed that she wasn't. He knew I'd drifted away from . . . but there were other . . . there were more important things to discuss –'

Beri took Lipot for long walks around Leeds, showed him the university buildings and lecture rooms, the parks and the synagogue and then, one evening while the two of them sat in front of the small coal fire in Beri's lodgings, Lipot told my father about the last time he'd seen Zori.

On disembarking from the train at Auschwitz she'd been carrying the three-year-old son of one of Beri's cousins in her arms, a little boy called Alexander. 'A guard stood at the entrance,' wrote my father many years later, 'who, with a silent movement of his forefinger, directed the able-bodied men and women to the right and the infirm, old and those with children, to the left. Carrying the child as she was, my mother was directed to the left.'

Can we ever truly know what other people have experienced or endured? This is a question I've often asked myself, particularly in relation to my father and grandmother. I'm fairly good when it comes to picturing strangers' lives, their joys and sorrows, highs and lows, but the way in which Beri lost his mother lies far beyond anything I can imagine.

I recall Peggy telling me of the terrible nightmares Beri suffered in the first years of their courtship and subsequent marriage. Peggy served in the WAAF (Women's Auxiliary Air Force) during the war and had had, as she herself described it, a wonderful time, one 'she wouldn't have missed for the world'. After she was demobilised she'd gone to work at The Board of Trade as a civil servant, at which point she'd met Beri at a university dance. Sixty years later, when asked if he could recall that first meeting, Beri described the dress Peggy wore – yellow with tiny white polka dots. Beri also recalled how, suffering terribly from the cold and living in spartan digs, he spent a lot of his time reading in bed, wearing bedsocks and gloves, with every available item of clothing spread on top of the blankets. For her part, my mother brought Beri lumps of coal from home for his small fireplace, dragging them across Leeds on the bus in an old green-and-red striped shopping bag.

'He never stopped complaining about how cold it was,' she said many years later. 'Nineteen forty-seven was not a good winter.'

She also remembered how, on the nights she spent with him, Beri would wake up shouting for Zori. 'He had these terrible nightmares in which he couldn't find her –'

These nightmares (in which his murdered aunts, Piri, Malvin and Rezi; uncles, Gabor and Erno, and grandparents, Sharlota and David, also appeared) occurred regularly during the early days of my

Peggy in Leeds, c. 1947

parents' relationship. How else, after all, does one deal with such an event? How else do you process the fact that the person you love most in the world has been murdered because there are people out there who feel that she and by association you and the rest of your family are, in the words of Primo Levi, 'biologically inferior'.

Some things are too difficult to describe. Their effect is felt in other ways. In what is not said.

It is a bedspread kept at the back of a cupboard.

It is a small black prayer book tucked away on a bookshelf.

It is an argument over a photograph.

BERI: What have you done with your grandmother's picture, the one that's kept in the cupboard up there?

SHELLEY: Nothing . . . I haven't been near it –

BERI: You must have . . . You know the one I'm talking about? In the maroon leather frame?

SHELLEY: Honestly, I haven't touched it –

BERI [suddenly – without warning – shouting at the top of his voice and slamming his hand down on the table]: BUT YOU MUST HAVE! YOU MUST HAVE. YOU'RE ALWAYS TAKING THINGS AWAY AND NOT PUTTING THEM BACK!

SHELLEY [trying to ignore the accusation, which she knows is accurate]: Okay, okay . . . let me take a look in the cupboard and if it's really not there, I'm sure I can find it –

BERI: Your grandmother was a very beautiful woman. It's a very beautiful photograph –

SHELLEY: I know. I love that photograph too. I'll find it, I promise –

And I did find it . . . eventually. Although – as Beri said – it wasn't in the cupboard where it had always been kept. Instead, after about half an hour of me hunting up and down the house, Beri suddenly recalled that he'd taken it out of the cupboard a couple of weeks previously in order to have it photocopied and, instead of replacing it where it belonged, he'd put it in his desk.

I hand the photograph over to Beri and the joy on his face says more about what happened to him and to Zori than all the volumes on the bookshelves by Sereny or Schlink or Arendt.

'She really was beautiful, wasn't she?' I say.

Beri nods. 'Yes, she was,' he whispers. 'She really was very beautiful.'

Zori, c. 1934

The blurred outline of trees and hedges and dykes. Scuffed drifts of willowherb alongside creamy ridges of hawthorn. Rain sluicing down from the hillsides. Rivers gartered by mists.

After learning of Zori's death, the consolations of the British countryside were many and varied. Foremost Beri was overwhelmed by the lushness of the fields and the softness of the hills surrounding Leeds. He and Peggy walked out together most weekends and it was during these hikes that Beri grew to love not only the girl accompanying him but also this landscape. The colours exceeded anything he'd experienced back in Senta or Palestine. Raw, milky and sodden, everywhere swished with rivers, foamed with trees. Beaten golds, greens and russets. Crashing, creaturely colours all swimming together. Beri had lost his mother and was only too aware that with that loss his world had been brutally diminished; yet here in Britain, in these verdant surroundings, he was also aware of new possibilities.

Dining Room

Having moved to the Borders in 1956, Peter Womersley later described it as a 'superb landscape to live in – ruined abbeys in wooded parks in the river valley, lonely lochs in the bare and desolate moorlands which ring the small group of textile towns for which the area is best known. A marvellous countryside to build houses in!'

Nowhere is this more true than the field chosen in which to build High Sunderland and nowhere within the design of High Sunderland is this better exemplified than in the dining room. Peter designed this space specifically to make use of the most breathtaking view over the fields and woodland towards the triple-peaked Eildon Hills.

Framed by sliding glass panels at the far end of the room, then re-framed on the outside by both horizontal and vertical beams marking the edge of the courtyard, the view of the Eildons becomes like a David Hockney 'joiner' landscape, all angles and shadows, divisions and subdivisions.

I can look at this scene for hours and still find it as exhilarating as if seeing it for the first time. A magical synthesis occurs where landscape and architecture combine to create something more uplifting than either element by itself.

To a lesser degree this relationship also occurs throughout the house between the glass and the shifting views beyond, because in whichever direction you look, whichever way you turn, you are aware of perfectly framed pictures. In winter, when snow falls and the world outside turns white, the effect is even more electrifying. House and landscape compete with one another over which sets the more beautiful scene.

BERI [looking out of the dining-room window]: Shelley! Come, come!

One winter's night when the snow lies eight inches deep in the garden, Beri calls me to take a look out of the dining-room window. A full moon is shining, which, with the reflections it throws up from the snow, makes it seem as if no glass exists between us and the landscape. I am disorientated and exhilarated at the same time. The room is awash with the same silky mooniness that lies outside, while I can also see into the studio room on the far side of the courtyard that, because of the play of reflections, is also transformed into a snowscape or – to be more precise – a snowroom.

> BERI: Have I ever told you about the Kiddush Levana – the Jewish sanctification of the new moon?
> SHELLEY: I don't think so.
> BERI: The Jewish calendar is lunar not solar – when the Jews fled Egypt, God told them to turn their backs on their oppressors and create a new calendar based on the moon and its cycles.
> SHELLEY: What's the prayer?
> BERI: I forget.
> SHELLEY: The general gist?
> BERI: That the Jews will be delivered from darkness into light – it's not a long prayer, but it has to take place on a clear night so that you can see the new moon. I seem to recall a lot of standing on tiptoe and moving up and down –
> SHELLEY: Like in a gym?
> BERI: Not like in a gym at all –
> SHELLEY: Good for the calf muscles, though –
> BERI: It's one of the nicer Jewish prayers; at least you get to look at something beautiful while you're chanting –
> SHELLEY: That's not like you to look on the bright side –
> BERI: I always look on the bright side –

SHELLEY [raising her eyebrows because she can't believe what her father has just said]: Are you sure you can't remember how it went?
BERI [smiling]: It's a long time ago now –

Beri's inability to recall the Kiddush Levana was understandable. He had not recited it for well over sixty years, but the fact that he might think of it periodically whenever he looked up at the night sky was the moment it dawned on me how huge the arc of his life had been.

I was only six years old when Neil Armstrong landed on the moon yet I can still recall how excited my father was as the flickering pictures were beamed into our living room. Twenty-eight or so years before that Beri had been living in Jerusalem at Rabbi Dushinsky's house, giving praise to God for creating this celestial object. Now man had done the unthinkable and set foot on it. This was a true 'moment in history'; a moment when people the world over must have reflected on how far man had come – not just in moon miles but from our Darwinian origins to the sort of technological age that allowed us to travel through space.

When I went to bed later that night I recall keeping the curtains open for a while in case I could see the men on the moon, only closing them again because I was scared people might be peering in at me, pressing their faces up against the glass. This was an occasional childhood concern – the fact that at night you couldn't see who was outside, but they could see in. There were witches and warlocks out there. Dangerous people with smiles that weren't really smiles. I frightened myself half to death with these visions; swore blind I could hear people whispering outside in the dark.

Given these childhood imaginings, it seems ironic that the only time I've ever been attacked was when I was seventeen years old, living alongside twelve other students at my sixth-form college in Oxford.

One night, when I was asleep in my upstairs bedroom, someone broke into the house and, possibly because my room was the first one you came to at the top of the stairs, this man entered my bedroom and sexually assaulted me. I remember waking and feeling instinctively that something was wrong, but not knowing quite what. Then, still half asleep, I saw this man standing in the shadows and before I had time to scream or shout out, he was looming over my bed, punching me several times hard in the face, hissing at me that he had a knife and that I was to keep quiet. I also recall he wore a stocking over his head so that there was no way of recognising him and that he threw my duvet on the floor so that I was lying on the bed naked.

I thought I was going to die. He put a pillow over my face and I thought either I would suffocate or he would stab me to death. Not being able to see meant I could only hear and guess what might be occurring or, worse still, about to occur. The man kept punching me to keep me quiet while at the same time, I felt him removing my tampon (I was having my period). 'This is it,' I recall thinking, 'now I'll be raped.' But instead, in between very long, unnerving periods of silence, I felt a warm liquid being dribbled on to my stomach. He was masturbating over me and the whole time he was doing this, all I could think of was that he would kill me when he was finished and how devastated Beri and Peggy would be.

Later, after my attacker finally left, I took the pillow away from my face only to discover that all the lights in the room had been switched on. Lying there under their blaze was humiliating. I was exposed; meat-on-a-butcher's-slab exposed, patient-on-an-operating-table exposed. Next to my bed lay a towel that I quickly wrapped around me. Had someone really just appeared in the middle of the night? Had someone really just broken in and attacked me? Nothing was real, nothing made sense, and it was in this half-dazed, somewhat bruised and broken state that I stumbled downstairs to the warden's flat.

Ten, maybe fifteen minutes later the police arrived with two huge Alsatian dogs to search the house. I don't recall a great deal after that except that I was hugely embarrassed that the police were going to see my bloody tampon lying on the mattress. Much later they said that the fact I was having my period was probably why I wasn't raped. 'Must have put him off,' I overheard one of the officers saying, which made me feel even more embarrassed, added to which they explained that they would have to bag the tampon to take back to the police station as evidence.

I gave a statement to a female officer, but when I came to read it through and sign it, all I could see were how many spelling mistakes the policewoman had made. I also recall being asked to give the policewoman the towel I was wrapped in as it was smeared with semen and then, just as quickly as the police arrived, they disappeared and my house warden gave me a sleeping pill before letting me doze off in her bed.

Over the following days the police came and went on a regular basis. I had bruises on my face and upper body where my attacker had punched me and cuts to my lips. I told the officers that the man had worn a stocking over his face yet despite this they insisted I look through several books of mug shots. Two male officers also took me driving around Summertown in north Oxford to see if I could identify anyone, but my house warden quickly put a stop to that, reminding them that my attacker HAD A STOCKING OVER HIS FACE.

'All they want,' she told me after they departed with a flea in their ear, 'was to drive around Oxford with a young girl in their car.'

It was creepy, but creepier still was that a couple of days later while walking down Lathbury Road, I spotted my then boyfriend and, running up to him, gave him a kiss. Later that day two policemen knocked on the door of the house and told me that a plainclothes detective had been sitting in a car on the street when I'd done this and that they did not think my actions appropriate. The police officers said there were far too many of us (school students) kissing outside on the Lathbury Road, walking up and down holding hands and that this sort of thing might have been what aroused my attacker. But instead of being outraged at what they were implying, once again I felt confused and embarrassed, not to mention terrified because this man was still at large.

And terrified is how I remained, although not so much by the physical act of the assault, more by the shock of waking up to find a stranger standing in the dark watching me.

Two days later Beri flew down from Scotland. My house warden, together with my parents, decided this was the best course of action as they agreed I needed positive male role models. As for me, I think I would have preferred my mother to visit. I think I would have wanted her gentle, abundantly comforting presence and I probably phoned to tell her as much. I can't really recall. On the other hand, Beri's trip to Oxford stands out clearly in my memory. I recall him arriving with a beautiful, hand-knitted oyster-grey garment as a thank-you gift to my house warden for looking after me. The two of them chatted for a time after which Beri took me for a meal in Little Jericho. He hugged me closely and I remember thinking I never wanted him to let me go at the same time as which my bruising was so painful I could almost have fainted.

Over dinner Beri told me how, when he was a student studying at the yeshiva in Czechoslovakia, he had been attacked by some men in the mikveh (pools used for ritual immersion) where he went daily. He spoke about it in a very matter-of-fact fashion before leaning towards me and holding my hand, telling me not to let what happened dictate how I lived my life in the future. 'You have a choice,' he said – advice I didn't fully appreciate at the time because I was so preoccupied with the thought that my attacker (who was never – as far as I am aware – apprehended) would be able to recognise me, whereas I could pass this man in the street and not know who he was. He was invisible and suddenly being seen and being able to see took on a whole new dynamic.

When I returned to High Sunderland for the holidays it was midsummer. Beri enjoyed sunbathing when the weather was good and quite often this meant he would pad about the house naked. This never used to worry me, but that summer I recall not so much being concerned by Beri's nudity as by the fact someone – the postman, our gardener, a passing hiker – might see him.

I did not want Beri being judged so I repeatedly told him to put some clothes on and was still doing so almost thirty-four years later.

SHELLEY [coming across Beri doing his morning exercises in the living room, in the nude]: Could you please put some clothes on?

BERI: Why?

SHELLEY: Someone might see you –

BERI: Who cares if they see me? I'm allowed to be naked in my own house –

SHELLEY: I could draw the curtains a little –

BERI [chuckling]: You think the birds might be offended?

SHELLEY: The birds, the squirrels and EVERY OTHER FREAK out there –

BERI: You're being ridiculous –

SHELLEY: What's ridiculous is me standing in front of my naked, ninety-year-old father at seven o'clock in the morning telling him to please put on some clothes!

BERI: Exactly.

It was ridiculous. I was ridiculous. It shouldn't have mattered. But glass houses, while beautiful, also have (as Edith Farnsworth discovered) a flip side. Like giant petri dishes or Skinner boxes, you can feel under observation, stripped of your privacy, stared at as if under a microscope.

My mind now flies off in another direction and I start to wonder if it's not too far-fetched to equate modernist architecture – that is to say buildings with stark, unadorned exteriors – with nudity. Perhaps that is why there's so much resistance to this type of house? Do people on some profound level think of them as unclothed buildings and therefore inappropriate? Do they prefer living in houses with solid brick walls and small windows because these buildings are 'clothed' and, consequently, not only safer but also more acceptable? Tom Wolfe in his wonderfully irreverent book *From Bauhaus to Our House* gently pokes fun at this idea. 'The bourgeoisie had always been great ones,' he writes, 'for false fronts [...] every manner of grandiose and pointless gesture – spires, Spanish tile roofs, bays, corbels – to create a dishonest picture of what went on inside, architecturally and socially. All this had to go. All masonry, all that gross and "luxurious" granite, marble limestone, and red brick was suspect unless used in obviously non-load bearing ways. Henceforth walls would be thin skins of glass or stucco [...] it was dishonest to make walls look as chunky as a castle's. The inner structure, the machine-made parts, the mechanical rectangles, the modern soul of the building must be expressed on the outside of the building, completely free of applied decoration [...] Astonishing! What virtuosity! How very nonbourgeois.'

For Beri, however, a naked building (whether 'nonbourgeois' or not) was a perfect building. Plain wood and glass were all he required, a building stripped back to its skin. Anything more ostentatious, that is to say houses barnacled in faux detailing, and we'd soon hear him muttering words such as 'pretentious', 'twirly' and 'twaddle' under his breath.

Yet despite Beri not caring if people saw him padding about the house in the altogether, it was an entirely different matter if he spotted something going on that wasn't to *his* liking.

> BERI [standing in the dining room, staring out of the window]: What's that in your bedroom?
> TEENAGE SHELLEY: What's what?
> BERI [pointing across the courtyard to where I had just Sello-taped a life-sized poster of Starsky – of *Starsky and Hutch* fame – on to my wall]: There. What is *that*?
> TEENAGE SHELLEY: A poster –
> BERI: I can see it's a poster, but what is it doing on the wall?
> TEENAGE SHELLEY: It's a P O S T E R. Posters go on walls, duh!
> BERI [half closing his eyes while considering my cheek]: Well … perhaps … you could hang this poster somewhere … else?
> TEENAGE SHELLEY: I doubt it –
> BERI: I'm sorry, sweetie pie, but it can't stay there.

In my defence I had not given much thought to who else might be able to spy my biggest crush since Davy Jones from The Monkees. Nevertheless, Starsky was not going down without a fight.

> TEENAGE SHELLEY: But I like it –
> BERI: How about I buy you a proper poster? We can have it framed and hung above that shelf there? A Chagall? You like Chagall –
> TEENAGE SHELLEY: I prefer Starsky –

BERI: So stick Starsky on the wardrobe door where I can't see
him –
TEENAGE SHELLEY: I can't see him from my bed if I put him
there. Besides, it's my room.
BERI [GROWLING LOUDLY]: Only up to a point –

Of course, glass has many properties other than being transparent,
the most notable amongst them that it reflects everything around it.
High Sunderland is a house of visual echoes. The trees that surround
the house are mirrored in the walls and depending on where you
stand, these reflections can be reflected ad infinitum.

Is this how memory works, too? One reflection leading into
another, each memory creating a network of glittering, intricate
threads that vibrates just under the surface of consciousness? Only
this morning while seated in the dining room eating toast and drinking espressos I talked to Peggy about marmalade because that was
what I was spreading on my toast. It was delicious. So sticky and
sweet. Marmalade! The condiment that Paddington Bear always
chooses to spread on the sandwiches he keeps under his battered felt
hat and immediately I was thinking of the hat Beri always wore when
he was out in the garden trapping moles and then suddenly – perhaps
because I was thinking of Beri and sunshine – I was in the South of
France – aged five or six – eating freshly baked rolls spread with apricot jam and Beri's cousin Suzanne was with us, dressed in a dazzling
pink and green kaftan, all zigzags and stripes, and without missing a
beat I found myself in Los Angeles looking down over the hazy city
that seemed to stretch out to the horizon from where I was standing
in Suzanne's cicada-filled garden, high in the Hollywood hills.

Paddington Bear, moles and cicadas – an invisible hinterland all
contained in this one room whilst munching on toast and marmalade.

W. G. Sebald, that master of the fragmented, dreamy nocturne, puts it far better in his novel *Austerlitz*: 'It does not seem to me,' he writes, 'that we understand the laws governing the return of the past, but I feel more and more as if time did not exist at all, only various spaces interlocking according to the rules of a higher form of stereometry, between which the living and the dead can move back and forth as they like.'

Of course, all houses are repositories of memory, but if a house is the container, who or what is it that lifts the lid on what Proust called that 'vast structure of recollections'? When I lived in Cornwall, I'd watch the fishermen from the shore as they flung their lobster pots overboard alongside brightly coloured flags and buoys that bobbed on the surface so that each fisherman knew precisely where to return in order to pull up their catch. After my mother and subsequently my father died, my brother, sister and I received a great many beautiful letters from friends and relations expressing condolences. Reading these letters I was struck by how kind people were to take the time to write to us and how these letters brought a great deal of comfort, but it was only recently whilst reading through them again that I realised just how many people mentioned the food my parents used to cook. My father's recipe for cucumber salad made a frequent appearance in their recollections, but there was also talk of other dishes such as Goulash, Hamantaschen, Chicken Paprikas, Nocken, Palacsinta ... In other words, food was a significant ingredient of life in the See-Through House because Beri took great pains to recreate the dishes he remembered from childhood, perhaps as a way of retrieving something of what he had lost. The smell and taste of paprika and poppy seed guided him back to his past just like the fishermen's buoys signalled to the fishermen where their pots were located. Not only that, but the older Beri grew, the more significant food became. In his nineties – if he felt under the weather – I'd watch him prepare soft-boiled eggs, which he'd crack into a tumbler, scooping out the warm silky yolk and barely cooked white before drinking it down with relish.

'Zori would make this for me whenever I was ill as a child,' Beri explained when I first witnessed this atrocity. It looked so disgusting, but for Beri it was comfort on a scale I couldn't even begin to fathom.

Back in Senta, Beri's family had always eaten well. Zori was an exceptional cook and because they occasionally holidayed in Rumania, Austria and Italy, the dishes she prepared reflected the countries they visited. In addition, Beri had an extremely sweet tooth – or as he liked to put it, 'a whole mouthful of sweet teeth' – so much so, in fact, that when he came to draw a map of Senta from memory, one of the first locations he recorded was The Vince Patisserie.

'Some of the pleasantest memories of my childhood,' Beri wrote, 'are connected to Vince's Patisserie as it took only a minute or two from our house to cross the road to reach it. My brother and I were, on special occasions, allowed to get cakes or ice cream from Mrs Vince for which our mother was later invoiced – we were not given any money to pay with. I have never, since then, tasted cakes like those in Vince's except on the rue de la Paix in Paris; and the smell of baking chocolate blended with brandy remains unforgettable.'

Coming to Britain shortly after the end of the war, when rationing was still in place, was – as he so often recalled – an assault on his taste buds.

Peggy's cooking was another assault. Over-cooked vegetables, watery stews, boiled tripe in white sauce. He quickly taught her to cook the dishes he loved, but having picked up the basics she subsequently became exceptionally skilled in her own right, collecting shelves full of cookery books including all of Elizabeth David's work together with a vast selection of Jewish and Hungarian cookbooks.

All these meals were consumed in the dining room, a space that is divided from the living room not only by the physical difference in height between the two areas but also by the trough of tropical plants and cacti, which Peter cleverly equipped with its own drainage system.

There is something wonderful in having so much greenery indoors, particularly in a house that has been designed in such a grid-like fashion, for it allows an informality and wildness to occur. The plant trough also advances the theme of bringing the outside inside in a way that no amount of yuccas stuck in ceramic pots and dumped in the corner of a living room do. At High Sunderland the plants are part of the architecture, as important to the overall concept of the house as are the walls, windows and floors.

The trough, however, does come with one unforeseen drawback: modernist houses are not ideal places in which to keep pets, especially when that pet is a cat that thinks an indoor garden makes for the perfect litter tray. Throughout my adolescence we spent an inordinate amount of time chasing our cats out of the trough or devising invisible barriers with metre upon metre of sewing thread, none of which worked.

⋆

In late 2013, in one of the last interviews Beri ever gave, he was asked by the interviewer, Paul Schütze, the question: 'How should a table sound?'

'Plentiful,' came back the reply.

The table around which we all sat to eat and chat every mealtime is long and rectangular and reflects the shape of the room. In addition, if any piece of furniture in a house containing only atheists might be labelled 'holy', this would be it. The dining- room table was central to life at High Sunderland much like – as Virginia Woolf puts it in *Moments of Being* – 'savages, I suppose, have some tree or fire place, round which they congregate'. In this respect the chairs, too, were sacred.

When Peggy and Beri first moved to the house, the chairs they brought with them were smaller and less imposing than those we sit on today, which were designed by Danish furniture designer, Hans Wegner.

Wegner – with his soubriquet of 'The Master of the Chair' – was one of a handful of Scandinavian designers (including Arne Jacobsen, Finn Juhl and Poul Kjærholm) who revolutionised furniture design in the Fifties and Sixties by inventing a fresh, new aesthetic combining the modernist principles of simplicity and functionalism with a joyful appreciation for the materials used thus infusing each piece with an overwhelmingly organic appeal.

'A chair isn't just a piece of furniture,' said Wegner, 'but a work of art made to support the human form.' Nowhere is this better displayed than in the chairs around the dining-room table. Made of oak and black leather, the smooth planes of the armrests together with their gently curved, black leather backs are – much like the Kjærholm – as close to sculpture as you can get. 'I was striving to make a thing which I could live with and hold and touch and which would have some sense of eternity in it,' said Barbara Hepworth of her work in 1967, but in many ways her statement rings true of Wegner's ambitions. The sense of eternity these chairs possess springs not just from their solidness, but from their tactility. You want to touch their surfaces, experience their warm grained armrests that, like the trees from which they are carved or like ancient standing stones or sculptures, contain an essence of timelessness, of having been here long before we were born and of existing long after we're dead.

Timelessness is also present in the places in which we all sat as a family around the table: Beri always at its head while my mother, brother, sister and I all sat (and continued to sit whenever we returned home) in our designated places too. This 'selected seating plan' also took place in Beri's childhood home with Lipot at the head of the table and Zori on his right-hand side. Back then weekday lunch was the main meal of the day with his parents inviting not only travelling businessmen to join the meal but also strangers, 'who had been brought to the shop by a volunteer local "guide" in order to beg for a contribution to whatever cause they were collecting money for: a daughter's dowry, money for a large, hard-up family, or some communal charity in a far-flung town or village'.

To gather around the table and share food was part of Beri's psyche. Consequently it played an enormous role at High Sunderland (albeit a strictly non-religious one). Mealtimes were sacrosanct and woe betide latecomers. To make Beri wait to sit down for a meal was dicing with death. On the other hand, both he and Peggy were very generous hosts and took enormous care in the food they prepared, often discussing the menu for days in advance.

I picture my father at the head of the table, which is laid with a pink linen tablecloth together with an array of matching pink napkins. Of the latter we have hundreds in every colour imaginable because just as Peggy had shoes dyed to complement every outfit in her wardrobe so the dining-room table had to be 'dressed' in individually dyed tablecloths with napkins to match.

Beri dishes up food, scooping broccoli, carrots and peas on to everyone's plates. The room fills with noise; my brother and Beri are talking politics. This is the Seventies so their discussion probably concerns the second miners' strike or Edward Heath's three-day week or perhaps Harold Wilson's recent re-election. Beri and my brother never see eye to eye about anything, least of all politics, so the talk soon turns into an argument with my brother growing increasingly incensed at what he perceives to be Beri's right-wing, capitalist ideals. My mother – always the peacemaker – is trying to keep the atmosphere calm. Now I see Peter and his mother (better known as 'Mumsie'), who often travels up from her home in Yorkshire for short holidays with her son, sitting at the end of the table. Peter is looking slightly bemused at the level of noise Jonathan and my father are making. My mother has prepared Peter's favourite, steak and kidney pudding, and now Peter is making some joke about a recently built housing estate he passed on the way over here, which is not to his liking. He picks up his knife and says that this insignificant object has had more thought put into its manufacture than the entire housing complex. A statement Beri seconds, adding that our local councils seem hell bent on replacing old slums with new slums. 'I believe,' he said once in a documentary made for BBC Scotland, 'that the environment begins just outside my skin, and everything beyond that is important. The design of all these things, the appearance of all these things and particularly in relation to me, and to the other people who use them, look at them and their relationship to each other, all these things matter. It's as simple as that.' Beri also adds that the knife Peter's just referred to has, in fact, been very carefully designed so as to be as functional and beautiful an object as possible. Ditto the fork and the spoon. Each is a work of dedicated craftsmanship – the stainless steel of the knives sharp and sleek, the scooped dips of the spoons smooth as tinned peaches. Design for Beri was not something that should ever be separated from life as it was lived. 'To design,' he wrote, 'means to care about people as individuals. Or, perhaps, it means simply to care.'

This sentence strikes a familiar echo and sends me scurrying back to the one describing Bezalel. 'Him has he filled with wisdom of heart to work all manner of work of the engraver, of the embroiderer, of the cunning worker and of the weaver.' Beri commissioned and subsequently filled High Sunderland with this same 'wisdom of heart', furnishing it not only with his own paintings and tapestries but also with curtains that he designed and wove in his own mill, cushions, rugs, bedspreads, kitchenware, upholstery fabrics and of course the clothes he created, which he, my mother, Jonathan, Gillian and I all wore at one time or another.

I can think of few other houses where this is the case. Charleston, perhaps, where Vanessa Bell and friends not only hand-painted the walls and furniture but also designed objects such as tables, bookshelves and pottery? Or Red House, which was commissioned, lived in and decorated by William Morris alongside a few Pre-Raphaelite cohorts including his wife and daughter, Jane and May Morris?

I pad around the house looking at all the things Beri created. Even the objects he didn't design have integrity. The crockery, for example. Especially the crockery.

A few days after Beri died High Sunderland filled up not just with family but also with a handful of my closest friends, who came to lend me their love and support. Amongst them was my oldest friend, Claire. Claire is not so much an English rose as a wild rose. Beautiful, scatty and slightly eccentric, over the past thirty-five years she has visited High Sunderland on many occasions.

On the second morning after she arrived, my sister came through to the dining room only to find Claire standing in front of one of the dining-room cupboards, camera in hand.

CLAIRE: Oh my God, you've caught me. This must look a bit odd, but I'm not a stalker, I promise!

GILLIAN: What on earth are you doing?

CLAIRE: I'm in love with this cupboard. Everything inside it is white –

GILLIAN [slowly]: O k a y.

CLAIRE: I wanted to take a photograph. I *am* a stalker, aren't I?

GILLIAN: It doesn't sound good.

CLAIRE: It's just that the contents of this cupboard are so beautiful. Every time I visit I have to take a peak inside. All those white plates and cups and everything –

GILLIAN: Can't say I've noticed –

CLAIRE: Really?

GILLIAN: No.

CLAIRE: But everything in there is so sleek and so –

GILLIAN: Perhaps you'd like to close the door now?

CLAIRE: Or I could just take the photograph? It won't take a second –

GILLIAN: I don't think it's very . . .

CLAIRE: Appropriate? It's not really, is it?

GILLIAN [shakes her head then walks away looking bemused]

The cupboard – which I have since christened the White Cupboard – has as far back as I can remember only ever contained white china, most of which was designed by the German company Rosenthal. The cups and saucers are particularly pleasing. Shaped like paper-thin water lilies, they don't so much sit on the table as float.

BERI: So why are you drinking out of that mug?

SHELLEY: How do you mean?

BERI: I mean we've the most beautiful cups in the cupboard –

SHELLEY: This mug's fine, thank you –

BERI: But it's got a [peering more closely at said object] . . . rabbit on it?

SHELLEY: Benjamin Bunny. I think it was Gilly's when she was little.

BERI [eying the mug with suspicion]: Really?

SHELLEY: You're not to throw it out –
BERI [holding his hands up in mock horror]: Did I say I wanted to throw it out? You're always accusing me –
SHELLEY: You put my coat on a bonfire –
BERI [looking puzzled]: What coat?
SHELLEY: You know very well what coat –
BERI [shaking his head]
SHELLEY: When I was …
BERI [starts snorting]: You looked like a tramp –
SHELLEY [indignantly]: It was a present from my friend –
BERI: What was his name again?
SHELLEY: Daniel Freiburg –
BERI: He had dreadful taste in clothes –
SHELLEY: You're not getting rid of this mug. This mug is part of my childhood –
BERI: I wouldn't DREAM of getting rid of the mug … I just think some people have better taste than others –
SHELLEY: Leave Daniel Freiburg out of this. His taste's as good as anyone else's.
BERI: I wasn't thinking of Daniel Freiburg –
SHELLEY: Yes you were –
BERI: The things I'm accused of!
SHELLEY: I'm right, though, aren't I?
BERI: You've a dreadful taste in men too –

Bunny mugs aside, nearly all the china in the kitchen is as white as that in the dining room, only here the serving plates, casserole dishes and teapots are by the Finnish company Arabia. But if white was the prevailing colour of the crockery at High Sunderland, there was something else each piece had in common – that is to say whether they were eggcups or ashtrays, a great deal of thought had been put into their purchase. This did not necessarily mean the purchase need be expensive, but three criteria had to be met:

1. The object had to look right.
2. The object had to function properly.
3. The object had to look right.

To this end the White Cupboard was blessed with an evil twin – a second cupboard into which my father shoved all the gifts he and my mother had been given over the years that did not pass muster. Two of these objects spring immediately to mind – the first being a clock made out of a large piece of highly lacquered rosewood on to which were glued penny-sized chunks of dyed turquoise and pink coral in a sort of oval shape while two gold hands engraved with black snakes marked off the hours.

The second gift was even worse than the first – if this can be imagined. Made out of white porcelain (so far so good) in the shape of an over-sized egg that is beginning to crack open, a pink and pur-ple-winged horse emerges out of the fissure. I can still see the mixture of horror and bewilderment on Beri's face as he was handed this gift and his querulous voice asking, 'What is it, exactly?'

Sadly, I can't recall the reply.

> BERI: Shelley, please try and remember that design always matters –
> SHELLEY: But what I think makes good design might not be what you do –
> BERI: Then please also remember that I'm always right.

I have the book that testifies to this statement. *Design Matters* contains many examples of what Beri considered not just bad design, but crimes against the word 'design' itself. A teapot with a handle in the shape of a banana decorated with 3D strawberries and cherries, geometric wallpaper, bed linen in headache-inducing patterns – in fact, anything fussy, anything kitsch, anything that wasn't streamlined, that wasn't a means of living a simpler, more beautifully realised life.

After Beri graduated from Leeds, his first two jobs were at factories producing knitwear and clothing fabrics, firstly as a designer at a company called Tootal Broadhurst Lee in Bolton and afterwards at a Scottish manufacturer, Munrospun in Edinburgh. It was here, on a freezing cold day in February while wandering down to the beach in Queensferry, that Beri spied a crab's claw washed up by the tide. Noting the claw's colours consisted of 'bone, smoky purples and a hint of coral' he picked it up and, hurrying back to the design studio, hand-wove a length of cloth reflecting these hues. Pleasure surged through him, not so much because the colours were bright or bold, they were in fact comparatively subtle, but because all of a sudden he had made a connection, admittedly a small one, but a connection nonetheless. To life, to his surroundings, to his place in the world.

I think again of Beri looking at photographs of his 'shabby, neglected' home back in Senta that was '[...] part of my past from which I had to learn to wrench myself free' and I also think of Lipot's description of his last moments with Zori at Auschwitz and the manner in which my father wrote about them. There was no sense of anger or bitterness in either man's words. Pain yes, sorrow certainly, but no outrage, no fury. Instead, in an interview he gave to Fiona Anderson, not long before he died, Beri explained apropos the Holocaust, 'If you live, it brings out the best in you.' The colours Beri worked with and created were this 'best'. Life affirming, celebratory.

Beri (fourth from left) apprenticing in a factory, c. 1949

But having moved up to Edinburgh and having begun to feel more at home, more connected, Beri realised there was another vital element, another 'best' that was missing from his life: Peggy.

On Beri's departure from Leeds, my mother had stayed behind with the rest of her family, but in August 1950 Beri persuaded Peggy to join him up north. This move was another 'not done' thing because at that time Beri and Peggy weren't married although shortly thereafter, on 30 March 1951, they headed off to Leith Registrars' office where, with the help of two firemen whom my father dragged in from the station next door to act as witnesses, my parents wed. Beri had to go back to work the following day, which meant the honeymoon did not occur until later that year when Beri, always with one eye on design matters, decided the Festival of Britain would be the perfect destination.

Nor were he and Peggy disappointed. 'Almost everything at the South Bank,' my father wrote fourteen years later, 'from dustbins to doorknobs had an element of newness, excitement or just plain fun. Nearly all the works were stimulating and we found the architecture, textiles, furnishing fabrics, rugs and carpets most exciting.' So cutting-edge and avant-garde were they that, on Beri's return to Scotland where he was still designing outmoded tweeds in the traditional style, he decided the time was right to branch out on his own.

By this point he and Peggy had been relocated from Munrospun in Edinburgh to the company's sister mill in the small manufacturing town of Galashiels. To begin with they rented a room in Plumtree Place from which, according to Beri, he could throw a stone from the window and hit three mills including the one he was working in. Some weeks later the young couple moved to a flat a little further up the hill on Magdala Terrace – another row of greyish-brown brick houses that wouldn't have looked out of place in a painting by Lowry. The flat was tiny; the kitchen so small that their prized possession – a brand-new Frigidaire – had to be placed in the living room. Nor did the flat have a bathroom, although it did sport an inside toilet, but any bathing to be done was to take place in front of the fire in a tin tub. Yet despite these small indignities, Beri and Peggy enjoyed setting up this their first real home together:

227 Magdala Terrace
Galashiels

29 April 1952

Dear Mother and Daddy
... Bernat bought a beautiful piece of printed material in Heal's when he was in London & he has framed it in a big rough

white frame & it looks quite lovely – he also bought some very nice china & pottery from Heal's. The material is modern and very good colours & although I can't describe it to you it really is beautiful framed like this (like an abstract painting) & it fits in with our house well.

The piece of fabric in question was *Calyx* by Lucienne Day, which Beri and Peggy had first spotted on display at the Festival of Britain. But Magdala Terrace inspired far more than just an admiration for other people's work, for it was also while living there that notions of Beri's first business, Colourcraft, sprang into being. Bored and not a little fed up of working for other people, in 1952 my parents took the decision to rent out a corner of a dilapidated, rat-ridden weaving shed within which Beri set up an ancient, power-driven pattern loom.

Colourcraft began small but grew rapidly. The first orders for lambswool scarves were made by chain stores such as Littlewoods, Woolworths and Marks & Spencer. Not only that, but these stores placed massive orders, one of which alone was in the region of 2,000 dozen pieces. The trouble was Beri couldn't afford to buy the yarn needed to fulfil such an order, nor did he own enough looms on which to weave them.

Step into the picture an extremely kind, local manufacturer, Mr David Colledge, who not only extended a huge amount of credit to my father but also organised for a lot of the dyeing, weaving and finishing of the scarves to be spread across several local mills, many of which were struggling to keep their machines running due to the post-Korean War textile depression.

Yet for all the help extended him, it soon became clear that with the growth of his company, Beri needed to invest in more looms as well as a larger building in which to house them, and so in 1956 he bought Netherdale Mill.

Long nights and early mornings. The joy of owning one's own business alongside the worry. Responsibility piled on responsibility. To oneself and to those you employ. Balance sheets and bookkeeping. Deadlines and deliveries.

Seven years after Beri bought Netherdale, in spring 1963, while sitting in his office he picked up the newest edition of *Elle* magazine. 'As usual I leafed straight through to the middle in order to reach the

Beri at Netherdale Mill, *c.* 1962

section dealing with clothes. To my amazement, there in front of me, in full colour and over several pages, was our newest cloth modelled by Chanel. I was too excited to speak or to realise at that moment the far-reaching implications.'

The fabric Chanel bought was inspired by a painting Beri had done while trying to capture the essence of my mother's favourite flowers: yellow roses. The picture has long since disappeared into a private collection, but photographs exist revealing the influence of my father's paintings on his textiles. The movement of colours and shapes across the canvas. Compressed blocks of yellow and gold vying for space with glittering edges of orange and green. The painting is a summation rather than a replication of the flowers; a rose abstraction translated into a tweed as light and bright as a bee's wing.

A spread for Christian Dior in *Art et la Mode*, 1964

By July that same year Pierre Cardin, Christian Dior, Louis Féraud, Guy Laroche, Nina Ricci, Yves Saint Laurent and Hardy Amies had all chosen Beri's fabrics for their autumn collections. These were heady times for my parents, days filled not only with joy but also with a quiet pride that at one and the same moment they were supplying both the British high street *and* haute couture, and all from the less than glamorous surroundings of Galashiels.

In her *Recollections of a Tour Made in Scotland A.D. 1803*, Dorothy Wordsworth described 'the village of Galashiels [as] pleasantly situated on the banks of a stream; a pretty place it once has been, but a manufactory is established there; and a townish bustle and ugly stone houses are fast taking the place of the brown-roofed thatched cottages of which a great number yet remain, partly overshadowed by trees.'

By the Fifties any remnants of what Dorothy Wordsworth had described as 'the brown-roofed thatched cottages' had long since disappeared and in their place stood the 'ugly stone houses' together with over one hundred mills. Built of whinstone rubble and sandstone, some of the buildings were as tall as high-rise blocks of flats. These were nearly always the spinning blocks while the rows of lower-slung buildings with their slate-hung roofs were the weaving sheds.

Entering the latter is like stepping into an alternative dimension. The noise of the looms crashes over you so loudly it's impossible not to shrink back at the assault. The sound is relentless, it's the clatter of industry, of things being made; it's a sound that vibrates through your body and belts you around the head, that grips you like no other sound has done before or will do again. At one and the same moment you are also overcome by the strong smell of raw wool. This is the lanolin, the waxy, oily substance that all wool-bearing animals secrete to keep themselves protected against the wind and the rain. The smell of the lanolin is strong and seeps under your skin; sharp, earthy and cold yet also surprisingly comforting. It's the smell of the hills on which the sheep graze, the lanolin absorbing everything around it, winter and summer rolled into one; soured milk, snow, sweat, ice, raw pine needles and honeybees. It's a smell I can't forget, that sends me hurtling back to my childhood and to the second mill my father set up in Galashiels having sold Netherdale in 1969.

All the men and women who worked in Waukrigg's (sometimes spelt Waulkrigg) weaving sheds had to wear headphones to protect their hearing. As a result, no conversations took place while the machines were in production so everyone either nodded or used some type of sign language to communicate whilst keeping their eyes firmly trained on the weave in case of flaws or broken wefts.

Nor were the mills confined to Galashiels. Nearly all the Border towns relied on the textile industry for employment: Selkirk, Hawick, Walkerburn, Innerleithen, Jedburgh. So large was the industry, in fact, that by the time Beri arrived, over one third of the population in the area was employed by it.

All the curtains at High Sunderland are made from a looped, cream-coloured mohair bouclé woven at Waukrigg. It has a wonderful, full-bodied texture, one that Beri occasionally used to admire by taking the fabric between forefinger and thumb and gently rubbing it to feel for its quality.

Cottons. Chenilles. Wool bouclés. Brushed mohairs and raw silks. My father identified them all by touch, much like a farmer identifies grain by rolling it between the palms of his hands. It was an age-old habit, something he had learnt from his parents, something Zori and Lipot did to test for a fabric's quality, something Beri did that kept him in touch with his past.

Patterns of memory? It intrigues me how so many of our habits are passed on to us via our parents. Zori and Lipot's affinity to the materials they handled in their shop travelling down through the decades. Woven inheritance? Watson and Crick's double helix like strands of yarn twisted together. I walk through the woods at High Sunderland with their worsted carpets of pine needles, their naps of red and pink campion, bluebells and foxgloves. If I am hefted to High Sunderland, I am also hefted to this landscape. I've learnt its secrets by following Beri, by seeing what he saw, forests marching for miles over dark hills, sods of bracken, moorlands bruised purple by heather, bashed yellow by gorse.

In London the apocryphal story is that you're never more than a foot away from a rat, whereas in the Borders it feels as if you're never more than a mile away from some form of water. Lochs, burns, waterfalls, marshes and bogs saturate the landscape while the rivers Ale, Tweed, Blackadder, Teviot, Ettrick, Yarrow and Leader slither across it like eels. Warm and misty in the summer, flapping with salmon in the autumn, the Borders are a fly-fisherman's dream with mile upon mile of unadulterated wateriness in which to stand and literally immerse yourself in your environment.

I lie face down on the banks of the Ettrick. This spot is called Paradise Corner – so named by my brother (alongside Badger's Palace and Strawberry Hill) because ... well, the name speaks for itself. My feet rest on the grass while my face hangs over the water, so close to its surface that the river tickles my nose. Below me in the shallows I spy a shoal of baby trout, each fish no bigger than a thumbnail, just visible against the riverbed, which is a jumble of greys, greens and browns. The fish barely move. They lie suspended in the water, silently gilling. I have to remain as motionless as they are, not something that comes naturally, but I've become mesmerised by the beauty of this underworld. At first I suspect the fish are nothing but a dull greyish-brown, but as I study them, I begin to detect all manner of silvers and golds and flushed rosy pinks. My mind starts to race. There is no choice but to immerse myself in the water. I can think of little else. Everything comes alight with sunshine and mud and the mesmerising green drift of this riveryness.

For Beri I think the same was also true; the Borders, their physical presence, awoke his senses just as mine are awake staring down into the river. Fields, trees, hills and lochs immersed him in their being. Colour and texture came alight; warps of gold and wefts of green, or wefts of blue and warps of turquoise, not to mention the silvers, greys and rippling oranges. In *Paradise Lost* Milton wrote, 'What if earth/Be but the shadow of heaven', but for Beri the Borders *were* heaven. The remainder of what little family he had left after the war found new homes in the Promised Land, but Beri's Promised Land was this, a place where he saw colours more brightly, textures more acutely and patterns more vividly than any place else on earth.

My father was in love with this landscape, with his life here and with the house he lived in, which in truth was nothing more or less than the representation of hope. Of light after darkness and optimism after the destruction of all he held dear. But over and over again I have to remind myself that his vision is not my vision. I cannot live his life for him. Although no doubt patently obvious to outsiders, this fact hits me like a bullet between the eyes: I am trying to keep Beri alive by continuing to live in his house. Why else would I still be at High Sunderland almost four years after he died? Why else would I be rattling around in such an isolated and isolating place if not to keep Beri breathing? In hospitals machines do this job for you. Keep the patient's lungs functioning, heart pumping, brain fully oxygenated. So is that what I have become: a life-support machine? And if this is the case, isn't it time to switch off the machine and sell up?

*

Abbotsford lies less than five miles away from the See-Through House. Built by the poet and novelist Sir Walter Scott in 1824, the building could not be more different from High Sunderland, yet despite Abbotsford being one of those wildly romantic, Victorian-Gothic buildings while the See-Through House remains steadfastly modern, the two places share something in common. Both owners loved their houses to the point of obsession. In particular, Sir Walter exceeded his budget when building Abbotsford and even when debts threatened to bankrupt him, instead of selling the house and managing his losses, he chose to write his way out of insolvency, a decision that almost certainly cost him his life.

Another house in the region that its owner appeared almost married to is that which sits at the centre of the country estate on which the See-Through House is built and from which it takes its name. Sunderland Hall is a baronial mansion more akin to a Wildfell or a Thornfield than anything hailing from the twentieth century. Like Thornfield the building comes complete with prickly turrets and crude crenulations that peak and trough around the roof's edge. The estate also boasts a family cemetery set in the middle of a wood so dark and misshapen it could well have been born of Angela Carter's imagination.

Once upon a time iron railings surrounded the gravestones, but these have long since been eaten away by rust or stolen and sold for scrap metal. In their place lie metal traps. The estate is fortunate in that it still boasts red squirrels, but they are hopelessly outnumbered by greys. The traps are for the latter, which, once caught, will be shot or more likely have their heads staved in by a gamekeeper with a large stick. The only other wildlife to inhabit the cemetery are the crows, which, as you enter the wood, rise up from the yews – blackened scraps of burnt paper.

In the mid Fifties, when Beri wanted to purchase land on which to build his new home, the estate was owned by Mr and Mrs Scott-Plummer (although Mr Scott-Plummer was later to die on the estate in a hunting accident). My father took me to visit Mrs Scott-Plummer once. I recall the house being as dark and damp as a coal cellar, so much so that when we walked up the stairs I missed a step, tripped and bashed my head so hard against a wall I'm certain I was concussed. When we left I asked why Mrs Scott-Plummer had failed to switch on any lights.

'I expect she didn't want us to see all the holes in the carpets,' Beri replied. 'She's not got a lot of money.'

In the Seventies the estate was put on the market. Selling up was not easy for the Scott-Plummer family; after all, they had owned the house and land for decades. But at some point everyone has to move on. We are all migrants within our own lives. Be it that what we are moving away from are parents, childhoods, jobs, dreams or homes.

Kitchen

When we are born we are laid, so says Bachelard, 'in the cradle of the house'. This building is our first universe, its rooms as vast and limitless as outer space. At High Sunderland the kitchen lies at the centre of the building much as the sun lies at the centre of the universe, while the living room revolves around the kitchen and the bedrooms – consigned as they are to the outer perimeters of the house – revolve around the living room like satellites or far-flung planets. The kitchen is the heart of High Sunderland and this is entirely appropriate given that it was the food Beri's mother cooked when he was a child that lay closest to his heart and consequently to the heart of our family.

Not that it was the position of the kitchen, as such, that was at the forefront of Peter's mind when he drew up the plans. Instead, his central concern was how to keep the kitchen separate from the main living space while, in Miesian terms, still maintaining the idea of an 'ultimate, simple open' area. To this end the kitchen is contained within a box-like central reserve with two 'hidden' doorways, one of rosewood that leads from the dining room into the kitchen and one of walnut that leads from the kitchen into the hallway.

As the *Daily Telegraph* noted in May 1961: '[Womersley] has an ingrained dislike of doors, knobs and corridors. So, doors are hidden in ingenious ways. Sometimes they slide, sometimes they are made of panelling to match the rest of the wall and sometimes they are made to double up as cupboards.'

The two kitchen doors at High Sunderland are almost invisible when viewed from the hallway and dining room, while the kitchen itself acts as a central reservation, subtly dividing the main part of the house from the 'children's end'.

With a tiled floor the colour of bluebells and large windows over-looking the back courtyard so that Peggy could keep an eye on us children when we played outside, the kitchen is also a functional space rather than the type of 'dream' kitchen one hears so much about these days on programmes such as *Grand Designs*.

For example, there is no large kitchen table at High Sunderland, no central island and definitely no snug corner in which to place a sofa or TV. In modernist houses, kitchens are for cooking in, not grandstanding one's social ambitions. As Le Corbusier so famously put it in his 1923 manifesto *Vers une architecture* (*Towards an Architecture*), 'A house is a machine for living in. Baths, sun, hot-water, cold-water, warmth at will, conservation of food, hygiene, beauty in the sense of good proportion. An armchair is a machine for sitting on and so on.' In other words, a well-designed house should enable its inhabitants to live more comfortable, productive lives simply by dint of the fact that everything within it works and serves a specific purpose.

This describes the kitchen at High Sunderland within which all the fixtures and fittings have been hand-crafted in wood and painted white, although the mahogany frames around each cupboard have been left untouched to reflect as well as emphasise the grid-like nature of the house as a whole. But does this lack of luxury mean this kitchen is a failure? Not so far as Peggy and Beri were concerned, for having both spent childhoods in houses where the cooking areas were either dark or damp or both, their Fifties kitchen was a bright, light-filled area that was stuffed with all manner of modern gizmos and gadgets.

'The Kitchen is quite magnificent,' wrote Elizabeth Kyle in a 1961 article about the house that appeared in the *Southern Reporter*, 'and has almost every labour-saving device. The colour scheme is white with a blue tiled floor. The large electric cooker is a Canadian one and has, apart from the oven, a warming oven.

'The gadget which intrigued me most was the Waste Master in the sink. Having no dustbins at High Sunderland Mrs Klein disposes of all the rubbish, except paper, down the sink drain. A switch puts the Waste Master into operation and it breaks and crushes the rubbish.

'Of her dishwasher Mrs Klein says: "It is really just a glorified dish drier. I prefer to wash them first and then put them into it to dry." There are also a refrigerator, electric mixer and liquidiser in the kitchen.'

The Waste Master was an insatiable beast with a belly full of rusty, steel blades. Why and when Peggy decided to get rid of it, I am unsure. On the other hand, one thing that still remains, which in many ways is the only item in the entire house to carry echoes of a bygone era, is a small enamel bell board with four red glass bubbles that light up according to which bell is rung (Front Door, Bedroom, Guest, Lounge). The bells still work and the board still lights up although these days, unless there is an inquisitive child in residence, only the front doorbell is used.

Another remnant from the past, but one that is far less obvious than the bell board, is the imprint of a child's hand on one of the huge floor-to-ceiling cupboards. The handprint is small and pale and was made by my two-year-old self because I hadn't dried my hands properly when I accidently pressed my palm against the cupboard's unvarnished surface. This handprint makes me think of buildings where paintings and mirrors have been removed from the walls only to leave an impression of what was once there, much like those ghostly handprints found in Indonesian caves that are thought to be between 35,000 and 40,000 years old.

Other recollections of the kitchen at High Sunderland are of the rich aroma of roasting coffee beans mixed together with hazelnuts; the buttery smell of fried onions and garlic, the waft of paprika, the bitter taste of Peggy's Cinzano Bianco which she always sipped whilst she was cooking (the almost indelible imprint of her waxy pink lipstick on the side of her glass), sweet sticky caraway biscuits that I sucked on as a baby and the steamy smell of roast joints of meat impregnated with thin slivers of garlic. But in particular roast beef, which, if it was to satisfy Beri's tastes, had to remain rare and bloody.

Of all the disputes my parents ever had, it was the ones over how long to cook roast beef that were the most insane.

Particularly if guests were invited.

> PEGGY: The beef weighs eight pounds, three ounces. The book says you should seal it at a 200° for fifteen minutes then cook it a further twenty minutes at 180° for each pound so that's one hour and forty minutes or thereabouts –
> BERI: You'll incinerate it, for God's sake! The book doesn't know what it's talking about –
> PEGGY: It'll be fine –
> BERI: If you like sawdust. The flavour's all in the blood –
> PEGGY: Darling, you can't serve our guests raw meat – they won't touch it –
> BERI: They'd prefer rubber, I suppose?
> PEGGY: There'll be gravy –
> BERI: MARGARET, be reasonable!

At this point a compromise – of sorts – was normally brokered. Peggy would say she'd cook the meat for half the length of time it said in the recipe book in order to keep Beri happy; however, surreptitiously, she would turn the oven up a notch or two in compensation. Sneaking into the kitchen while Peggy was laying the table in the dining room or arranging her hair in the bathroom, Beri would turn the oven down to practically zero where the temperature would remain until some time later my mother would return to the kitchen, detect the subterfuge and whack the temperature right back up again. In and out of the kitchen they both went. In one door and out the other. Round and round like a comedy sketch. Continental Europe versus Great Britain.

The same thing occurred every Christmas when it came to cooking the turkey. Not that Beri insisted on raw turkey, but he couldn't abide it when the meat was dry, it had to be succulent. In and out of the kitchen they trotted. Round and round in circles. Switching the temperature up and down. Up and down until finally, when the turkey was 'done', it would be placed on the table for Beri to carve. I hated this moment. I did not want Beri to be disappointed with his meal, but nor did I want Mum to feel that she hadn't cooked things correctly.

My loyalties were divided.

I'd hold my breath.

Things did not improve either when I returned home to take care of Beri two years after Peggy died. Cooking for someone who not only loves to eat but is also an excellent cook himself is not easy.

BERI: I thought I'd help you chop up the parsnips –

SHELLEY: Thanks, but I'm fine –

BERI: I'd like to help –

SHELLEY [deeply suspicious]: Okay . . . if you really have to –

BERI: The thing is . . .

SHELLEY: WHAT THING?

BERI: Calm down, I'm just saying that recently . . .

SHELLEY: What? What recently?

BERI: . . . that recently I've noticed you've been chopping the parsnips too finely.

SHELLEY: I've chopped up parsnips for years without any complaints.

BERI: Perhaps I can show you?

SHELLEY [snapping]: No, I'm fine, thank you. Besides, you've never said anything before –

BERI: I was being polite. But things are getting worse –

SHELLEY: This isn't a Greek Tragedy! We're talking PARS-NIPS –

BERI: Badly sliced parsnips –

SHELLEY: This is unbearable –

BERI: Stop exaggerating, all I'm saying is –

SHELLEY: I just want to chop up my parsnips in peace –

BERI: But when you chop them up too finely and put them in the oven, they get burnt and go hard and I'm breaking my teeth on them.

SHELLEY: Now who's exaggerating?

BERI: All I'm saying is –

SHELLEY: That I'm incapable of chopping up a parsnip.

BERI: If you say so.

OR

SHELLEY: What would you like for dinner?

BERI: You decide.

SHELLEY: How about a nice salad?

BERI: Salad's not a meal –

SHELLEY: It will be if I roast some vegetables. I'm famous for my salads. We could put some hard-boiled eggs in it as well or some chickpeas?

BERI [looking suspicious]: Chickpeas don't belong in a salad . . . [querulously] do they?

SHELLEY: They can do –

BERI: How about some duck breasts?

SHELLEY: Try the salad. I think you'll like it –

BERI: I'd prefer duck; we could do it with red cabbage, apple and caraway? You like that –

SHELLEY: But I've everything here for the salad and besides I haven't time to go out and buy duck –

BERI: If you'd started earlier we could have had a nice goulash or some of those meatballs I like –

SHELLEY: I was working.

BERI: Really?

SHELLEY [ignoring this comment]: Duck with red cabbage? That's what you'd like?

BERI [beaming from ear to ear]: If you wouldn't mind?

SHELLEY [monosyllabic]: Fine –

BERI: Then we could have one of your *famous* salads tomorrow.

Once, when I was on holiday for a few days, my brother came up to look after Beri. I normally called them from wherever I was at some point during the week, just to check everything was okay. On this occasion when Beri came on the line and I asked him how things were going, he made a sort of harrumphing sound.

SHELLEY: What's the matter?

BERI: It's just very difficult –

SHELLEY: What is?

BERI [whispering]: You know –

SHELLEY: Are you two arguing?

BERI: He doesn't know how to cook spaghetti –

SHELLEY: Of course he does. Jonathan's a great cook –

BERI: He doesn't put enough water in the pan. You've got to have a lot of water –
SHELLEY: Does it taste the same?
BERI: That's hardly the point –
SHELLEY: What is the point then?
BERI: He won't listen to me –
SHELLEY: That sounds familiar –

Similar disputes broke out at regular intervals over what was and what was not allowed to 'decorate' the kitchen. Beri insisted all work-tops remain clutter-free save for a glass bread bin, a wooden knife block, a coffee machine and a kettle. There were to be no vases of flowers, no cookery books unless one was in use, no bowls of lemons or bunches of parsley. All condiments were to be kept in the cup-boards, ditto all pots, pans and bowls. After the first meal I cooked on the night I came back to live at High Sunderland, I dutifully washed up the pans, dried them and stacked them away in their various cup-boards. I wiped down the worktops then placed the cloth next to the bottle of washing-up liquid beside the sink.

Next morning I spent half an hour playing hunt the Fairy Liquid, eventually locating it two cupboards down, behind a huge saucepan.

Disappearances of this nature occurred regularly. Often while I was still cooking. Beri would appear by my side under the pretence of fetching a glass or some such other excuse, only for me to turn around in order to use a bottle of wine or a tin of tomatoes to discover it gone.

'I thought you were finished with it,' he'd say, all wide-eyed and innocent.

If I went out to buy a Sunday newspaper there was no point leav-ing it on the dining-room table because the second I turned my back, the paper would be gutted.

SHELLEY: Where's the Travel section?

BERI: Why on earth do you want to read that? You're not going anywhere –

SHELLEY [mouth opening as if about to say something then slowly closing again as she realises – on some deep psychological level – Beri has spoken the truth. She is stuck. She is going nowhere. She is a forty-seven-year-old woman living in a see-through house on top of a hill somewhere in Scotland with only her beloved, impossible father for company for as far into the future as she can see . . .]

But for every frustrating thing that happened in the kitchen, twice as many good things emerged. Zabaglione, Sachertorte, Leberknödel, goulash and my all-time favourite, poppy seed cake. When I lived in Cornwall several of the latter, swathed in bubble-wrap and brown paper, winged their way to me through the post, care of Beri, alongside jars of home-made pickled cucumber and boxes of apples and plums from our orchard, all individually wrapped in tissue paper so they wouldn't touch one another and grow mouldy.

Beri also went through a jam-making phase, filling jar after jar with raspberry, strawberry or plum jam. I found one of these containers at the back of a kitchen cupboard only a few weeks ago with Beri's distinctive (i.e. barely legible) handwriting scrawled across it. *Plum Jam, 1998*. Plum jam was my father's favourite because it was made from our own Victoria plums, but given the date on the jar, I didn't dare open it. Instead, I sat peering through the thick glass to see if I could detect any signs of deterioration. Preserved in that small container was a moment in time, an autumn during which Beri had gathered the plums, washed, peeled, stoned and boiled them with lemon and sugar before pouring the liquid into glass jars and sealing the lids.

And there sat the last one, a microcosm of the house in which it sat except that the house is not sealed so I cannot preserve its contents, only memorise them.

Memory was also how Beri recreated the food from his childhood. In every other area of his life he was loath to look at the past, but not when it came to food. Maybe that is why, when I think of the kitchen, I see a small procession of my father's relatives marching from one end to the other.

This is the odd thin-again, thick-again looping weave of history. All the people who have passed through this kitchen creating a pattern of sorts, a world where past and present are woven together. For instance, here is 'Auntie' Vera, who is not a real aunt but one of my father's several cousins who spent most of the war hiding in a cupboard somewhere in Budapest. And here is Vera's mother, 'Auntie' Illonca, and her mother's sister, 'Auntie' Yoli. Then there is 'Auntie' Suzanne (also one of Beri's cousins) alongside Uncle Moshe with his wife Auntie Hannah who doesn't speak any English, only Hebrew. The women gather in the kitchen insisting Peggy remain on the sidelines while they busy themselves making all manner of dumplings and schnitzels and blintzes to present to 'their' Beri.

But of all the visitors to the house, it was Suzanne who made the biggest impression. On 3 June 1959 Peggy wrote to her mother:

> [...] we've been having a spate of Bernat's relations here just now. We've had an aunt & child and a cousin and tomorrow another aunt & cousin come for the weekend ...
>
> The cousin – Susan – was a very nice girl – 29 years old. She lives in America now having escaped Hungary during the recent revolution. She was very pretty and good-natured and easy-going, which is a change for Bernat's relations, who are

usually slightly mad perfectionists. Bernat says she's on his mother's side though and they were a very sweet & kind family; while his father's side were Tartars!

What a life she's led though. She & her mother were taken to Auschwitz & her 10 yr old brother was sent to another camp from which he never returned. Her father went to another labour camp. She was only 14 then herself but she is a big girl & she says that is what saved her as she was big enough to work. She has a huge wide scar right under her armpit & across her chest where she was beaten with a strap with iron nails in it – for picking up an acorn to eat when they were marching along to work. She had her feet broken. And the worst thing – she can't have children as they gave the women pills there to stop their periods. She was very ill afterwards in Sweden where she was taken when the camps were released.

In actual fact, Suzanne had had an even worse time than Peggy's letter suggests, as she was chosen by the most notorious of all Auschwitz's figures, Josef Mengele, to be experimented upon in his laboratories while Suzanne's younger brother Laszlo and their father had been taken away and murdered immediately upon entering the camp.

It seems odd, but these days when I talk to people about Beri's past, I usually speak of my grandmother and other members of the extended family as having 'died' in Auschwitz or at the very worst having been 'killed' there, but I rarely if ever speak of them in terms of being 'murdered'.

'Murder' seems such an intimate word. Personal. It's green with envy and red with rage and it's something that happens to other people, something you read about in newspapers. It's not something that occurs to eleven million people (six million Jews and five million men, women and children made up of communists, homosexuals, gypsies, the mentally and physically disabled). Murder never felt that close to home. No doubt this is because Beri rarely talked about this part of his life and was able to protect us from the long shadow of his family's experience, unlike many children of the victims of the Holocaust who feel defined by their parents' suffering and unwittingly pass on that trauma, even if they did not experience it firsthand. In America this has been given a name: 'second generation complex'. But whether Beri would have given this idea traction is unlikely. He was not the type of person who believed in digging into the human psyche too deeply. His entire life was based on a conscious decision not to pathologise the past.

> SHELLEY: Did you ever experience anti-Semitism?
> BERI: Not that I can think of –
> SHELLEY: None?
> BERI: Not really. Perhaps with Chanel –
> SHELLEY: As in Coco?
> BERI: She bought a lot of our fabrics across several seasons and because it was such a success our agent asked if she'd like to meet me. I was prepared to fly over when the reply came back a definitive, No. There was a lot of reading between the lines. We concluded it might have had something to do with my name ...
> SHELLEY: You didn't ask?
> BERI: I didn't care –

When Peggy was alive I recall her talking about a dinner party that she and my father attended shortly after moving to the Borders. They were sitting at the table alongside the other guests when the conversation turned to the war and from there to the 'Jewish situation'.

'Quite a lot of unpleasant things were being said about them,' my mother told me many years later, 'and in particular by the man sitting next to me so I said, "You do realise my husband is Jewish, don't you?" The man didn't say a word after that.'

Dinner parties, cocktail parties, parties designed around fashion shows, my sister's wedding reception, my father's ninetieth birthday party – over the years the kitchen at High Sunderland catered for all these occasions and with great success. Beri also enjoyed many successes in his life although there were low points too, but the lowest was the death of my mother.

I had only seen Beri cry once before, at the funeral of his daughter-in-law – my brother's first wife, Kirsten, who died from cancer. The second occasion was after Peggy's death, but even then Beri cried only briefly (that I know of) and I don't believe he realised my sister and I were watching. The affect was, however, profound. I wanted to protect him from feeling so sad, I wanted to make things better for him, which I realise now was not only unhelpful but also misguided. As if I could have saved him from his own emotions, as if he *wanted* saving from his own grief. That said, I believe this need to help was one of the main reasons I returned to High Sunderland. I needed to look after Beri, not out of any sense of duty but because I loved him and because I knew he could never live anywhere else. To expect him to do so would have been cruel.

As anyone who has ever cared for a parent knows, this is one of life's more challenging roles, even when that parent is mentally alert and physically able.

Most of the time I felt like Goneril or Regan, or a combination of both. I certainly wasn't Cordelia.

When I lived in Cornwall I led a selfish life. Within limits I did what I liked with my time, my space, when and where I worked, how I dressed, what I ate and when I ate it. I did not have a partner or children to worry about or care for, but even if I had had, I have never been a person who lives by routines.

Beri was.

Routines made him happy. You knew where you were if you had a routine. So to begin with I tried my best to follow suit.

We had breakfast at 8 a.m.

We had lunch at 1 p.m.

We had dinner at 5 p.m.

This last almost broke me.

Normally I would not eat my evening meal until seven or eight in the evening. Eating at 5 p.m. meant stopping work at around 3.30 or 4 p.m. in order to begin preparing food. I had barely digested lunch by 4 p.m., let alone felt hungry enough to begin cooking again.

When friends came to visit I warned them about the hours we kept although, to be fair, Beri would allow me to postpone dinner a little. That I never asked him if we could eat at 6 p.m. or, God forbid, 7 p.m. on a permanent basis says more about me than it does about him.

The moment I moved back to High Sunderland and stepped over its threshold, I turned into a hybrid creature: half child, half adult. This must happen to a greater or lesser extent to most people if they return home to live with their parent(s). We know that we're adults, we know that we hold down jobs, run houses, have children, husbands, wives – yet the moment we step over the threshold of the parental home, all is as dust. I could no more insist on eating a few hours later each evening than I could tell Beri that I wanted to get rid of my single bed, the bed I'd been sleeping in ever since I was a child, so that I could buy a new king-size one. Consequently, just as children all over the country were sitting down to enjoy their tea at 5 p.m., Beri and I sat down to eat our evening meal.

Is this what they call washing your dirty linen in public? The last thing I want to do is make Beri out to be the type of person who refused to take others' needs on board. As human beings we are complex, we all contain a multitude of good and not-so-good character traits and behaviours. That is what makes us human. Besides, as I said, it is more a reflection on my character than it is on his.

> SHELLEY: How come you never picked me up from school, not once?
> BERI: I was working –
> SHELLEY: So was Mum, but she always did it. Every day –
> BERI: Fathers didn't pick their children up from school in those days –
> SHELLEY: That's not an argument ...
> BERI: Surely you haven't been holding on to that all these years?
> SHELLEY: No ... Maybe ... But you never picked us up or cooked us tea or –
> BERI: You remember too much –

He was right, I do remember too much. I cling to memories like a hoarder struggling to fit into their house because of all the old newspapers and carrier bags and ...

Having finished my MA in photography at Goldsmiths, I took a weekend job on a stall at Camden Lock Market selling Doc Martens. It was fun working there despite the long, cold winter months, but I didn't earn enough money to keep me going all week. Instead, while looking for a permanent position in a publishing company, I took a variety of part-time jobs. I worked in a second-hand bookshop on the Gloucester Road in Kensington a couple of evenings a week, as a home tutor for children struggling with basic English and Maths, as holiday cover for a receptionist at the Commonwealth Institute and, once, as a temp for the Metropolitan Police in Bow. I also accepted a position with a woman who required someone to help de-clutter her house.

'What I need you to do,' she explained over the phone, 'is tell me I don't need twenty-three milk pans or thirteen spare lampshades.'

I agreed. I said, 'It does seem rather excessive.'

'Not excessive, but you'd be doing me a favour if you could come over once or twice a week to help me decide.'

When I turned up, however, I was horrified to discover the hallway impossible to negotiate unless you walked down it sideways like a crab due to the thousands of old gardening magazines stacked up from floor to ceiling.

'So perhaps we should start with these?' I suggested. 'It's not as if you're going to need them all now, is it?'

But F— disagreed.

She said they might still prove useful. She said that she might need them in order to look up an article for her job.

'You're a nurse.'

'I know, but ... nursing and gardening aren't so far apart.'

'How d'you work that out?' I said and then just as quickly, 'You know, it doesn't matter; we could start here instead?' This time I pointed to eleven or so sandwich toasters lying in a pile by the kitchen door.

'But a lot of those are brand new.'

'No one makes that many toasted sandwiches.'

All of a sudden F—'s phone rang and while she took the call I peeked into one of the rooms next to her bedroom. Inside, piled almost up to the ceiling, were hundreds of boxes, each one wrapped in beautiful wrapping paper, some with ribbons and bows tied around them from which labels dangled. 'Darling F,' read one. 'Happy Birthday, Old Thing; with love and kisses, Mum.'

'I don't like opening presents,' F— said when she saw what I was doing.

'Didn't your mum ever ask if you liked what she'd given you?'

'She understood.'

'How about opening one now?'

F— shook her head.

'Just one?'

Needless to say, my job was short-lived. F— could no more open any of her gifts than she could discard a single belonging.

'Don't you feel claustrophobic?'

'I like feeling like that.'

I didn't know how to answer.

Eventually I said, 'I feel trapped.'

Trapped is also how I began to feel living with Beri. The daily routines grew ever more stifling. I moved through rooms free of detritus yet felt as if I were stubbing my toes on all the things that needed to be done to keep Beri's life running smoothly. Worse, it felt at times as if the house was colluding with Beri in order to rein me in. It was transforming itself into a prison. Suddenly its bold lines, square courtyards, neat right angles and unflinching symmetry weren't simply a question of aesthetics, they were metaphorical barriers to spontaneity.

I couldn't leave the house on a whim, but needed to let Beri know not only that I was going out, but where I was going and at precisely what time I would return. It was not his fault. I didn't want him worrying where I was and if – perish the thought – something went wrong he would need to know my whereabouts, but this meant having to explain myself every time I popped out, even if only for a few minutes.

Not that it was always daggers drawn. There were days when the funny side of parent-sitting broke through the frustration. Like the day I asked if he'd like to come for a short walk with me by the river in Melrose where there was a tarmacked path that would be easy for him to negotiate. To my surprise Beri said 'yes' so half an hour later we were on said path with Henry dashing in front of us in and out of the river.

After a while I saw a man walking towards us carrying a lead. There was no dog in sight but I'd seen this man before and knew his dog wouldn't be far behind. Sure enough, just as he passed us, he began calling out for it.

Beri leant towards me.

> BERI: I hope you don't bump into him often?
> SHELLEY [puzzled]: What d'you mean?
> BERI: How can you ask, what do I mean? He's crazy! He's making the sound of a fire engine …
> SHELLEY: You've lost me … I don't understand what you're … [but then the man began shouting out for his dog again].
> MAN: NINA! NINA! NINA!

But episodes of this type were infrequent. Everyday life got in the way. Small observations metamorphosed into large battlefields.

> BERI: I've noticed you're drinking a lot of whisky these days –
> SHELLEY: I like whisky.
> BERI: It worries me that you need so much of it –
> SHELLEY: Not so much, just a couple now and then –
> BERI: Now and then meaning every night?

SHELLEY: The thing is, if I wasn't living with you, you wouldn't know how much I was drinking so perhaps you could pretend I'm not here?

BERI: But you are here –

SHELLEY: Hence the inclusion of 'pretend'–

BERI: You don't want to become an alcoholic, do you?

SHELLEY: I've a long way to go before that –

BERI: Not from where I'm sitting –

SHELLEY [pouring herself another large whisky]: Then sit somewhere else.

And then there were the never-ending appointments for the dentist, doctor, audiologist, Parkinson's clinic, heart clinic, podiatrist, optometrist … I didn't want to be a full-time carer. Not that Beri needed full-time care, least ways not in the way that a lot of the elderly require it because of Alzheimer's or other devastating illnesses. Nor did Beri want me to care for him. He was fiercely independent, quite happy to spend his days painting or reading or snoozing. But the fact was I had moved back to High Sunderland and therefore I was, like it or not, on hand twenty-four-seven.

In an article called 'The Good Daughter' in the *New Statesman*, the journalist Janice Turner wrote that while her mother was staying with her after a spell in hospital, she hired a private carer to look after her for a few weeks so that she (Janice) could continue working. 'This lovely woman,' writes Turner, 'was boundlessly kind, calm, patient, unfazed: I am none of these things. Ask me to fix the car, get sense from a doctor, shout at the council: I'm Action Daughter, at your service. But expect me to sit still in a room making nice for hours and I'm crap.'

That is precisely how I felt. Crap. I was crap at being Beri's companion. Crap at conversation. Crap at giving my life over to this man whom I loved, but who nonetheless drove me insane. In addition I could not help but think that little had changed since the age of the Victorian spinster; that is to say, those times when unmarried daughters renounced their own lives in favour of looking after their widowed mothers or fathers.

Unhelpfully those of my friends and family who had children added to this equation by delighting in telling me that now I would know what it was like being them – as if somehow I was due some sort of comeuppance for not giving birth. But looking after a parent is not comparable to bringing up a child. A sort of despair overwhelmed me and I began making dark calculations. If Beri lived to be 101, I'd be sixty years old when he died – if not an elderly woman, then certainly on the wrong side of fifty. I didn't want Beri to die, but nor did I want him to live for such a long time that old age was waving at me from next door. Which meant I *did* want Beri to die. I wanted my father to die. Of all the thoughts I've entertained in my life, this was the darkest. I was disgusted at myself. On the worst days I felt like punching myself in the face. I felt a violent self-hatred. On other days I wanted to escape High Sunderland, put a fist through the glass, watch the glory of something so rigid explode into a thousand, billion pieces.

I did not do this (of course). Instead, my urge to destroy the fabric of the house developed into daydreams of running away – not to a circus but to a hotel room where everything was white. White linen sheets, white counterpane, white curtains and carpet: a place where I could lock the door behind me, curl up on the bed and go to sleep. Thinking of nothing, listening to nothing, doing nothing for as long as I wanted.

Days, weeks, months, years . . .

Instead, I ended up in Tesco's car park.

After I finished the shopping on a Tuesday evening, I would sit in my car and watch as the youth of Galashiels used the place as a racecourse. Round and round they drove, revving up their engines, racing each other to the exits. Even when the council put in speed bumps, it didn't stop the boy racers. It was peaceful watching them. The car park was covered so there was no mobile reception once you had parked up and that meant no one could phone you. It was the most non-place ever, with no view, no radio reception and nothing to do except sit and watch the cars going round and around. Or the occasional pigeon. I wanted to be nowhere and this was the best bit of nowhere I knew.

Nor was the irony lost on me when – after Beri died – I was free to run away whenever I chose. But by then escaping, being nowhere, was the last thing I wanted to do.

Master Bedroom

When the phone call came it was the middle of a cold April night. I'd half been expecting it, yet I was also convinced everything would be okay because past experience said that it would.

Six or seven months previously, while my sister and niece were visiting High Sunderland, we'd all had to rush to the hospital when Beri had fallen seriously ill. Sitting in the relatives' room for what seemed an eternity, a doctor finally came and fetched us and said they had put my father on a machine to squeeze some fluid out of his lungs, but we were to prepare for the worst because they did not think he would make it.

But he did.

Next morning when we visited Beri on the ward, he was sitting up in bed, bright as a lollipop.

> BERI [beaming with pleasure]: They said they didn't expect me to survive –
> SHELLEY: Can you remember us being there? We were there with you in the room?
> BERI: Vaguely. It was very uncomfortable but I don't remember so much. They said they didn't expect me to survive –

Three days later I was still visiting him in hospital, my sister and niece having returned down south.

'The doctor wants to talk with us,' Beri said as I sat down next to his bed.

Moments later said doctor appeared and pulled the curtains around Beri's cubicle.

'We'd like to send you home tomorrow, Mr Klein. You've done really well.'

Beri nodded and smiled. He looked pleased as punch.

'But,' said the doctor, half-closing his eyes, 'your defibrillator?'

Again Beri nodded.

'We think it might be best ... that it might give you a more comfortable ... it's not very nice for you when it goes off, is it?'

'No, it's not a good feeling,' my father agreed.

'So,' the doctor said, taking a deep breath, 'we think it might give you a more peaceful death if we switched it off. Of course, it's entirely up to you, it's your decision and you can take as long as you want to think about it and talk it over. It doesn't need to be done straight away, but if you were to have another heart attack we don't think you'd survive and the defibrillator would go off and like you've said to me just now, it's not a pleasant sensation ... '

His voice droned on endlessly.

Unlike my heart, which felt as if it had stopped. I did not want to be privy to this conversation. If this was transparency, I wanted obfuscation. I wanted walls thick as forests, I wanted windowless houses, I wanted –

'The thing is,' Beri said, 'I've had a very good life so on balance I think you should switch it off.'

I left the ward, shattered.

So, on that dark April night when the final phone call came, I should have been expecting it. Except that I wasn't. A few hours earlier, at around midnight, Beri had rung his night bell to say he thought he was having another heart attack. He was still fully conscious although his breathing was raspy and 'wet'. I phoned for an ambulance and having been assured one was on its way, I gathered all of Beri's medications together and fetched his overnight bag, which was packed and ready to go for just such an occasion. Then I sat down on

210

the edge of Beri's bed and held his hand. As far as I can recall we barely exchanged a word. Beri was concentrating on his breathing. I was concentrating on staying awake. I remember us both smiling and nodding at each other a lot, but otherwise the room was silent.

Silence, peacefulness – both are qualities the master bedroom exudes. Don't ask me why because, being at the front of the house and consequently nearest the main road, it should be the least quiet room in the building and yet it's a cool, peaceful haven with views across lawns and pine trees.

Originally this room had a dusky green carpet that blended in with the greenery outside. Perhaps this is why as a child it felt like entering a forest – an impression that must also have been influenced by the dark walnut panelling behind the beds and the paler, honey-coloured, walnut-trimmed limba wood of the inbuilt cupboards and drawers that run down one side of the room. Branching off from here are two further spaces, a dressing room and bathroom. The dressing room belonged to my mother and it was there she hung all her most beautiful garments – long evening skirts in waterfall blues, coats the colour of kingfisher wings.

But other than that, the bedroom was sparsely furnished. Indeed, the only pieces of freestanding furniture were the bed and a small fabric-covered stool that stood in front of a full-length mirror. I can't recall any ornaments decorating this room, nor clothes ever scattered across the floor. There were certainly never any mugs of coffee or glasses of water left on the shelves. Only after my parents died did I hang one of Beri's paintings on the wall. I know he wouldn't have approved. This was a room like all the others in which nothing was meant to distract the eye or disturb one's thoughts, a concept nowadays approved by proponents of 'clean sleep', but which, as always for Beri, was an aesthetic decision rather than one based on science.

Of course the *inside* of the cupboards at High Sunderland was a different matter and, as with the kitchen drawers, Peggy's cupboards were never organised or tidy. On the rare occasions she asked me to fetch something from one of these spaces, the overwhelming joy at being able to rummage about in the intimate tangles of brightly coloured stockings and jewellery, of discovering little nests of multi-coloured jumpers and socks, was like being let loose in an Aladdin's cave, especially as mixed in with the clothing I was also likely to uncover small presents Peggy had squirrelled away and forgotten to give people; tins of toffees, bottles of perfume, alongside a tiny nugget of gold that she kept hidden inside a matchbox, hairgrips and hair rollers, packets of bath salts and, on one unforgettable occasion, stuffed right at the back of her jumper drawer under piles of fluffy blue and green mohair – a copy of *The Joy of Sex*.

I was shocked. Not by the fact that my parents were still having sex, but because the man in the illustrations sported a beard. How had Beri reacted on seeing this picture? Or perhaps my mother never told him she'd bought the book? Perhaps it was another of her secrets? Naturally I never asked, but instead whenever my parents left me alone in the house, I'd go and sneak another look at all the different ways 'it' could be done until the day I opened the drawer only to discover the book no longer there. It had vanished, never to be seen again, which came as something of a relief as I found the bearded man a bit creepy.

But besides the disappearance of *The Joy of Sex*, the master bedroom remained much the same as it was on the day my parents moved in to the house save for replacing the green carpet with one in cream.

It was on this carpet in 2008 that my mother collapsed. By chance I was at home at the time, something I'm eternally grateful for as I don't believe I would have coped half so well with her death if I hadn't been there. Beri quickly alerted me to what had occurred at which point I tried to give my mother mouth-to-mouth resuscitation, but even while I was doing so, I knew she had died.

Watching Peggy's body being pushed out on a trolley across the front courtyard before being loaded in to the undertaker's vehicle reminded me of all the times I had said goodbye to my parents thinking it might be the last time I'd see one or both of them alive. My reluctance to leave home seemed knotted to this thought whilst at the same time it reflected Beri's own unwillingness ever to depart his beloved home, the house he had so very carefully shaped and cared for over the years, not only as a defence against what he perceived as the chaos of the outside world but also, on a deeper psychological level, perhaps as a defence against death itself.

As a family we often joked about Beri's reluctance to leave High Sunderland saying it was because he might disintegrate if he did. That was the feeling my father conveyed, that the house's boundaries were under a magical spell that if broken would result in disaster. If he had to go away on business trips (which he frequently did) the tactics he employed to delay departure, including 'losing' his passport, meant he frequently missed flights or only caught them by the skin of his teeth. If we were going on holiday, the same applied. Even when we had to leave the house to go to a party, his eagerness to return home as quickly as humanly possible is marked in my memory by the heated exchanges between himself and Peggy that took place in the car on the way over.

> BERI: So, can we just agree a time we can leave?
> PEGGY: Darling, we haven't even got there yet –
> BERI: Roughly?
> PEGGY: We'll leave when we leave – I'm not setting a time limit –
> BERI [silence]

PEGGY: Besides, you always enjoy yourself when you get there –
BERI [puzzled]: Do I?
PEGGY: Yes, you do –
BERI [staring out of the window]: Okay, but how about we have a signal? I could touch your shoulder, nothing too dramatic –
PEGGY: BERNAT!

But here's a question I've often asked myself. Did Beri's desire to stay put at the house stem from an unconscious longing never to leave home again? Had his early derangement encouraged a need to put roots down so deep, they could not be dislodged? I don't know. What I do know is that it always felt to me like I was Beri's emotional amanuensis. For example, I recall the day Beri told me the news of Peter's death [Womersley died in London, in 1993, at the home of his niece]. Beri and I were sitting at the dining-room table when he leant over and told me what had happened, adding that he was very sad because he'd wanted to visit his old friend, but Peter had requested no visitors.

'I just wanted to let him know I was there for him,' my father said, shaking his head sadly. 'That I was thinking of him.' Beri was dry-eyed, but tears coursed down my cheeks and for days afterwards whenever Beri and I were in the same room, I felt a profound, tangible sadness.

And when it came to Beri's dislike of leaving High Sunderland, I believe I absorbed this too. Perhaps it was a sort of osmosis or transference of everything he feared? Whatever the case, as a child I found even the notion of staying a couple of nights at friends' houses filled me with dread.

*

'Should I go with him?' I said to the ambulance-men when they arrived. 'I could follow you in my car?'

'I'd wait until morning,' one of them replied. 'Nothing will happen tonight.'

And he should have been right. We'd been through this routine so many times before and Beri was always okay the next morning.

The ambulance doors closed and I went back to bed. Seconds later – or so it seems to me now – I awoke to the sound of the telephone and a woman's voice asking if I could get to the hospital as quickly as possible because my father was going downhill. Did I have someone who could drive me?

'I can drive myself.'

'Please don't drive too fast,' she said.

I think I knew then that he had already died.

Hospitals – especially rural hospitals – are silent places at night. I walked through the sliding doors into the empty, over-lit Emergency area. I rang a bell and from what seemed like out of nowhere, a nurse appeared and directed me to the small, comfortless relatives' room where 'a doctor will come and talk to you soon'.

I don't recall much of what happened after I returned home. Except for two things. The first was that High Sunderland was still there. Somehow a part of me thought the house might have vanished now that Beri was gone. I don't think I'd have been surprised if it had. In fact, I believe I would have been relieved because to walk back inside knowing Beri was dead was unbearable.

And the second thing? The second was attached to the first and it was how very ordinary everything felt. The clock in the kitchen still made the same soft, slow, ticking sound. The kitchen tiles were still the same dull blue. The living room was exactly as I had left it barely an hour before.

I stared at the house and it stared back at me, glassily. It had the eyes of a dead animal. The house might have looked alive, but it wasn't. It was a con.

The irony of losing someone. You feel dead without them. You are the ghost while they live on in your memory. The following days were a blur. I can't recall when or even if I stripped the sheets from his bed or whether I left this job to someone else. I probably did.

I do remember having to go back to the hospital the next morning to pick up the death certificate, being driven there by a friend. On the way home I screamed at her to stop the car because I was about to be sick. I threw up in the middle of Selkirk, just outside Grieves Snack Attack in the main square, with people staring at me as if I were drunk. In their place I probably would have thought the same. I wiped my mouth then fumbled around in the back of the car trying to find something with which to mop up my vomit, but nothing came to hand. Shortly afterwards we arrived back home.

For the second time in twenty-four hours I had to walk back through the front door knowing that Beri was not going to be there. Nine times out of ten he'd be sitting in his chair at the dining-room table, standing at his easel or lying down on the top couch reading a book. I can see him there now. All three spaces are imprinted with the memory of him. Today, as I write this, I am sitting at the dining-room table in the same chair I have sat in since I was a child. There are seven more chairs here – all of them empty – yet I can see Beri sitting at the head of the table, with Peggy on the other side of me, in her chair to my right.

Echoing pools. High Sunderland is awash with them. Although often the pools feel like tar pits.

Sitting around the dining-room table with my brother, sister and undertaker. The undertaker slides a plastic folder across the table in our direction containing a collection of laminated colour photographs picturing a selection of coffins. Why is this necessary? Why is there this hierarchy of coffins from cheapest to ludicrously expensive? Wouldn't it be better if there were no grading at all, simply a plain wooden box in which to carry the body so that no one need feel guilty for choosing something modest? I flick through the pictures, bewildered at the over-abundance of gold plate, wood veneers, white satin interiors, beading and breastplates.

'Dad wouldn't be seen dead in one of these,' I whisper in an attempt at a joke.

The undertaker stares at me.

Undertaker. I've never considered this word before. The person who undertakes something – in this case the funeral – or the person who takes something under? Is the man sitting in front of us in his relentless grey suit a modern-day Hades, Greek god of the underworld, who dragged Persephone down into his kingdom? According to myth, Persephone's mother, Demeter, wandered the earth in search of her daughter, her grief causing all living things to wither and die. In one version Zeus sends his messenger to bargain with Hades for Persephone's release, leastways for half of the year thereby creating the seasons with spring and summer signifying Persephone's return to the light, autumn and winter her descent back into darkness. High Sunderland is Persephone's spring and summer, a building that frames and highlights the rolling greens of those seasons, the see-through walls creating modernist ballets in which rhomboids of light dance across floors. But Greek myths aren't the only ones to focus on what lies beneath. The Borders have one of their own.

Sir Thomas of Ercildoune (better known as Thomas the Rhymer or True Thomas) was a thirteenth-century poet and 'prophet' who lived in what is nowadays known as Earlston, which lies about eleven miles from here. In several ballads Sir Thomas is the central protagonist who, having been kidnapped by the Queen of Elfland, is taken down into her underworld beneath the Eildon Hills. There he remains for seven years before being returned to the 'mortal realm'. Thomas then spends the next seven years making predictions that, although none were written down by Thomas himself, appeared in later history books. 'On the morrow,' reads one, 'afore noon, shall blow the greatest wind that ever was heard before in Scotland', which supposedly predicted the death of Alexander III in 1286. However, having served seven years prophesying the future, Sir Thomas disappeared once again, presumably returning to the Eildons' shadowy realms.

The undertaker stares at me as I turn my head to catch sight of these hills through the window. Majestic. Magical. Other-worldly. Today they are a soft, sooty black although when the light changes, they can be green, turquoise or gold. That is their beauty. The Eildons are geological chameleons. But today they are black and I think of Sir Thomas curled up underneath the full weight of their soil and suddenly a chord is struck, an echo of my own crushing heaviness for underworld myths suggest like nothing else does the subterranean agonies of those left behind. The stranded. The abandoned. The grief-stricken.

'We're not burying Dad,' I tell Auntie Suzanne in Los Angeles. 'He's being cremated . . . like Peggy.'

Gillian and I have chosen a favourite suit for him to wear, in addition to which we've also decided he should be wrapped in Zori's blue and white cotton bedspread.

'I didn't know this existed,' my sister said when I took it out of Dad's cupboard to show her.

'Neither did I. He only told me about it last year.'

'He's being cremated,' I repeat down the line to Suzanne. 'It's what he wanted.'

'But after everything that happened … to Zori … and everyone else? It doesn't seem right … ' Suzanne's voice trails off.

'I understand,' I say, although, of course, I don't understand because I can't say it's occurred to me to link cremation with the ovens at Auschwitz. To me the idea of fire has always appealed because it's transformative, besides which, I don't like the thought of lowering Beri into a grave, of piling earth on top of a coffin and leaving him all alone in the dark. But this wasn't the reason my father didn't want to be buried. Over his lifetime both he and Peggy had made it very clear they wanted to be cremated because for them burial was analogous with religion, with vicars and rabbis and graveyards, none of which was for them. Besides, if there was any place in the world that represented their lives, who they were and what they both stood for, it wouldn't be marked by a headstone. It could only be marked by High Sunderland.

I write this down then glance up from my computer only to catch sight of the Eildons again. According to geography books these formations take their name from the Old Norse word *eldr* meaning 'fire' because the Eildons are the remains of volcanic eruptions that occurred millions of years ago. Suddenly a thought springs to mind. Why not set fire to High Sunderland? I've always liked the idea of Viking funerals where the dead are placed on longboats, set alight then pushed out to sea. Besides, I don't want anyone else to own High Sunderland. I want to keep it unsullied. I want – like a child hoarding its toys – to keep it all for our family so I go down to the living room, pick up a box of matches and begin lighting them one by one, watching as they flare and burn then blowing them out before the flames catch my fingers. If only I could do it. If only I could set light to the house. That would be the best ending of all.

Echoing pools. The inner seethings of loss. I begin getting headaches. Some days I find it hard to swallow, other days I start to shake.

I see black dots in front of my eyes. Sometimes these dots merge together in shapeless, amoeba-like splodges. I continue to write only I find myself putting words down on paper which come out as other words. I take paracetamol and Nurofen, Nytol, codeine; anything I can obtain over the counter rather than asking my doctor for help. I drink too much and sleep too little. All I want to do is walk into the woods, curl up under the trees and close my eyes. But even sleep isn't peaceful. Every night for a week I find myself walking across a loch, the surface of which has turned to ice. The world is frozen. Glebs of frozen water cling to the bulrushes. I know the ice is unstable yet I keep walking and then I hear the first crack. It echoes through the woods surrounding the loch. Cold as a sledgehammer to the back of my neck. A second crack then a third and my foot is gripped by what feel like teeth. Ice slices my flesh. Suddenly I am going under, falling through, being consumed by black water. I'm not frightened; part of me wants to be submerged by the darkness; part of me yearns for it.

I start putting a gun to my head. An imaginary gun, lighter than swansdown. Over and over again, when the pain gets too hard, when I can't breathe because I'm sobbing so much. When the edges of my body dissolve and I'm thinner than watercolour. I put this gun to my head.

I feel like I'm going insane. Not straitjacket insane. I'm not bound for cuckoo-nest land, not yet, although I hate to admit it, but I've begun to envy those people whose minds have taken them so far from reality.

Back in the Nineties I lived in a flat in the centre of Soho opposite what was then an overnight refuge for homeless women. Most of the time the activities in this building were kept securely behind its featureless walls. But occasionally I'd be awoken at two or three in the morning. Someone would be laughing or shouting outside and I'd peer through the curtains. One night I spied a tall, broad-shouldered woman with long brown hair, dressed in what appeared to be a knee-length nightgown. She was swinging around a lamp-post, laughing maniacally to herself. Bertha (my nickname for her) became a permanent fixture of my time on Greek Street. During the day I'd occasionally spot her outside a cashpoint at Barclays either begging for coins or squatting beneath the cash dispenser taking a pee. Bertha had no inhibitions, no ties to reality. But I was nowhere near Bertha insane. My mind was simply trying to fill a space that was short-circuiting crazily. All kinds of bizarre thoughts entered my head, the strangest of all being that Beri had killed himself. Had he secretly taken a cocktail of drugs to bring on a heart attack? Or deliberately not taken his drugs? Had he done this because he knew how much I was struggling to look after him? And why did I keep hearing footsteps on the roof? Every time this happened I rushed out to see who was up there, but of course no one was there. I was hearing someone who didn't exist and, in the words of the American poet William Hughes Mearns, 'He wasn't there again today'.

I lost precious objects and hunted for them for weeks on end before my mind began telling me that someone had broken into the house and stolen these objects. I searched for my set of spare house keys, which I kept outside in a 'secret' hiding place but then couldn't remember where that place was. I changed all the locks on the front door. Two weeks later I found my 'stolen' items exactly where I'd left them, on the top shelf of the cupboard where Beri stored his boxes of oil paint.

During a daytrip to Edinburgh, I came to a standstill in the middle of the St James shopping centre. Suddenly, for no apparent reason, or none I could discern, I lost all sense of my bearings and for a couple of minutes didn't recognise I was in Edinburgh, let alone in a shopping centre. I saw people walking past me, heard them talking and whispering. In the distance bagpipes were playing, but I couldn't move or anchor myself in time or space. Was this Galashiels or Selkirk or someplace else? I felt dizzy. Odd. Then someone came up to me and asked where the loos were.

I pointed to the left.

Moments later someone else wanted to know if I could direct him to Thorntons.

'Yes,' I said and gave him directions.

'I'm looking for Sports Direct?'

'It's ... ' I answered, turning around to where I thought the shop might possibly be. Only then did I spot a large sign above my head that said, HELP POINT.

Help was what I needed the most, particularly waking in the porcelain calm of those cold spring mornings. Sometimes I'd have been crying in my sleep and I'd find my pillow soggy, but even on the mornings when the pillow was dry, from the second I opened my eyes, a huge weight lay on my chest. The weight was black and it was not simply lying on top of me, it was growing into my skin, had put its roots out which were now spreading through my chest and each root was filled with such heavy blackness it was impossible to breathe. The black roots squeezed my lungs, they were tearing their way through the soft skin on my back, sewing me into the mattress.

Outside I heard lambs bleating. This was April and at 5 a.m. each morning the neighbouring farmer zoomed into the field below the house on his quadbike, bellowing and roaring while at the same time racing around at top speed, scattering sheep in every direction. I knew why he was doing it: he needed to make the sheep stand up in order to spot if any were sick or dead. But all I could think of was: there's no one to check up on whether I was too sick to move or whether I'd died in the night. There was no one I had to get up for; no one was waiting for me to kiss them good morning. No one needed me to prepare breakfast or lay the fire, or order their meds. One day I calculated I could lie there for two days straight before my sister realised anything was amiss. Gillian was calling every evening to check I was okay, but there was a possibility she wouldn't think anything wrong until maybe the second or third evening. In fact, the only thing that prevented this from occurring was the fact that about a year before Beri died, I had taken the enormous decision of buying a dog.

Henry arrived as an eight-week-old puppy. He was the first dog I had ever owned, the first dog ever to live at High Sunderland where previous to this we'd only ever been allowed cats and even their introduction to the house wasn't simple as I'd had to sign a 'Cat Contract' with Beri before so much as one feline paw was allowed over the threshold.

Beri had softened somewhat since those early days and when I returned to High Sunderland from Cornwall bringing my two cats, Pootle and Porridge, with me, he instantly fell in love with them both. But dogs were a different matter altogether. Neither Beri nor Peggy had had dogs as children. In Beri's case, he said this was because his parents were far too busy being religious to own dogs. Cats, yes, because cats caught mice and therefore served a purpose. But dogs? No purpose to them whatsoever unless you were a farmer . . .

> BERI: Which we aren't –
> CHILD SHELLEY: But Bella has dogs –
> BERI: Her parents are *farmers* –
> CHILD SHELLEY: And Pippa?
> BERI: Farmers –
> CHILD SHELLEY: How about Anna?
> BERI: Her father's a psychiatrist so that doesn't count –
> CHILD SHELLEY: That's not fair! You're changing the rules –
> BERI: Sweetie pie –

CHILD SHELLEY: Okay, what about Alison?

BERI: Who's Alison?

CHILD SHELLEY: I don't know, but there's got to be an Alison out there with a dog whose father isn't a farmer OR a psychiatrist –

Yet, despite my skills at debating, it still took me almost forty years to finally get what I wanted.

I first informed Beri of the decision to buy a puppy while driving him into Galashiels for a dental appointment.

BERI: That's a terrible idea!

SHELLEY [instantly irritated]: Why?

BERI: You don't have enough time to look after one –

SHELLEY: But you're always telling me I should get out more –

BERI: Am I?

SHELLEY: Yes.

BERI: The house isn't big enough for a dog –

SHELLEY: The house is massive. I'm not buying a Dobermann –

BERI: It's a terrible idea. You should definitely not be getting a Dobermann.

SHELLEY: Do you even know what a Dobermann is?

BERI: A dog of any description is a terrible idea –

SHELLEY [snapping]: But I wasn't asking you if I could get one. I was telling you that I am!

When we got home I wrote this conversation down in my notebook. Imagine Beri thinking the house was too small for a dog! How on earth did his mind work? Then it dawned on me that Beri's house *was* too small to fit a dog inside because Beri's house, his Bachelardian snail shell, was fully occupied. *By him*. By how he lived and what he expected. And this is what had made me feel so infuriated because it also characterised all the tensions, the claustrophobia, the constant monitoring, the feelings of being trapped. It seems simplistic to state that when we're children there's (more or less) room for us in our parents' houses because, figuratively speaking, we're still attached to them so they have to accommodate us, but as adults this equation no longer works, we're separate beings and the tensions that consequently arise from this can be agonising.

This also explains why at times, the relationship between my father and me felt like a fight to the death: either that he had to die so that I could move in to the house properly or that I had to kill myself in order to escape it. Looking after a parent or parents is both blessing and curse, a time that brings you face to face with some extremely unpleasant parts of yourself, reflections you might well not want to confront.

Three weeks later Henry arrived: a warm-bellied, wet-nosed puppy of pure deliciousness who duly proceeded to turn everything upside down. Including Beri, who – as he had done with the cats – fell in love with him instantly. Every night Beri insisted on coming through to 'my' part of the house to wish Henry goodnight. And every morning when I went through to the kitchen to make breakfast, Beri's first enquiry was always, 'Did Henry sleep well?'

I adored Henry, too. In spite of the fact that he chewed holes in every jumper I owned.

> BERI: You know how much you love that dog?
> SHELLEY [staring into Henry's big, dark eyes]: Of course I do, I'd do anything for him.
> BERI: Well, that's how I feel about you.

I recall that sentence and something inside me caves in. How did I respond? I can't remember what I said or if I said anything at all. If I could go back to any moment in time, it would be that one. 'And I love you too,' I say over and over – 'And I love you too.'

Henry was the only reason after Beri died that I dragged myself out of bed every morning. He'd breathe his soft, doggy breath into my face, press his velvety muzzle against my cheek, nudge me over and over with his nose until finally, finally, I moved and we would shamble through the woods together. If I was having a good day I would share in his heaven, watch him sooling through the undergrowth, racing between the pine trees at a hundred miles an hour. Sometimes he'd swim across what I began calling 'Henry's Pond' in order to terrorise the local wildlife.

But if I was having a bad day I saw none of these things because none existed. On mornings like that I did not want to live.

I tried talking to a friend about it. We were walking through Crow Wood at the time, kicking up leaves.

SHELLEY: I'm finding it a real struggle. The pain's relentless; some mornings I don't want to carry on, it would be so easy to start swallowing pills and not stop –
FRIEND: You shouldn't talk like that –
SHELLEY: It's how I feel. I'm not going to kill myself or anything but –
FRIEND: So why say it?
SHELLEY: Because talking about it helps –
FRIEND: You shouldn't talk about suicide. Not if you're not going to do it –
SHELLEY: You'd rather I kill myself?
FRIEND: I didn't say that –
SHELLEY: As good as –

FRIEND: It's like the difference between being a professional actor and being involved in amateur dramatics –
SHELLEY: Wow!
FRIEND: That didn't come out right –
SHELLEY: Too right it didn't –
FRIEND: I just don't like talking about suicide –
SHELLEY: Neither do I . . . !

My friend Chris tackled me from a different angle. Ever since Beri died, he called me from whatever bus he was catching to or from work.

CHRIS: Are you up yet?
SHELLEY: Of course I am –
CHRIS: It's quite obvious you're not –
SHELLEY [silence]
CHRIS: Don't make me come up there. Because I will. I'll catch the next train up and drag you out of bed –
SHELLEY: By my reckoning it'll take you all day to get here, longer perhaps – by which time it'll be evening and I'd be going to bed anyway –
CHRIS [ignoring my logic]: Where's Henry?
SHELLEY: Next to me.
CHRIS: He needs walking –
SHELLEY [silence]
CHRIS: Are you still there?
SHELLEY [(choking back tears, whispering] I can't talk . . .

'No one ever told me . . . ' These are the opening words of *A Grief Observed*, a book C. S. Lewis wrote after his wife, Joy Davidman, died in 1960.

No one ever tells you how lonely grief is.

No one ever tells you how numbing grief is.

No one ever tells you how BORING grief is.

After my mother died I had immersed myself in other people's words and it had helped me through the pain. But this time, instead of reading other people's books, I begin writing my own. Only a few words at first. Then a few more. I fill one notepad full of scribbles then buy another, only this time I choose one with a cover the colour of egg yolks. I start jotting my thoughts down as and when they arise. Sometimes this occurs during the night when my dreams wake me up. Sometimes it's during the day while light tips through the windows.

I start doing some research into Beri's life, try to unravel the bits I don't know while attempting to weave other bits into some kind of pattern. I spread out every newspaper article I can find on Beri and Peggy and Peter – scatter them across the dining-room table in a giant configuration of documents before trying to familiarise myself with the varying accounts and events. It's irresistible to see writing and weaving as sharing something in common. Both draw different strands and threads together and if you go wrong, it's easy to unpick the fabric, unravel the stiches, delete the paragraph and start over again.

I take a trip in to Edinburgh and notice a new housing estate on the A7 just outside Bonnyrigg. Brand-new buildings that have yet to be lived in – carpet-less, furniture-less spaces. High Sunderland was a new-build once, too. A blank canvas. An empty space on to which its new owner could make his mark, leave his impression. After Beri's death I found several blank canvases propped up behind his easel. When he was alive they spoke of promise, of the future, of something yet to be realised, but now that he's dead they describe nothing other than the space into which he has vanished. They are un-paintings, not-pictures.

'And what will you do now?'

This question is posed two weeks after Beri dies. By a woman who barely knew my father and certainly doesn't know me. She's wearing too much make-up, her cheeks glow with rouge and her purple lips glint scarily under the strip lights within the room in which we are standing.

'I don't know,' I say, a surge of anxiety rising inside me like vomit.

'What about the house?'

'The house?'

'Are you going to carry on living there?'

'We've ... ' I stutter, before realising that 'we' – that is to say, my father and I – was no longer applicable. 'We' no longer existed. Yet this is a trap I fall into over and over again. I begin speaking a ghost language, talking about Beri in both present and future tenses when in fact he exists in neither. Limbo is a place that lies between heaven and hell. The language I speak after Beri dies is similar. It is transitional, a nowhere kind of language in which my father passes through tenses as if they are invisible walls, existing and not existing at the same time.

'Will you stay on at High Sunderland?'

The question reverberates in my ear and (okay – I'm not entirely proud to remember this) I recall wondering, if I were to 'accidently' push into this woman, could I do so hard enough to knock her into the glass display case standing behind her? Would the glass shatter? And if it did shatter would the shards pierce her skin? Perhaps a piece might become lodged in her neck? Her neck would be a good a place. The glass might sever an artery?

Blood pools stickily over the floor.

'Will you stay on at High Sunderland?'

'Perhaps ... I don't really know yet, it's too early to think about stuff like that ... '

'Take your time,' someone else chips in. 'There's no hurry, is there?'

'None I can think of.'

And the truth is, there isn't. There's no hurry to do anything, which comes as a massive relief. And yet I've always known that once Beri died, we (my sister, brother and I) would need to sell High Sunderland.

When Beri was alive this thought never carried much weight. Instead, I imagined myself leaving immediately after the funeral, running towards a new life. But after he died nothing was further from the truth. With each day that passed I clung tighter and tighter to the house, wanting to bind myself to it. At night, with eyes closed, I imagined storms out at sea and how sailors roped themselves to the decks so as not to be washed overboard.

I began wearing Beri's jumpers. Bernat Klein's Bernat Kleins. Angoras in soft, sugar browns. A mohair sweater in deep copper-rose. Liquorice-black cashmeres and thick cream Arans.

I made lists of colour transparencies, cleared out drawers of pencils and paints, placed prints in thin glassine envelopes.

I took all of Beri's paintings (about 200 in total) and placed them about the house, propped them up against chairs and tables and cupboards, and then began hanging one or two on the walls, swapping them over until I felt I'd hit the right balance. This was another way of communicating with Beri, of continuing a dialogue with him and filling the silence around me. Possibly it's also why I began caring for High Sunderland in ways I never thought possible.

One morning when I get out of bed, I decide it would be a good idea to clean the house's exterior framework. I tell myself it will make the house look brighter for when prospective buyers came round, but the enjoyment I take from scrubbing the house is also suffused with the pleasure I know Beri would have gained seeing this taking place. I climb my ladder, clear away all manner of cobwebs and leaves before swabbing the woodwork down with gallons of hot soapy water. It is satisfying work. Then the windows need washing. It takes me two full weeks to get around the outside of the house, but I do these too before making a start on weeding the front and back courtyards. The whole summer goes by and I am still cleaning and scrubbing and painting. I buy a pressure washer and begin maniacally hosing down the paving stones. Sixty years' worth of lichen and moss get sluiced away. It is the most gratifying feeling in the world, a bit – I imagine – like removing a layer of dirt from an old oil painting only to discover how bright the colours are that lie underneath. We can't sell the house – or so I keep telling myself – if it looks unloved; besides which, all this physical activity helps me to sleep. Nor am I unaware that I've swapped caring for Beri for caring for his house. The ritualised washing of a dead person's body – the lifting of each heavy limb, the gentle attendance to skin, hair and nails, the affording of dignity to someone even in death.

When he was alive Beri took enormous pride in his appearance. Caring for his house is one way of carrying this forward, one way of continuing the relationship between myself and my father although in reality I am doing a far better job of the latter than I ever did caring for Beri, the knowledge of which fills me with guilt.

Guilt is the perfect partner for depression. If they were to read each other's profiles on a dating website, they'd fall in love instantly. Every day after Beri died I felt a gnawing anxiety. Could he see through my bad moods, my grumpiness, and know that although I had griped and groaned and snapped, I loved him in a thousand different ways?

But alongside being the ideal partner for depression, guilt is also a pugilist and as such the punches keep coming.

I didn't do –

I should have done –
I could have been –
Why didn't I?–
I snapped –
I ignored –
I shouted –
I blamed –

SHELLEY: You sent me to boarding school. I hated it –
BERI: It was the best education available –
SHELLEY: I wanted to stay here –
BERI: What can I say? We thought we were doing our best –

And what can I say now, thinking back on how childish I was to lay that grievance at his door? Worse still, I am now thinking about selling his house.

No sooner does this thought spring to mind then something else pops in to my head. Who will I be if I no longer live at High Sunderland? For so long now it has been such a major part of my life. Unlike Jonathan or Gillian I have never owned my own property, only rented them, and although I have put my own stamp on these places, you never make a rental property your own. Not that High Sunderland is mine, but at least I feel I belong here. It's as much a part of me as my childhood or the colour of my eyes or my surname. The house explains who I am, not to other people, but to myself. 'Buildings,' wrote Juhani Pallasmaa in *The Eyes of the Skin*, 'enable us to structure, understand and remember the shapeless flow of reality and ultimately, to recognise and remember who we are.'

So will I fall apart without High Sunderland? Will I go through the grieving process a third time? The thought of packing up all the furniture and ceramics and books – carefully placing them into boxes

– feels wrong. They belong here. In this building. Taking them someplace else makes me think of organ transplants: the removal of hearts, livers and lungs from one person and embedding them in another. But sometimes the new organ won't take despite the surgeon's best efforts. Despite medications pumped into the new body to fool it into thinking nothing has changed. Is that what will happen when I pack up High Sunderland? When I take all these objects to a new home?

And what about me? Will I ever feel right living someplace else? Suddenly I find myself spending night after night on eBay, buying objects Beri designed, lengths of fabric, balls of knitting wool, old skirts and dresses, back catalogues and magazines with articles in them about his work. I know I'm shoring myself up against the loneliness of being left behind, but this gathering of miscellanea is also a type of ballast against the oncoming tide of the future, a future where the house will no longer belong to us. Or will it? Possession is nine-tenths of the law; that's the saying, isn't it? But I've discovered something else since putting my mind to the sale of the house. That no matter who ends up buying the building and what the person or persons eventually do to it, High Sunderland will always belong to Beri, Peggy, Jonathan, Gillian and myself.

I have good evidence for this claim, for although Beri's much-loved Studio was – on top of being his workplace – also one of his greatest pleasures, suddenly in the late Eighties, owing to the recession, Beri was forced to sell it. Subsequently it was bought by Scottish Borders Enterprise who themselves sold it a few years later to a property developer who, having begun work to make the space into two separate flats, suffered a set-back in the form of a burst water pipe that flooded the building, ruining ceilings, floors and electrics, after which all work ground to a halt.

The Studio,
1992–present day

Standing in front of The Studio, weeds funnel their way out of cracks in the once white now slimy-green concrete. Water drips from crumbling ceilings. Pathways are clogged with dead leaves while legions of stinging nettles and brambles push up against the outside walls. In places the enormous glass windows are cracked, while on occasion people force the locks and break in.

Over the last few years of his life I tried at all costs to avoid driving Beri past The Studio, but if it *was* necessary to go in to Selkirk, I'd put my foot down hard on the accelerator. Beri hated seeing this once stunning building not only abandoned but allowed to deteriorate. Indeed, so affected was he that recently, while sorting through some of his books, I noticed he'd underlined the following remark by the architect Berthold Lubetkin while in conversation with Rowan Moore (architecture correspondent for the *Observer*) on the subject of why he hated revisiting his buildings: '"It is like seeing an old girlfriend," [Lubetkin] said, "who was beautiful, but has now become wrinkled and lost her teeth."' Next to this in the margin, Beri had scribbled the following words: 'The Studio!' In essence, the building has metamorphosed in to the See-Through House's neglected twin: a hideous monster; a symbol of decay, rack and ruin.

2016 was designated 'The Year of Innovation, Architecture and Design in Scotland' and as part of this celebration a photograph of The Studio appeared on a poster for an exhibition called 'Grey Gardens' that aimed to examine the 'interplay between concrete forms and nature'. The photograph was of The Studio in winter when all the leaves had been torn from the trees and lay in piles against the filthy, fogged-up windows. It's an image worthy of a Gothic horror story with a brutalist twist – Frankenstein's monster made concrete.

'Grey Gardens' is, of course, also the name of a famous documentary made in 1975 about a crumbling mansion in West Hampton, New York, owned by two remarkable women, Edie Bouvier Beale and her mother Edith Bouvier Beale. Whether intentionally or unintentionally the poster for the Scottish exhibition echoes the American *Grey Gardens*, only no one inhabits The Studio save maybe a few spiders and mice. But here is the thing: even though we no longer have keys and even though it has not been owned by us for over twenty-five years, I still think of The Studio as ours. How could it be otherwise when I still see Beri standing upstairs carefully studying swatches of fabric or waving and smiling at me through the windows as I turn to walk back up to the house?

And if the time comes when I have to sell High Sunderland, the same will apply, only one-hundred-fold. Not that the new owners will be aware that I'm there. How could they because they won't be able to see me? Nonetheless, I'll be walking around every room, sitting on chairs, lying on sofas, cooking in the kitchen and sleeping in the bedrooms. In summer if they feel a sudden breeze blowing through the rooms, that will be me opening a window to take a walk outside. Or perhaps they might smell a faint hint of smoke because I've decided to light the fire and am sitting in my favourite chair in front of it, glass of whisky in hand. I am not a ghost; don't get me wrong. I am not a Rebecca come to haunt her Manderley. I do not want to instil High Sunderland with evil.

Beri only returned to Yugoslavia once, to visit a cousin who lived in Belgrade.

'Will you visit Senta while you're over there?' I asked before Beri left on his trip.

'I don't need to go back,' he replied.

Only now do I understand what he meant. The idea of revisiting his past was impossible because it would obliterate his childhood memories and for once he didn't want to replace the past with the present. He did not want to see who was living in his house or how they might have reconfigured the rooms, or even how the street might have changed. Sometimes the passage of time is unsettling and there is nothing to gain by returning somewhere to see how things have progressed. Does anyone ever find it rewarding? I trawl my mind for an example. *Brideshead Revisited* is perhaps the most famous and then I recall something Jean Rhys said about going back to Dominica years after she had left the island and how she found all the rivers polluted. Whether metaphorical allusion or reality, journeys back to the landscapes of our past always seem to spell disaster, disappointment or both.

Beri never returned to Senta, but when I was in my late teens, I did. I wanted to see for myself the place where my father was born and grew up so – while staying in Belgrade – I took a train to Novi Sad and from Novi Sad another train across to Senta, arriving in town at around midday on a shimmeringly hot afternoon. The town was empty; everyone was taking a siesta, or so an elderly gentleman standing at the entrance to the station informed me.

Meandering down the dusty main road, Senta resembled a pint-sized Vienna or Paris with wrought-iron balconies and a warm golden glow. The acacia trees lined the streets and occasionally I caught a glimpse of a tiny courtyard filled with dusty orange flowers in earthenware pots.

Before I left on this trip Beri told me I must walk down to the Tizsa as this was where he spent two to three hours each day during the long summer holidays, swimming and sunbathing. Horse chestnut trees lined one side of what was a very wide, flat stretch of water with – every few hundred yards or so – small wooden piers jutting out on to which boats could be tied or from which children could dive.

Back in my father's day he recalled there being a wooden bathhouse 'anchored at the centre of the embankment with dozens of slim, multicoloured, privately owned rowboats tethered around it like petals around the centre of a giant, oblong daisy'. He recalled how Uncle Mishka (who – like all our paternal aunties – wasn't a 'real' uncle) used to dive into the water, pull off his swimming trunks then, while still upside down, push his bottom up above the surface. This was called doing a 'yellow melon' and it was one of Beri's happiest memories.

He had countless others; some of which he told me while the two of us sat together in the evenings at High Sunderland, others of which he wrote about on and off over the years, but every reminiscence always came back to Zori because, as he put it, 'What would have otherwise been a drab if righteous house was, through her, a light, bright, warm and gay home with new joys waiting for us children every day. [...] She was deeply, instinctively and spontaneously involved in the enjoyment of life in all its facets and cared intensely but calmly about the appearance of things; as a result our house was one of the most beautiful, clean and comfortable homes I have known.'

No wonder he didn't want to go back. What end would it have served to return and have to ask permission to gain entry to a house that was no longer how you remembered it? Why superimpose your memory of a treasured time with something else? I didn't enter the house either. Instead, I stood outside on the street and listened to some starlings gathering overhead, screaming and swooping over the dusky, early-evening landscape in huge loop-the-loops.

Visiting someone else's past is a strange thing to do. When he lived in Senta, Beri had no idea I would exist in his future. Now there I was, standing outside his old home trying to locate the small boy who had once lived there. The sky darkened and turned a deep violet gold. Twilight is made for moments like this. It's the hinge between two worlds, the point at which things dissolve, grow blurry and liquefy. There's diffusion at twilight. I thought about the See-Through House back in Scotland and how it contained photographs of this house and how, in turn, this house was linked to the one back in Scotland. All these different threads connecting the past to the future and the future to the past. All these different reflections bouncing backwards and forwards. In this respect The Studio embodies this too. It's the See-Through House's doppelgänger, a shadow of what it once was. Yet it's still a beautiful building. Still striking, perhaps, *because* it's in a state of disrepair as much as in spite of it. Part of me wishes this was not true – that is to say, I wish I didn't find its emptiness so appealing – yet I have to accept there's a profound beauty in the dilapidation of some-thing so solid. More than that there should be a space for it in our lives just as there should be a space for grief.

In Virginia Woolf's novel *To the Lighthouse* she acknowledges the idea of decay in a section called 'Time Passes'. The Ramsays' holiday home, around which all the action of the novel has so far occurred, is locked up for an unspecified number of years during which 'Nothing, it seemed, could survive the flood … ' Mrs Ramsay dies, Andrew Ramsay is killed in the First World War, Prue Ramsay first marries and then dies during childbirth. Time marches on and the house 'was left like a shell on a sandhill, to fill with dry salt grains, now that life had left it'.

Death stands at the novel's centre and is memorialised in the vision of the empty house. It's the 'shell on a sandhill'. The Studio is also a shell, one I pass daily while out walking Henry. On rainy days water drips from the ceilings. On sunny ones I notice layers of dust gathering across the floors and two days ago there was something else – someone had taken a brick and smashed in one of the doorways leaving a hole, which if I ducked my head, was large enough for me to climb through.

It felt strange being back inside. All the flooring had been removed leaving only bare concrete so that everywhere I went my footsteps echoed. I walked over to the fireplace where someone, a squatter perhaps, had left one of those tinfoil, barbecue trays with the charred remains of something unspeakable inside while upstairs I found several empty beer cans and a mattress lying on the floor. Empty shells attract interlopers. I was one myself, but so was Beri, for The Studio, as it slowly crumbles and dissolves, is like emotional origami. Time folds in on itself. Two photographic negatives sandwiched together. Beri is in his mid-fifties, he is standing at the far end of the room playing with bright cones of yarn while cracks appear in the windows, blisters of plaster peel away from the ceiling.

Empty buildings, no matter how beautiful, don't make cheery viewing; they indulge melancholy, encourage it even; however, there was another building my father once worked in – Waukrigg – which might still show some signs of life.

It's a typical Scottish summer's day, the day I decide to visit Waukrigg. Cold, wet and dark, even though it's only eleven o'clock in the morning. I haven't been back to the mill since it closed in the late Eighties. I've driven past it often enough while on the main road into Galashiels, but the mill itself has, over the years, become obscured by a handful of new buildings, mainly low-rise, pre-fabricated warehouses and offices.

I drive past the car park at Aldi's then catch a sign I've not noticed before saying, 'Gala Bank Industrial Estate'. Underneath are printed the names of all the companies that occupy this area. I glance down the list, wondering which of these businesses occupies Waukrigg. Perhaps it's Dingbro – Distributors of Motor Components? or Ingeus Ltd – Provider of Employment and Training Services? Or maybe it's Momentum Scotland – a charity that provides services to people with brain injuries? I continue driving along the empty road. This is Sunday and the only people about are a few stray dog-walkers, although why they are walking their dogs through a business park as opposed to a real one is a mystery.

What did Waukrigg look like thirty years ago? This is what I'm trying to recall as I drive. There was a narrow canal in front of it or behind it, which normally sported a few ducks, and there was always a loud, thrumming sound coming from within the building itself, much like the humming of an industrial beehive.

The mill was where Peggy worked. Having helped Beri set up his first company and having taken over the designing of the knitwear patterns, my mother also took over the running of Waukrigg Mill. Even for a man this would have been no mean achievement, but for a woman it was doubly so, for in the Fifties and Sixties, women in industry were few and far between. Nevertheless, Peggy did not balk at the challenge. She had an extremely good head for figures as well as people management, added to which I never once heard her complain about the long working hours or the mill environment, which was a million miles away from those my father enjoyed at The Studio. Put simply, Waukrigg was as ugly as The Studio was beautiful. Built of red brick with a grey slate roof, it was nothing more than a Victorian weaving shed with skylights instead of windows, bare concrete floors and a cavernous yarn store that stood alongside a mazy collection of pokey, plywood offices.

But today as I drive down the road at the far end of which Waukrigg stood, I realise with a sickening jolt to my stomach that only part of the building – a squat, brick, three-storey tower (now converted in to flats) – remains, whereas the long weaving shed that my parents occupied has been entirely demolished. I clamber out of the car, notebook in hand, and wander aimlessly towards what has replaced it, namely a low-lying, grey structure that looks like an elongated Porta-Loo but which, according to a sign nailed to the wall, is Limelight Childcare. Opposite Limelight stand three much larger, even greyer buildings belonging to Ross Electrical, SBS UPVC Building Products and City Electrical. Rain begins to leak down the back of my neck and the longer I stare at these buildings, the bleaker I feel.

It's not even that Waukrigg was a huge part of my childhood. Besides which, these days I barely give it a second thought, yet suddenly its absence seems to stand for everything that is now missing from the Borders.

Once upon a time there were over twenty-five mills in Galashiels:

> Abbots Mill
> Beechbank Works
> Botany Mill
> Bridge Mill
> Bristol Mill
> Buckholm Mill
> Buckholmside Skinworks
> Comelybank Mill
> Deanbank Mill
> Gala Dyeworks
> Gala Mill
> Galabank Mill
> Ladhope Mill
> Langhaugh Mill
> Mid Mill

Netherdale
Riverside Mill
Rosebank Mill
Tweed Place Mill
Victoria Mill
Victoria Dyeworks
Waulkmillhead Mill
Waukrigg Mill
Waverley Mill
Wheatlands Mill
Wilderhaugh Mill

Now, although some of these buildings have been remodelled to function as residential flats or business premises, there are (to the best of my knowledge) no longer any working establishments. Waverley Mill, for example, was demolished in 2006 to make way for the likes of retail giants such as Tesco, Clarks, New Look, Next and Boots. There's a plaque commemorating the mills that used to stand on this site (obligingly placed at such a height that it's impossible to read unless you hoist yourself up on to a brick wall in front of it) with old black-and-white photographs of all the beautiful Victorian buildings and little write-ups beneath each one saying things like: 'This mill was still in use in 1968, and the water turbine was still supplying power for the machinery. It remained an integrated spinning and weaving mill, making high-quality tweeds and other worsted cloths.'

Not now. Now all you see is the retail park with – ironically, given that a lot of its woollen products were once woven in Galashiels – a spanking new Marks & Spencer selling clothing manufactured for the most part in China. Beri's own business, alongside so many others, went into liquidation during the recession of the late Eighties and although he carried on designing, it was on a much smaller scale. An entire industry was wiped out; that is what the empty mill buildings and giant Tesco and M&S represent. Everything is now either retail or a service provider and suddenly it strikes me that none of the buildings that have replaced the old mills and none of the businesses that have moved into the industrial parks manufacture anything. We are losing touch with touch itself, with the pleasure and skill of crafting and making things, of being able to understand the world through our senses.

I used to take Beri food shopping once a week in Tesco, a task that always took – or so I believed in my impatience to get back to work – twice as long as it needed to because Beri insisted on loitering in the fruit and veg section, methodically picking up melons, peaches and pears in order to smell and squeeze them to test if they were ripe. Vacuum-packed fruit and veg never got a look-in. Not on his watch.

'How can you know what you're buying if you can't touch it or smell it?' But increasingly everything is so securely packaged in plastic we can't get anywhere near it. Or we buy goods online while traversing virtual arcades, viewing neon-bright images of things winking and blinking at us from the far side of our computer screens, distant as starlight. In a world rife with instant connectivity, where are the connections? Where is the man who stops by the side of a road to study a field of ploughed earth? Its colours and textures. Who tastes the astringent aroma of forests when he bites into acorns? The very lifeblood of the world feels cauterised and cut off, leaving only dead limbs, which is how Galashiels feels too. Dead.

I walk through the centre of the town and the impression is of a place on its last legs. People drive through it, but rarely stop. There are seven charity shops, three e-cigarette outlets, two pound shops, two tattoo parlours, numerous barbers, the Pavilion cinema, Crollas Takeaway, Iceland, Argos, three funeral parlours and on my last visit – like a gap-toothed grimace – six retail units standing empty. There's also

Gala Fairydean – a football stadium – although this is positioned at the other end of the town.

Fairydean is an extraordinary structure – a stark, rough concrete zigzag of a building designed by none other than Peter Womersley. Much like everything else in Galashiels, however, Fairydean is not what it once was; its interiors have been allowed to deteriorate or have been altered beyond recognition. That said, recently there have been murmurings that the building might be renovated, but I'm not holding my breath. In any other country, America or Australia, for example, Fairydean would have been cherished, praised, championed as a shining example of a unique and adventurous mind. But in Scotland its only champions seem to be a few enlightened individuals

Fairydean stadium

245

whose passion for buildings other than those 'of yore' means they consistently try to ensure it's preserved.

I continue my walk around the town centre. On a sunny day Bank Street Gardens shine with regimented rows of marigolds and geraniums, but today everything looks tired and grey. My bleak mood is colouring my view of this place, but it's more than just mood. Galashiels' decline has been going on for decades and continues to do so despite a new railway linking the Borders to Scotland's capital, Edinburgh.

Work on this line began in 2012 (it was closed in 1969 thanks to the infamous 'Beeching cuts') and in 2015 the first passenger trains began running. But rather than bringing tourists in, it appears to be taking locals out. And who can blame them? Get off at The Interchange in Galashiels and what are you met with? A Somerfield's car park, a bridge over Gala Water blooming with carrier bags, empty beer cans, metal shopping trollies. An Argos. The Grapevine café and some of Galashiels's empty retail units.

I'm not saying there aren't scraps of what used to be a thriving mill town still dotted around here and there. But the odd gift shop or exhibition displaying a Victorian spinning wheel are scraps only – odd bits and pieces such as you might find in the remnant bin at Cloth Warehouse. In fact, until very recently, if you drove over to Hawick you were greeted by a sign that read 'Hawick: Home of Scottish Cashmere', but like Ozymandias's pedestal with the words 'Look on my works, ye Mighty, and despair!', very little remains of this 'Home'. Pringle of Scotland moved their entire production line to Italy in 2008 with the loss of eighty jobs and five years later, in nearby Innerleithen, Scotland's oldest textile mill, Caerlee, also shut down.

Something has drawn to a close here, something has ended. What the state of Galashiels says, alongside the abandoned Studio and the non-existent Waukrigg, is that it's time for me to move on. Even

High Sunderland is not what it once was; it's the geographical location of loss rather than the living embodiment of all that is present and consequently it's time to look forward rather than back. But that's one of the biggest differences between Beri and me. Whereas I'm always glancing over my shoulder, Beri consistently looked straight ahead. I don't want to become a modernist Miss Havisham. I don't want to turn High Sunderland into a hermetically sealed timepiece, but I haven't inherited Beri's horror of monumentalising the past.

When my father talked about the time he lived in Mea Shearim he always described it as if it were a mosquito in amber, a Pompeii where both buildings and people were trapped not by ash but by something more deadly. Religion.

Why move forward when you can stand still? That's what Mea Shearim seemed to suggest. That it's safer to wall yourself in, to ignore the ebb and flow of the life occurring around you. In the outside world you never step into the same river twice. In Mea Shearim you always do.

'Life,' Beri once wrote, alluding to his time at the yeshiva, 'was to be looked at as an unlucky interlude between periods in heaven; to be spent in repentance of sins committed here and now or, if there was a shortage of these, in repentance of misdeeds from previous incarnations and for full measure in repentance for Adam's original sin.'

By deciding to leave and join the art school, what Beri experienced was the evolutionary equivalent of a fish sprouting feathers and turning into a bird, but without any steps in between. Barely half an hour's walk from each other, the two buildings were, in truth, two hundred years apart. In one short journey Beri stepped from a religiously obsessed eighteenth-century world into an emancipated twentieth-century one where rather than being engaged with 'abstract mental exercises to do with worlds that I never knew', he was thrust into an environment where everything was 'painfully tangible'.

His teacher at the Bezalel, a man by the name of Mordecai Ardon, had trained as an actor before studying at the Bauhaus in Berlin where he was taught by, among others, Paul Klee, Wassily Kandinsky and Johannes Itten. It was through Klee in particular that Ardon began a lasting love affair with colour, one that saw him using it as an abstract tool rather than a symbolic vehicle as played out in the Old Masters. And it was this way of using colour that Ardon encouraged in his students while also inspiring in them a dedicated curiosity and 'the determination to satisfy [this curiosity] in the world of the eye'. Once bitten by this way of seeing, there was no turning back. No glancing over his shoulder.

Not so me. Not so Beri's youngest daughter. Because, for every day of his life my father put behind him, I did the opposite, amassing memories and storing them for the both of us until I had built an entire edifice out of the past.

*

Peter Womersley, even at the height of his career, was never a prominent name in Britain, not in the way a Sir Basil Spence or a Dame Zaha Hadid – to take but two examples – have been. But recently there has started to be some interest in Peter's work, one that has caused my email box to begin filling up with requests. One such was from the Royal Incorporation of Architects in Scotland (RIAS) asking if High Sunderland could be included in a tour of Womersley buildings that was being organised.

'We're envisaging about thirty to forty people wanting to come on the tour,' Colin, the event coordinator, said.

'You think it'll be that popular?' I asked, somewhat incredulous that so many people would want to spend £50 to walk around a handful of mid-twentieth-century buildings.

'You'd be surprised. We'll have an expert on Womersley's work giving a lecture up in Edinburgh in the morning and then a coach will bring everyone down to the Borders to look around Fairydean stadium, Peter's house in Gattonside, your father's studio and finally High Sunderland. It's good to see things in the flesh, so to speak.'

'Sounds great,' I said, perhaps a little too enthusiastically, because over the next several weeks the original estimate of thirty people somehow metamorphosed in to seventy descending on my front door.

'It's very kind of you to open up your home to us like this,' one lady kindly said as she stepped over the threshold.

'It's my pleasure –'

'Is this where you were brought up?'

'Yes, the house was built in nineteen fifty-seven and I was born in 'sixty-three . . . '

And, so began several hours of me acting as tour guide, showing people around my past.

'Yes,' I heard myself saying, 'the builders thought the living room was going to be a swimming pool . . . No, my mother did not find the kitchen too small . . . It is a very old television set, isn't it?' I had the information down pat, little snippets about the family, Beri's idiosyncrasies concerning what he would or would not allow to be put on display, minor alterations that had been made to the building over the past sixty years, Peter's dislike of doors; the stories came flooding out.

Most of the visitors were very nice and extremely courteous, but one or two managed to wriggle under my skin.

'Would you mind not going into that room?' I requested as, out of the corner of my eye, I spied a woman opening the door to my bedroom.

'But we've paid to look around your house –' she sniffed.

'It's only my bedroom; it's not very interesting –'

'I,' she said, rising to all five-foot-two of her, 'will be the judge of what's interesting or not –'

'Well, I'm sorry, but I've put a large sign on that door saying "NO ENTRY" so perhaps . . . '

'They wouldn't do that at Longleat –'

For a moment I didn't know whether she was joking. Then I realised she wasn't so I said, 'But this isn't Longleat –'

'That's pretty obvious,' she snapped back. 'There'd be lions if it was –'

For every rather odd visitor, however, there were many more enthusiastic ones who made up the difference. In particular, one man caught my attention because, as I made my way through to the kitchen, I found him stroking one of the small, stainless-steel catches on the windows.

'It's so beautiful,' he crooned as he continued to stroke it.

'They always make me think of earlobes,' I said.

'Would you mind very much if I photographed you touching one?'

I hesitated then heard myself saying, 'I don't think that's really appropriate, do you?'

The man smiled and wandered off with his camera towards the living room where about thirty people or so were milling around snapping photographs of the Bakelite dials on our old record player, alongside the couches, vases and paintings.

I'd deliberately tidied away all the framed photographs of the family that, ever since Beri's death, I had scattered around the place to remind me of happier times, nevertheless it was an odd, dislocating experience, watching people studying the house as one might study a historical building.

People continued to walk to and fro through the rooms taking photos and chatting to each other and then as quickly as they had arrived, everyone disappeared.

*

'How did it go, then?' Chris called me from a bus somewhere in London a few hours after the tour of High Sunderland finished.

'Better than expected,' I said flatly.

'Don't go overboard. You wouldn't want to die of enthusiasm.'

'Okay,' I enthused, 'how about this: someone baked a loaf of bread and brought it with them on the tour in case anyone got hungry and I had a slice and it was delicious?'

'Of course there's a thin line between enthusiasm and being absurd.'

SILENCE.

'It's just the whole thing was a bit odd.'

'Of course it was odd. It would've been odd if it wasn't odd.'

'I'm living in a museum. How on earth did that happen?'

'Darling, you've been building that ever since Bernat died.'

'It's time to leave, isn't it?'

'Is that a question?'

'I really hate endings.'

'That's not what's wrong with you. Your problem is you had too good a start.'

Chris is right. I did have too good a start. Or to be more precise, I've idealised my start so that nothing else compares. Indeed, my whole adult life seems to have been spent pitting the joy and wonder of my idealised early years against the reality of my later years, trying to come to terms with the difference between the two so as to create somewhere special of my own. Have I succeeded? A couple of times I've come close, but while High Sunderland exists in my present, nothing else can compete. Now it's time to move on. I have to let the See-Through House go. Then another realisation hits me. An age-old fear.

Once I leave, I can never return.

Garden

BERI: Come. Come and help me pick the sticks up off the lawn? It's looking very untidy.

SHELLEY: I'm just doing something, can it wait a second?

BERI: An hour each day and we'll have it done in a week –

SHELLEY: I'm just doing something –

BERI: Stop being so lazy –

SHELLEY: What's so urgent about picking up sticks? They're not going anywhere –

BERI: Not if we don't pick them up –

No one's childhood is perfect. But some are more perfect than others. I was one of the lucky ones. I wasn't beaten, I wasn't abused, I wasn't so lonely that I needed to invent invisible friends. It's only now that I've started talking to people who aren't really there. Okay, I'm the one making up what Beri and Peggy say, but always in the spirit that I know they would say it in. As long as I am alive, they are too.

A visitor arrives at High Sunderland, a young architectural student who is writing a thesis on Womersley's work. The student is in his mid-twenties; he's neatly dressed in black jeans, a black crew-neck sweater, has neatly clipped red hair and is also sporting a long, intensely red beard.

BERI: Is he crazy?

SHELLEY: It's the fashion these days –

BERI: There's a fashion for wanting to look like an idiot?

SHELLEY: I think he looks pretty good; in fact, I like the way he looks –

BERI: You're sitting opposite van Gogh and you're telling me you think he looks good?
SHELLEY: I like van Gogh –
BERI: So do I, but not his beard, for God's sake! Look at it! It nearly reaches his stomach –
SHELLEY [whispering]: Keep your voice down, he might hear you –
BERI: Van Gogh's deaf, remember –
SHELLEY: Ha, ha.
BERI: You see, your father's not only clever, he's funny as well –

Beri's voice rings in my ear. I hear him almost every day now. Chiding me, advising me, encouraging, praising, disagreeing … Sometimes I think of myself as an aquatic creature being pushed and pulled by the element in which it lives. I am a fish suspended in a see-through tank, nudged in one direction by my memories, stirred towards another by the past. The house eddies around me, its emotional currents dictating my life.

Beri continues to whisper (loudly) in my ear as I give the student a tour of the house.

SHELLEY: Yes, that's one of my father's earlier paintings –
BERI: I suppose we're lucky he's not wearing dungarees –
STUDENT: Did your father and Womersley talk much about how the interior of the house would be furnished?
BERI: Of course we talked!
SHELLEY: I think my father allowed Peter free rein, but over the years he changed stuff. The marble, for example – there was a lot of black marble right at the beginning –
BERI: I ask you – black! All architects love black – so predictable!

STUDENT: Is the floor in the kitchen original, the blue tiles?
SHELLEY: Nothing's changed in the kitchen since the house was built. All the units are Peter's design.
STUDENT: What about the outside of the house? The garden and stuff?
SHELLEY: It's all much as it was –
STUDENT: No flowerbeds?
SHELLEY & BERI [speaking in unison]: NO! They'd spoil the line of the house –

Another object banished from within sight of High Sunderland was my Wendy house. Aged around seven or eight, all my friends – or so it seemed at the time – were having them erected on their front lawns or in their back gardens and so in turn – most likely after weeks and weeks of pestering – Peggy and Beri bought me one too – a Hansel and Gretel affair that, naturally enough, Beri didn't want anywhere that he could see it. Instead, the Wendy house was built at the very top of the garden, at the back of the orchard. A Formica floor was laid, a small table and chairs purchased, hooks were nailed into the walls on which I could hang some china cups from my dolls' tea service. In addition my sister made me some red and white gingham curtains for the windows and all manner of other things were dragged up from the playroom to decorate my new home.

But I barely used it because I was too frightened.

It was too far away from the house, too close to the darkest part of the wood that loomed behind it, an evil presence full of maleficent creatures. If I so much as heard a leaf falling outside or a twig snapping, I was convinced I was about to be murdered.

Leaving the Wendy house to return home – a journey of approximately forty-five seconds – was even more traumatic. I'd run as fast as

The Wendy house, c. 1970

I could past the trees, back down the lawn with all kinds of dark creatures pursuing me.

SHELLEY: Did you realise how much I hated playing up there when I was little?
BERI: What are you talking about? You were up there all the time –
SHELLEY: I wasn't. I'd say I was going up there, but mostly I was in my room –
BERI [looking puzzled]: Really?
SHELLEY: I was terrified. The Wendy house felt like it was miles away and the woods were too close – I really hated it up there.
BERI: You never said. I'd have changed it if I'd known, built it a lot closer –

SHELLEY [laughing]: No, you wouldn't!
BERI [laughing too]: You're right; I'd never have done that –

The garden was as sacred a space to Beri as the interior of the house, perhaps even more so as it is through the garden that you first spy the building and first impressions count. To this end the sign reading 'High Sunderland' that sits at the end of the driveway is so discreet, so unobtrusive, that unless you're really looking for it, it's almost impossible to spot. Nor can you see the house from the main road, so that even people who have lived in the Borders all of their lives and who have driven past the house hundreds if not thousands of times, on first arrival declare surprise that a building even exists. The drive isn't in fact that long, but with woodland stretching out on either side of it and with no gateway or formal garden to speak of, the house remains hidden. Until very recently there weren't many flowers either, except for in spring, a wild scattering of daffodils and snowdrops and, from April to May, the parrot tulips. However, after Beri died and in complete contravention to what I knew he'd have sanctioned, I decided to buy some large, square, concrete containers that I planted with lupins, foxgloves and poppies. I also planted a square section of grass at the front of the house with similar flowers. I didn't think of it as an act of rebellion so much as my own need to have something to tend by way of a garden. In Cornwall I had made a point of creating a large flower patch directly outside the front door of my cottage that I stuffed full of alliums, sea thrift and lavender. I had missed it, missed digging my hands into the earth, watching things grow.

But other than that one small transgression, nothing has changed outside. Everything is still lawn and trees: silver birch, ash, beech, oak, Scots pine, spruce, larch, horse chestnut, hazel, apple, pear, plum, which sounds like a lot, but as with the interior of the house, the over-all impression is always one of limitless space.

I love the garden almost as much as I love the house. I can't think of the one without the other and nor could Beri, who took this rela-tionship one step further in a mosaic he made for the front of the building. Constructed out of five horizontal panels, each one is con-ceived as a reflection of the surrounding beech trees as they turned golden in autumn. The top panel – a mixture of turquoise and blue – represents the sky; the second from the top the oranges, yellows and golds of the leaves and so on, down to the bottom panel, which is a mixture of dark browns, blues and blacks representing the earth. The synergy here is not simply of the interplay between light and shade, but between building and environment. The importance of the one to the other being as vital to Beri as the warp was to the weft in his textiles. Inside the house he painted on canvas, while outside in the garden the house itself was his canvas. This blending of materials was central not only to Beri's work but also to the manner in which he lived. 'Many people,' he wrote, 'may consider clothes and colour unimportant and trivial; in isolation and taken out of context, they are. But as part of a full life, which to me means a life composed of many simple, small pleasures, clothes and colour are at least as impor-tant as food and drink but perhaps nearer, in their source and in the senses that they satisfy, to music, poetry and painting.' Of course, a home is only ever a building, but to Beri *and* to me the See-Through House was (and still is) so much more than that; it is an integration of art and life, of the visible and the invisible, of hopes for the future and reflections on the past and in this way High Sunderland – or at least my version of it – is as much fiction as it is fact.

I realise this must be the single most truthful thing I've said or written about the See-Through House. That this version of it exists solely inside my head, that it is a reflection of reality only, which

Beri painting in the garden, c. 1968

makes me think, once again, of Princess Alexandra Amelie's glass grand piano for as much as High Sunderland swallowed me, I have swallowed it. It is a part of my internal world, along with all it involves, all the relationships and other fragile parts of myself. An object I will always treasure, clear and exquisitely beautiful but also, paradoxically, as strange, dark and complex as any Gothic novel.

STUDENT: Did Peter ever express any opinions about furnishings?
SHELLEY: Not that I recall. I think a friend asked him once what he did when people wanted his opinion on a room he disliked. Peter replied that he'd make his way over to a window and then tell them what a wonderful view they had.

BERI: Fine, so long as you're not staring at a brick wall –

SHELLEY [turning to the student]: What would you like to see next?

STUDENT: The bedrooms?

BERI: Oh God ... have you tidied?

SHELLEY [hissing at Beri]: Naturally –

BERI: There's nothing natural about your bedroom ...

SHELLEY [opening the door to her room, which is immaculate]: As you can see, it's a very simple space ...

STUDENT: Beautiful. Wow, great wardrobe too – Womersley did storage well, didn't he?

BERI: Ask her what's inside it. Go on –

SHELLEY: Shhhh –

BERI: You can't avoid what's in there, not for ever –

SHELLEY: What are you talking about?

BERI: You know what I mean – the boxes?

SHELLEY [feigning ignorance]: Boxes?

BERI: Get them out of that cupboard and get on with it, will you?

SHELLEY: Dear God, you've been dead for three years and I'm still running around after you –

BERI: Sweetie pie, that's ridiculous. You've never run anywhere in your life –

The boxes in question are those containing Peggy and Beri's ashes. As soon as I'd collected the former from the undertaker, I'd put it straight into my wardrobe. And when Beri died I did the same thing. His ashes went straight into my wardrobe too, alongside Peggy's. And there they remained for three or more years. Nor did this seem odd or maudlin. I didn't dwell on the fact that my parents were tucked up in my cupboard alongside my knickers and socks. Indeed, where Peggy was concerned I felt she'd enjoy being there because she'd never really been – apart from our agate-hunting excursions – the outdoorsy type. She hated all sports and could never see the point in walking anywhere, particularly when she owned a car. She'd even drive down to The Studio rather than walk the few hundred yards through the woods.

'If we scatter her ashes over the lawn,' I said after her funeral, 'that'll be the closest she's been to the garden in fifty years.'

It's a beautiful afternoon in late August when I remove the boxes from the wardrobe and plonk them down on the dining-room table next to a bowl of pink roses.

'Are you certain you want to do this?' my sister asks and I nod.

'I'm fine,' I say and to my surprise I *am* actually fine. Back when first Peggy and then Beri died, the thought of scattering their ashes had been too much to bear. I hadn't wanted to go through another farewell. My edges were too blurry with tears.

But now ... I stare at the bowl of pink roses, their delicate petals dashed with sunlight. Two magpies hop around the courtyard outside, wings stamped like piano keys. Everything is sharp and clear and in focus and I realise that although the boxes sitting in front of me contain my parents' remains, these remains are not my parents.

Or are they?

I can't seem to process this thought. The ashes either are or are not Beri and Peggy. They can't be both at the same time ... and yet ... my mind stalls. I've never been good at this 'the cat is both dead and alive' sort of conundrum so instead of trying to figure it out, I quickly remove the urns from their packaging and hand one to my sister and one to my niece, Zoë. Then we leave the house and walk across the lawn to the edge of the garden beyond which lies the view of the Eildons. It couldn't look more beautiful than it does this evening, the air milky and warm and bathed in soft sunlight, the field beyond the garden thick with a mixture of summer grasses, thistles and meadowsweet.

I unscrew both lids from the urns and peek inside. For some reason I've always thought ashes would be soft, like ashes from our fireplace. But these are dark grey and gritty and not soft in the slightest. In fact, they're not like ashes at all and briefly it occurs to me that that's exactly what they might be, i.e. not ashes at all but some fake product from China or Taiwan sold to crematoriums up and down the UK to cut down on the expense of firing up the furnaces. Of course this thought, much like the 'are the ashes really my parents?' thought is totally pointless, besides which my sister is ready to begin the scattering so I pick up Dad while she picks up Mum and Zoë stands to one side under a tree. Zoë is expecting her second child and because I'm worried that handling the ashes might contaminate the pregnancy, I've advised her not to touch them. 'Health and safety,' I say, which is also the reason Zoë's husband, Richard, has taken my one-year-old great-niece, Robyn, back to the house so that she can watch us from behind the dining-room windows without breathing in any dust.

'Shall we start?'

I take a handful of the grit and Gilly does likewise and then both of us throw our handfuls into the air where a breeze immediately catches them and blows them straight into Zoë's face.

'Thanks,' Zoë says. 'Now I've swallowed Granny and Gran'pa.'

Briefly, Gilly and I giggle, but even as we do so, we continue the scattering. We're in a rhythm now, a pattern, a drumbeat. It's as if we're sowing the air with seeds: poppies and pink campion, daisies and cornflowers . . .

'You take Mum now and I'll take Dad,' my sister says, so we swap over urns. The breeze grows stronger and although the heavier bits of ash fall to the ground, there are millions of lighter particles that lift up in great sifts of white and, despite not believing in things such as spirits or souls or an afterlife, there is something about the way Peggy's and Beri's ashes appear to join together quite purposefully that is magical. Then they blow away and dissolve in the uppermost branches and leaves of the beech trees.

I take a walk around the garden today. First I pick some plums in the orchard. Cold, pink and sweet. Then I walk past the Scots pine in which the honeybees nest before making my way back down towards the house. It looks so beautiful against the plate blue of the sky. Green and gold everywhere. Woven together. A moment to savour. A moment Beri would have appreciated.

When he was alive I used to glance through the windows just to check he was okay. Usually he was sitting by the fireplace reading or dozing. One day I banged on the windows to get his attention, but he couldn't hear me. I banged a bit harder, but he still didn't turn around. He was close enough to touch, but unreachable. There and yet not there and I hated it. Witnessing his isolation. His total seclusion. It made me think of those paintings by Edward Hopper, *Nighthawks*, *Room in New York*, *11 A.M.* – each one a saxophone solo of loneliness. I dashed inside to go and sit with him.

But today when I think of this, something else strikes me. If High Sunderland was the lens through which Beri saw the world, it is now the lens through which I am catching sight of my future.

I am finally ready to leave.

Acknowledgements

At the heart of this story lie a handful of very dear friends who have all, in their individual ways, supported me in writing this book and so I would like to thank: Jennifer Higgie, Christopher Rickwood, Paul Schütze, Claire Willats and Elizabeth Hume.

I am particularly indebted to my agent, Felicity Rubinstein, and to my editor, Clara Farmer. The enthusiasm they both showed for this book and the support they have given me has been far in excess of anything I could have expected. In addition, I am indebted to Charlotte Humphery and Alison Tulett for their editorial expertise and fine eye for detail.

Thanks also to Fiona Anderson for her kind permission to use a quote from an interview she conducted with my father, to Vivien Womersley for an early conversation about Peter and John Womersley and to Elise Bath, Senior International Tracing Service Researcher at The Wiener Holocaust Library who provided me with an invaluable glimpse of life in Senta under Hungarian and German occupation.

Finally, without the constant support of my family, writing this book would have been impossible to contemplate. Gillian, Jonathan and Zoë – each of you is a much-loved presence in my life.

High Sunderland, April 3rd

A final drink before leaving.

List of Illustrations

All photos, unless otherwise stated, are used by kind permission of the Klein family.

First plate section

High Sunderland through the birch trees, *c.* 1990

'Mace', Bernat Klein tweed sample, *c.* 1961; Image © National Museums Scotland

Bernat Klein Scotland catalogue, featuring High Sunderland, *c.* 1964

Bernat Klein space-dyed mohair yarn sample, 1960–80; Image © National Museums Scotland

Princess Margaret in a Bernat Klein velvet tweed as she leaves the WAIF Ball in Hollywood, 1965 © Reginald Davis / Shutterstock

Infinite Blue (oil on canvas), Bernat Klein, 2011; Image © Liz Seabrook

Sketch of the Living Room at High Sunderland © Peter Womersley, *c.* 1956; Image © Liz Seabrook

Co-ordinated colour guide, Bernat Klein Design Consultants Ltd, 1971; Image © National Museums Scotland

Beri considering colour guides in the Studio, mid 1970s

Second plate section

Tulips in the Living Room (oil on canvas), Bernat Klein, 1976; Image © Liz Seabrook

Terlenka advert featuring a Bernat Klein fabric design, *c.* 1969; Image © Jeff Morgan 09 / Alamy Stock Photo

Bernat Klein tweed with specially-dyed brushed mohair yarn, *c.* 1962–4; Image © National Museums Scotland

Tulips 3, Bernat Klein, *c.* 1961; Image © National Museums Scotland

Beri painting *Lichens 2* in the Library, 1963

Elle Collections cover featuring Bernat Klein tweeds, *c*. 1961

Beri in a coat of his own tweed, *c*. 1962

Reflections: the views through the See-Through House © Shelley Klein, 2015

Text images

xii   High Sunderland, *c*. 1959

9   Fashion show at High Sunderland, 1963

11   Klein family group, *c*. 1927: Front row, left to right: Lipot Klein (Beri's father) with Moshe (Beri's brother) on his knee; Ochi Hauer (Beri's cousin) with hoop and Ochi's father, Beri's Uncle Jozsi; Bernat Weiner (Beri's cousin) sitting on Beri's Aunt Julishka's knee; Ochi's sister, Eva (Beri's cousin). Back row, left to right: Zori Klein (Beri's mother); Beri's Aunt Helene (Jozsi's wife); Beri's Uncle Gabor (Aunt Julishka's husband) and Beri's Aunt Piri. Beri was hiding at the back of the group and nothing would persuade him to come out and be photographed.

20   Hallway, 2016 © Taran Wilkhu, courtesy of The Modern House

23   Watercolour design for High Sunderland © Peter Womersley, *c*. 1956

25   Beri and baby Shelley, 1963

32   Middle Bedroom, *Ideal Home*, *c*. 1966

40   Living Room, *Ideal Home*, *c*. 1966

53   Zori, Moshe, Beri and Lipot, *c*. 1930

71   Peter Womersley, *c*. 1961

76   The Studio, *c*. 1972

78   Beri with loom at Netherdale Mill, *c*. 1966 © Denis Straughan/ The Scotsman Publications Ltd.

Further Reading

Gaston Bachelard, *The Poetics of Space*, Presses Universitaires de France, Paris, 1958

Christopher Breward & Ghislaine Wood (eds), *British Design from 1948: Innovation in the Modern Age*, V&A Publishing, London, 2012

Bernat Klein, *Design Matters*, Secker & Warburg, London, 1976

Bernat Klein, *Eye for Colour*, Collins, London, 1965

Adolf Loos, *Ornament and Crime*, Ariadne Press, California, 1998

Simon Mawer, *The Glass Room*, Little Brown, London, 2009

Rowan Moore, *Why We Build*, Picador, London, 2012

Andrew Motion, *The Pleasure Steamers*, Carcanet Press Ltd, Manchester, 1978

Juhani Pallasmaa, *The Eyes of the Skin*, Wiley-Academy, Chicester, 2005

Michael Webb, *Architecture in Britain Today*, Country Life Books, Middlesex, 1969

Peter Willis, *New Architecture in Scotland*, Lund Humphries, London, 1977

Tom Wolfe, *From Bauhaus to Our House*, Farrar Strauss Giroux, New York, 1981

JOURNALS

'Architects' Approach to Architecture' (May, 1969), article by Peter Womersley, *Riba Journal*, vol. 76, no.5

FURTHER INFORMATION

The Bernat Klein archive is held at the National Museum of Scotland, Edinburgh https://www.nms.ac.uk/bernatklein

www.shelleyklein.co.uk

www.themodernhouse.com

www.wienerlibrary.co.uk

A Note on the Type

This book is set in Dante, a font designed by Giovanni Mardersteig and first used in a 1955 publication of Giovanni Boccaccio's *Trattatello in Laude di Dante* by the Officina Bodoni. It was adapted for mechanical composition by Monotype in 1957, the same year that High Sunderland was built.

Univers, the sans-serif font used for chapter titles, running heads and captions, was also released in 1957. Designed by Adrian Frutiger and released by Derberny & Peignot, it has been available since its launch in a comprehensive range of weights and widths. This typeface family was notably one of the first to fulfil the idea that a typeface should form a family of related designs, allowing for greater artistic consistency.

Bernat Klein's *Eye for Colour*, published in 1965, was also set in Univers.

penguin.co.uk/vintage